Library of
Davidson College

COLLECTED PAPERS ON SOUTH ASIA

RURAL SOUTH ASIA

CENTRE OF SOUTH ASIAN STUDIES
SCHOOL OF ORIENTAL AND AFRICAN STUDIES
UNIVERSITY OF LONDON

COLLECTED PAPERS ON SOUTH ASIA

1. RULE, PROTEST, IDENTITY: Aspects of Modern South Asia
   Edited by Peter Robb and David Taylor

2. POLITICAL IDENTITY IN SOUTH ASIA
   Edited by David Taylor and Malcolm Yapp

3. THE CITY IN SOUTH ASIA
   Edited by Kenneth Ballhatchet and John Harrison

4. BUDDHIST STUDIES
   Edited by Philip Denwood and Alexander Piatigorsky

5. RURAL SOUTH ASIA
   Edited by Peter Robb

6. RURAL INDIA
   Edited by Peter Robb

7. INDIAN RELIGION
   Edited by Richard Burghart and Audrey Cantlie

COLLECTED PAPERS ON SOUTH ASIA NO. 5

RURAL SOUTH ASIA
LINKAGES, CHANGE AND DEVELOPMENT

Edited by
PETER ROBB

CURZON PRESS

First published 1983

Curzon Press Ltd : London and Dublin

© Centre of South Asian Studies, SOAS 1983

ISBN
0 7007 0160 5

ISSN
0141 0156

Printed in Great Britain by
Nene Litho, Wellingborough, Northants.

CONTENTS

Contributors		vi
Preface		vii
1	Introduction: The External Dimension in Rural South Asia *Peter Robb*	1
2	The Plantation System and Village Structure in British Ceylon: Involution or Evolution? *Eric Meyer*	23
3	Wage-Gathering: Socio-Economic Changes and the Case of the Food-Gatherer Naikens of South India *Nurit Bird*	57
4	Economic Dislocation in Nineteenth-Century Eastern Uttar Pradesh: Some Implications of the Decline of Artisanal Industry in Colonial India *Gyan Pandey*	89
5	Rural Labour in the Bombay Textile Industry and the Articulation of Modes of Organization *Dick Kooiman*	130
6	The Role of the Broker in Rural India *Walter C. Neale*	163
7	Two Karnataka Villages and the Outside World: Internal Characteristics, Movement Linkages, and State of Development *H.G. Hanumappa and John Adams*	179
8	'Decentralized' Planning in a Centralized Economy: A Study of Sarvodaya Programmes in a Taluka *Ghanshyam Shah*	204
9	International Rice Research and the Problems of Rice Growing in Uttar Pradesh and Bihar *Paul R. Brass*	229

CONTRIBUTORS

Professor *John Adams*, Department of Economics, Maryland.

Mrs *Nurit Bird*, Department of Social Anthropology, Cambridge.

Professor *Paul Brass*, Department of Political Science and School of International Studies, Washington (Seattle).

Dr *H.G. Hanumappa*, Institute for Social and Economic Change, Bangalore.

Dr *Dick Kooiman*, Institute of Cultural Anthropology and Non-Western Sociology, Free University (Amsterdam).

Dr *Eric Meyer*, Centre d'Etudes de l'Inde et de l'Asie du Sud, Paris.

Professor *Walter C. Neale*, Department of Economics, Tennessee.

Dr *Gyan Pandey*, Centre for Studies in Social Sciences, Calcutta.

Dr *Peter Robb*, Department of History, School of Oriental and African Studies, London.

Dr *Ghanshyam Shah*, Centre for Social Studies, South Gujarat (Surat).

PREFACE

This volume results from an international symposium which I organized in December 1980 under the auspices of the Centre of South Asian Studies at the School of Oriental and African Studies, London. Further papers from the same symposium and an earlier meeting in June are being published separately under the title *Rural India: Land, Power and Society under British Rule* (Collected Papers on South Asia No.6).

The present book comprises those contributions which bore particularly on questions of change in relation to economic development. The intention is to concentrate on linkages between localities and the outside world, and in general between what may be defined as intrinsic to a given society and what may be called external. The essays are illustrative of the subject; this volume does not pretend to be a survey and has no pretensions to being regionally or thematically comprehensive. Four papers, those by Eric Meyer, Nurit Bird, Gyan Pandey and Dick Kooiman, examine the response of South Asian societies specifically to the introduction of 'modern' features of production: plantations, foreign imports or capitalist industry. Four more papers treat aspects of external linkages in particular relation to economic development: that by Walter Neale on the role of the money-lender as 'culture broker', that by H.G. Hanumappa and John Adam on the physical communication between villagers and nearby towns, and those of Ghanshyam Shah and Paul Brass on recent development efforts and different responses to technological advances.

The conference and therefore this publication would not have been possible without the financial assistance of the Projects Committee at the School of Oriental and African Studies, and that assistance is gratefully acknowledged.

The presentation of the papers has been standardized to a point but absolute uniformity has not been attempted. The use of italics has been avoided as far as possible, for example after the first appearance of less common but repeated words. A problem arises with transliteration where words are or were current in Anglo-Indian usage (in English): to apply strict conventions to such words is to give them a misleading 'indigenous' quality. I have therefore left all transliterated words in the forms used by the different authors.

P.G.R.

INTRODUCTION:
THE EXTERNAL DIMENSION IN RURAL SOUTH ASIA

Peter Robb

The symposium from which this volume is drawn had the title 'The external dimension in rural South Asia: linkages between localities and the wider world'. It was concerned to focus attention on processes of integration and exchange between the levels of government, central markets or regional and metropolitan culture, and the level of the villages of South Asia. The essays which follow treat aspects of these questions in their own way. Several continuing themes may be discerned. First there are methodological points. The papers show a clear preference for making assessments according to function rather than form, and on the basis of a complex of roles or a society in the round. As a consequence two general conclusions seem possible: that the 'traditional' systems may not be seen as a set of hierarchical isolates, for linkages of various sorts are not peculiar to so-called modern societies, and that the categories of our analysis - such as 'political', 'social' and 'economic' - are misleading because Eurocentric, conjuring up distinctions and divisions which do not exist in South Asia. Divisions there are, of course, but the categories which they provide are mostly hybrids ('sociopolitical', 'socio-economic' and so on) according to our terminology. Secondly the papers provide some substantive hypotheses. They recognise that communities differ in their response to stimuli, that in general adaptation is preferred to transformation, and that imperfect linkages are an important inhibitor of or barrier to change.

We may dispose of the methodological points first. The paper by Neale encapsulates them: he examines the moneylender, by which he means the 'external' bania visiting the villages to trade, according to his function and not his reputation, as a broker mediating between different economic cultures, and he stresses that the bania did not operate wholly in the economic sphere or seek economic rewards above all others. The more detailed papers embody similar ideas. Hanumappa and Adam stress the variety of relationships and the multiplicity of function for institutions and actions in the villages they study. Meyer, on Sri Lanka, begins by trying to understand the traditional ecosystem, and thus abandons the idea of static or closed villages which was implicit in accounts of areas of perpetual cultivation and permanent occupations: he sees the interplay between 'outfield' reserves of land and 'infield' paddy fields and gardens. Nurit Bird, too, stresses the pattern of work, consumption and trade in the life of the food-gatherers before they became involved with labour on a plantation, and Pandey pushes back in time the market-involvement and dependence on intermediaries of the weavers he studies, while also judging the impact of trade in manufactured goods in terms of the rural economy as a whole. Kooiman adopts Neale's strategy in analysing the functions of the 'jobber' who provided labour for the Bombay mills in terms of the services he provided. Shah's essay exemplifies the discontinuity between rhetoric and practice, between the Gandhian 'decentralization' which he sees as yet another in the series of strategies intended to defend the supposedly isolated village from outside influence on the one hand, and the practical needs of and constraints upon development agencies or the desires and expectations of local people on the other hand. Brass's questions too are very much of the genre 'how does it work?' in preference for 'how does it look?'; his explanations of the relative failure to improve rice yields in Bihar depend upon the connexion between agricultural profitability and ecological constraints, especially problems of water management.

The studies thus tend to emphasize pre-existing conditions and often enough resistance to change. To Meyer the essential feature maintaining the balance of the society was the flexibility provided by chena cultivation, that is, occasional crops of paddy and millets on so-called waste land. This was destroyed by plantations, land-grabbing and government policy. The villager's response was to substitute other sources of income and flexibility, for example by opening his own plantation or more commonly by trading with or working for the Europeans with their Tamil labour force. Bird's tribals, similarly, take from the plantation, its wages and the market, those features which best suit their previous life-style. Pandey's weavers, too, fit into established patterns. Pandey, anxious to distinguish between the impact of British trade on different sections of the population, argues that in the seventeenth and eighteenth centuries even lowly textile producers were already involved with entrepreneurs who captured most of the profits, and that the fortunes of different production centres fluctuated even then from time to time.

The External Dimension

Thus Pandey sees the loans and advances made under the East India Company and to a lesser extent the subsequent rise and fall of weaving communities as partially continuing the past: the region and its trade were already open to whatever damage was inflicted on them by the advent of European manufactures. Moreover, faced with the challenge, people did not suddenly change their habits: factory-products could be readily substituted for most of the finer qualities of cloth but not for coarser handloom (the demand for which continued into the present century), and local manufacturers of fine cloth attempted to save themselves by cornering the market wherever imports could not compete, and ultimately in cotton saris for local sale.

A second conclusion is that adjustment is usually preferred to revolution. Kooiman's jobbers were newcomers, urban-based, dependent for their position on knowledge and physical strength. To the employers they were both contractors for and managers of labour. But to the workers they were patrons, the 'mukadam' or traditional leaders. They were not of the village but they were from it, in the sense of recruiting through kinship and common origins and of reproducing, in the factory, conditions which accommodated to the understanding of the villagers. They were recipients of bribes or tributes; they were creators of vertical solidarity. Just as the mill-owner abrogated to the jobber the right to hire and fire, so the workers gave up any pretensions of entering a wage contract or combining as a class. The jobber was, in short, a culture-broker in the sense that Neale uses the term: he provided for capitalist enterprise a 'non-capitalist' face in the villages, and for the worker both a channel and a filter. Meyer's villagers required different aptitudes to meet the challenge of the plantations and therefore there was some change in the people who were successful, but none the less their involvement with a capitalist system may be represented merely as the substitution of one outfield for another; its function for the village had not changed, and therefore the underlying structure remained the same. Bird makes this explicit with the notion of 'pre-existing pattern' by which she accounts for the continuities to be found in the customs of the Naikens, and which may be seen to be the equivalent of the cultural conservatism described in all the papers. In stressing the importance of function, Bird reminds us, as Neale does also, that social, economic and other features do not exist independently of the uses to which they are put and the ways they are perceived. Integration with the plantation or the money economy did not imply for a Naiken what it would imply to a North American: Bird's concept of 'wage-gathering' is thus not paradoxical, because she does not understand wages to imply the system of values and customs which surrounds their payment in some other societies, but rather sees them as an objective feature whose functions are peculiar to the society in which they occur. For the Naiken indeed the wage is not a currency at all - that role is filled by debt - but a substitute for forest-products, and it is gathered when needed just as they were in the past.

The dynamic element in these explanations is also important, and central to some of the papers. Change, it is clear, is not a necessary consequence of contact, for contact of some sort is a perennial feature. Change is a necessary consequence of the right mix between an innovatory contact and a receptive society, or between internal needs and pressures and an appropriate input. The extent to which defence is possible, as in the substitution practised by Meyer's villagers, Bird's tribals and Pandey's weavers, depends on the ability to accommodate a change of content within existing structures, and that will depend, for example, on the degree to which the 'outfield's' characteristics are or are not peripheral, and in general on the nature of pre-existing arrangements. The Naikens did not 'develop', because the plantation represented a change with which they could cope, and also because they were not predisposed to seize upon the opportunities for economic maximization which it could have provided. Pandey's weavers were protected to some extent not by isolation but by the persistence of old tastes, the inappropriateness of some of the finer cloths for some of the consumers, and most of all by the continuing need for surplus income and the opportunities provided as an adjunct to cotton-growing. Indeed the claim is that weavers had probably always operated at or about subsistence level and that the true losers to foreign competition were probably those agriculturists who needed to supplement inadequate incomes from cultivation; they substituted migration. On the other hand, the weavers in some communities were not disposed to change their ways by producing in factories, even though they had long been involved in the market and dependent on middle-men. Here, I think, and in contrast with Kooiman, the 'de-industrialization' argument runs into difficulties. Arguably change would become endemic rather than epidemic, at the point at

The External Dimension

which intolerable conflict arose between the weavers' self-image and sense of identity, and the conditions with which they had to fit in. So too the half-way house represented by the jobbing system discussed by Kooiman is possible precisely because such a crisis had not occurred: the village may have been 'subordinated' to the factory but if so it was not because of the dominance of the capitalist mode of production but in the sense that villages were made to serve certain purposes for the mills, chiefly as labour pools; and indeed, on the contrary, the existence of the jobbers rendered the mills imperfectly 'capitalist', prevented them from undermining village society, and even perhaps caused them to perpetuate existing social relations.

In seeking fuller explanations of dynamic processes, these papers look first at the linkages themselves. Neale argues that the lack of suitable brokerage may have rendered ineffective some attempts at modernization and development. Hanumappa and Adam, concerned to analyse the 'hiatus between ... infrastructure and ... village structure', believe external connexions to be instrumental in development. Their two examples, one 'growing' and one 'declining' village, admit of differences of opportunity (proximity to towns, availability of water) but suggest that these are not sufficient explanations of the differences of performance. Rather the range and nature of outside movements may be correlated with the economic position of the villages and of individuals within them. The differences may have had underlying causes, as for example in the caste composition of the villages, one of which had a large number of tribals and the other a large number of the locally-dominant caste; but however the differences in receptivity originate they are, it is claimed, instrumental in development or decline. Other essays too take up this point by looking beyond the substitution and adaptation which we have seen as the initial reaction of non-receptive communities. Kooiman sees the adjustment represented by the jobber as a transitional arrangement: the interchange occurred at first without any concurrence of customs or attitudes between the parties, and the worker remained migratory, attached to his village which he sought to re-create as far as possible in the unsanitary chawls where he preferred to live: but, as the discussion of trade union development shows, this worker could be harnessed through the jobber into new forms of association, and vertical solidarity could be translated into without being superseded by horizontal mobilization. The fact that 'pre-existing patterns' are not at first disturbed does not mean that fundamental changes never come, merely that they are delayed. Kooiman's jobbers came to need or to want what outsiders could offer them, the political brokerage of administrative skills and the articulation of grievances in a political idiom; ultimately the jobber and the village could be superseded, by means of the linkages which were in existence or created.

Shah's account leads in the same direction. He shows how a development agency is dependent on external forces however committed it may be to internal uplift. The need for capital formation and certain political pressures invite centralization; but more than this much of the response to the external which distorted the Gandhian ideals was derived from the local people themselves. When the agency tried to emphasize agriculture and crafts in their school they found people demanding English and science, as vehicles for an escape from the status of manual workers and farmers. Cooperative preparation of papad, a vegetable product, flourished because it provided jobs for women who would not work in the fields, but its commercialization offended the Gandhians. The picture is of a tension between internal and external forces, certainly, because the development workers were unable to change the pattern of land-holding, the customs and attitudes which created local conditions, or the decisions of governments and aid programmes which provided the external inputs: thus the technocratic improvements evoked a ready response but were not to the advantage of small and marginal farmers, while the development of the dairy industry, diamond-cutting and paper-manufacture was dependent on the demands of external trade. But the picture is also of a tension that is being resolved, for Shah concludes that internal resistance has weakened as the external forces, particularly integration with the market, become stronger. The Gandhian ideals were first compromised and then rejected : so this agreeably sardonic essay reveals.

Such arguments have wide ramifications, for Gandhi's view of the Indian village was not an original one. Many years ago Daniel Thorner, in an appreciation of Henry Maine, remarked that his 'ideas may have been modified in a number of respects but they are very far from having been completely disproved or entirely displaced',[1] and this is still true, not just among Gandhians but generally. The essays in this volume however belong to a trend which has brought displacement nearer.

The External Dimension

Criticisms of Maine's egalitarian *ur*-community and of single-line evolution have been well-digested, but the present tendency is also to question the extent to which village structure was, in pre-modern conditions, largely or essentially unaffected by outside influence, or that communities were 'left to modify themselves separately'.[2] There is little autochthonous development to be found in the pages of this volume, and also little sense that the character (as opposed to the extent) of the most important exchanges between the village and its environment has altered in the dramatic sense in which Maine believed. It is true that in an essay which was before our symposium but which has been published elsewhere, Gilbert Etienne rejected the 'village republic' ideal on the basis of the lack of dynamism in the model, arguing that any system of production has its 'inner rationale' so that there comes a time when its 'maximum productivity has been reached'.[3] But this rationale so far as it is reflected in this volume seems to be the result of exchanges between external and internal conditions: it is itself a source of the dynamic, for conditions are constantly changing. Etienne proposed population pressure as an example (perhaps *the* example) of the crisis that generates advances in technology and a change in the system of production, or else leads to some catastrophe which preserves the existing system by a demographic check. But other essays suggest that change may result or be avoided through a range of influences, at once wider than this because reflecting the ways in which the village is embedded in its environment, and narrower because specific to each case.

We are groping then towards a fundamental explanation of historical change. We appear to accept the pre-eminence of ecology over culture without denying the resilience of the latter. It is after all only as a theoretical construct that we see behaviour resulting merely from man's accommodation to physical conditions, that we attribute entire social structures to pre-determined responses, in the way that the origins of *bhaiachara* communities have been traced to insecure agriculture.[4] The last paper in the collection makes this point clearly. Brass denies that lack of enterprise explains the failure to increase the productivity of rice cultivation in north and east India, and refers instead to problems which specifically affect paddy in many parts of Asia. The peasant, to Brass, is a rational producer who rejects the additional input required for high-yield varieties in situations of high climatic risk. But Brass does not ignore cultural explanations altogether. He emphasizes the importance of understanding ecological *and* human factors; and in the cultural sphere he notices particularly the impact on goals of a farming system geared to subsistence and not marketing. The size of holding is an important factor here, as is the ability to enjoy surplus, but so too are cultural preferences, though none of these is immutable. Indeed diversity is a theme for Brass and others.

In treating particular examples the papers in this volume have thus, it seems to me, some common conclusions. I shall attempt here to expand upon these points, to relate them to the questions with which we began, and to assess their significance. The interpetation will be my own, but based on the aspects of the papers already described. When I was asked to clarify the starting-point for our discussions, I explained that I sought a range of factors likely to be significant, mechanisms likely to operate, characteristics receptive or hostile, where there is externally-induced change. It seemed necessary to ask how internal and external worlds relate in general, to encompass continuity as well as change. There were two different kinds of question. The first was one of definition, which is, in South Asia, peculiarly complicated by point of view and assumptions: variations and contradictions present more than the familiar problem of deciding what is general and what is specific. We have to distinguish between reality and rhetoric. We can, for example, easily see the difference between varna theory and the practical operation of a jati. But how can we be certain that we are not, in our analyses of rural society, merely repeating the equivalent of a Brahmanical view? Moreover we cannot escape our definitions: our terminology must be general to the extent that we wish to communicate with others and relate our findings to theirs. In the last century the drawing of the boundaries depended upon certain preoccupations about society, evolution and race: thus we had tribes and castes as the imposed categories of analysis. Today we see that all the boundaries - the very study of ethnography, the idea of locality or the identification of a region - depend upon distinctions as difficult and arbitrary as those which historians have long worried about in the case of periodization.

Our first problem therefore was to describe and delineate externality and internality. We might, for example, map out the extent of operable relationships, find out how far regional influences extend, how wide

The External Dimension

are the networks within which a village is placed, and which aspects of life are subject to the general trend and which to particular variation. These are in the last resort questions of fact. The second problem, however, concerned interrelation - not just the identification of a shift in the external environment to which internal change might be a response, but the interaction of one culture with another or between general and specific aspects of a single culture. The interface between internal and external is a point of movement, of exchange and causation, whether we are analysing change or stability, for the first results from exchanges which tend to subvert and the other from exchanges which tend to confirm. And here the questions (what mechanisms determine which it is to be?) were wholly ones of interpretation. The problem goes deeper than merely choosing one or even a set of 'causes' when all seems interdependent. If there is no road, except the examination of the particular case, along which to seek the relative importance of factors that were generating or resisting change, it is a road that leads into familiar cul-de-sacs. It is agreed, perhaps, that change and continuity result from a mix of internal conditions and external environment. Go beyond this assumption, to questions about what the mix is likely to be, and agreement ends. We may see this in development terms: at some stage sufficient of either incentive or opportunity will induce change, but it is difficult to define the sufficiency. Just as we ask at what point lack of incentive will be overwhelmed by magnitude of opportunity, we have to consider when it is that internal forces are sufficiently favourable or external sufficiently dramatic, to induce change.

Hence it was that at the outset I asked for the independent examination of the ways things interact. Broadly speaking, are there kinds of institution which are resistent to change or kinds of influence which are bound to prevail? The inquiry had already moved on, therefore, from those old controversies about the nature of the village community which depended on the theoretical establishment of original forms in order to understand how relations 'ought' to be (before changing or protecting them). We were concerned rather with the terms on which various forms develop and decline, with what I made bold to call a 'systematic study of connexion'. It was not to be expected that any symposium would address itself wholly to the questions with which it began; but the essays presented here have, it seems to me, consistently abandoned any idea of a kind of moral supremacy for past or original social forms, discarded indeed any idea of isolation in which a single original form could appear and be sustained over time, and turned instead to the roles played by various forces at any time, moving societies in different directions from diverse starting-points. Moreover, to my mind, the essays reinforce certain conclusions, in particular that change will be induced within a society either when influences are so strong as to produce an environmental revolution, in which case change may be said to be independent of the social or value system, or when influences are so appropriate as to be readily accepted, in which case change might be said to be dependent on the existing culture.

One lesson of the papers is thus that we ought to escape the obsession with the cultivator in his isolated village. A second lesson is that our terminology still needs attention, damaged as it is by the observation of how groups function and interact. The return of the peasant to South Asian history has been rightly hailed, by a great and greatly lamented exponent of this trend,[5] but sometimes it seems as if it is a nineteenth-century view of the peasant that has come back. The term may imply the isolated and independent subsistence producer who is so much at home in those isolated villages. But who is this peasant? Is he the small-holder of the Mali type who grows vegetables for a limited market? Is he the surplus cultivator whose attention quickly turns to those 'capitalist' activities of rent-collection and usury? The term supposes an equilibrium in landholding and land-use which perhaps did not exist, and a broad and important section of the population on which we should be concentrating our attention. A peasant role no doubt existed, but perhaps it was not wholly identified with a single group, differentiated internally only by relative wealth and independence.

Furthermore, we are led to ask whether or not this *is* the role on which we should concentrate if we are interested in change. An economy and equally a society or a polity depend (I would argue) upon connexion, and it may be seen (as suggested by Walter Neale in this volume) that there are two roles which may be played in this regard in the South Asian countryside. There is brokerage, whose importance depends on the ability to translate, to be different things to different men, and there is patronage, the key to which is the supply of necessities in return for services. The underlying

The External Dimension

feature of the one is exchange, and of the other dominance or dependence. Here too we have to attend to the role and not a type or an individual. The money-lender who takes coin from the town and makes it available to the cultivator (for rent or revenue-payments) is acting as a broker. He may also be a patron if he supplies seed and food grains in return for control over the disposal and sharing of the harvest. The prosperous cultivator who lends cash or grain or draught animals to his fellow-cultivators, in return for their labour in his holdings, is also performing either or both of these roles. Our analysis of connexion therefore depends not on the use of categories such as bania, dominant peasant or zamindar, but on examination of the impact and operation of those who performed certain roles, regardless of their status.

These observations lead us on, or so it seems to me, to those further lessons about the nature of change already discussed. Our conclusions may be taken as representing a new stage, in contrast with some of those of the past. Not just in recent discussions but since the debates of the nineteenth century, 'colonialism' has cast a long shadow over 'development'.[6] Thus are postulated indigenous structures and external forces, the latter seen as having penetrated the former.[7] Such interpretations inhibit understanding, for in their Eurocentrism they imply a whole series of further conclusions: that movement comes from outside not just in the sense argued here but in the sense of across continents and cultures, and that internal or indigenous features are bound to be weaker than external or foreign ones, a weakness that results from isolation and segmentation, a strength that is attained and transmitted through improved communciation. Refinements of these ideas - Furnivall's pluralism or Boeck's dual economy [8] - have tended merely to add sophistication to the old dichotomy between East and West, fatalism and rationalism, sufferers and actors. So too Marx bequeathed to his followers an imprecise but potent image of backward Asia: of primitive communism, a despotic political and social system derived from communal property; of isolated communities where all divisions of labour (and those into producers and controllers) were unalterably fixed, in stasis, for want of class conflict; of a milieu in which production for consumption prevailed over production for wealth, only the latter demand being insatiable and thus dynamic. Nineteenth-century debates and also some of those conducted more recently, are dominated by a model for which Adam Smith was ultimately responsible, one in which development resulted from the displacement of inefficient peasants by landlords and capitalists, and of fragmented economies by more integrated ones. Some condemn the process; others object to its being interrupted. Only the heterodox argue that because social groups and economic roles were interdependent - the merchant or money-lender or zamindar needing the cultivator as much as the cultivator needed him - there was no certainty that the predicted development would take place and no safe identification of individuals with the Smithian or indeed the Marxist categories. Of course we can hardly, today, escape Smith or Marx, any more than our predecessors could; and we are bound to measure economic progress in comparison with the rise of the capitalist economies of Western Europe: certain kinds of economic change presuppose particular changes in the means of production and the allocation of resources. But we can allow the theory to take us in rather different directions from those in which it has taken many people in the past: in particular we need not assume that inefficient peasants are necessarily displaced by the operations of capitalists and proto-capitalists; or that integrated economies necessarily take the form of those which exist in Europe; or that, indeed, localized, 'traditional' economies are static isolates, unlike capitalist or centralized-bureaucratic economies. We are encouraged to avoid the assumption that one set of characteristics implies another. We are encouraged, moreover, to endorse the assumption that there are, in all societies, internalized features, which tend to reinforce existing patterns, and that change depends on the resolution of an equation in which the two variables are the resilience of the internal features and the strength of the external, subversive pressure. The argument is that the inate tendency in any society or system is towards stability, to variation within a specific range, and that development is generated by the breaking of the mould. All societies constantly experience interchange between the internal and the external, in this sense of the terms, and the status quo is itself therefore a long-term movement. But equally some societies are more open to influence than others, or in some periods are more exposed to influence. All evolutionary theories propose some necessary or likely progression; we postulate various results from the fortuitous matching of pressure and response.[9]

It may seem that the argument is circular, dependent on the particular definition of 'internal' and 'external' features; rather, I would argue, the terminology, which is not wholly satisfactory, is not material to the general conclusion. What is essential is first acceptance of the idea that every society represents an optimal formulation in respect of its environment. Take for example the concept that there are appropriate customs of inheritance. It is true that the absence of primogeniture may be said inevitably to involve fragmentation of rights in land, though not necessarily of working units; this is the case provided the rights are individually heritable and regardless of any increase in population. But we may reasonably argue that if this fragmentation had been seriously disadvantageous then some other expedient would have been adopted; and that perhaps on the contrary joint and equal inheritance had beneficial effects on the provisional of agricultural labour, especially for rice cultivation and in general where rainfall followed the Indian pattern of monsoon and drought and thus prevented a steady demand for work, or that it played its part in unifying the family's and the clan's claims over land in conditions of political insecurity or variable cultivation. The British of course tended everywhere to provide someone with a definite legal title over specific pieces of land and to guarantee that title for an individual and his heirs. For various reasons, moreover, land gained in value. The opening up of waste land and of alternative employment, and the slowness with which British laws came to be effective in practice in rural areas, may have masked what was happening, but it is clear that steadily the incentives for solidarity in land decreased and the advantages of separation grew. Family quarrels or opportunism thus led increasingly to the expression of the fragmentation of rights in terms of a sub-division of land. The development may even have been exaggerated because the poor were most vulnerable to the famines and epidemics which kept down the overall population, while those who had most land were most affected by a rising birth-rate and possibly an improved survival-rate: their cultural patterns, especially the age of marriage, still depended on the expectation of early death. Partitions may also have had debilitating effects, in the longer term, especially on productivity (though a debate turns on this question). None the less, however, the change may be seen as fitting with our general model: it is produced by a sufficient change in external conditions, and partition or fragmentation, however motivated, represent *responses* as much as did joint inheritance; this observation does not depend on the resultant pattern of land-holding continuing to be effective, though of course effectiveness must be judged overall by the widest social and economic criteria, and what seems detrimental inertia for the many, in terms of the total economy or some moral judgment, may well represent continuing advantage or the minimising of disadvantage for the few, those able to effect change.[10]

That societies represent optimal compromises is not to say that they result wholly or largely from rational or utilitarian decisions, or indeed to imply any significant degree of human control: often enough what is meant is merely 'making the best of a bad job'. But the argument is that the compromises will be sought and that they will persist until conditions change. The stimulus for such change may seem at times to be internal, coming from an innovating farmer, for example, but general or significant application of new methods or technology implies an input whereby an idea is *brought in* and *taken up*. If, as I argue, men are mostly content to imitate and are not striving constantly to improve methods or even to avoid effort then a catalyst is needed to prompt widespread response to innovation: it may be leading individuals who provide linkages to outside information or resources, and by their own example demonstrate advantages; or it may be the pressure of need, from some demographic, climatic, economic, political or ideological change which has altered the ground rules on which existing practices were based. It does not seem to me fruitful or possible to single out any one of these types of change as prime mover in theory: for any significant movement they are likely to appear in combination, and their relative impact depends on the nature of the society on which they impinge - concentration on connexion rules out single causes or mono-directional change. By the same token, moreover, while change may be seen as resulting from some impetus, outside the range of exchanges promoting continuity, it may not be seen as necessarily induced by outsiders; it is arguably more likely to result from reactions by insiders. The point is merely that societies tend to reproduce and not to reform themselves, but that it is difficult for customs or attitudes to persist unchanged in an environment in which they are disfunctional.

There will be, however, an element of lag, differing from society to society. In the short term customs may show great and even enhanced resilience, and this may be distinguished from persistence in the face of damage as a

The External Dimension

result of, say, a preference for social over economic goals. We approach what our discussions showed to be a hotly contested issue, however, when we argue that societies differ in their conservatism or adaptability. One side of the argument, indeed, stresses objective factors in such a way as to suggest that any cultural emphasis is a crude reiteration of nineteenth-century racial stereotypes. But let us, for the sake of argument, admit that there are differences between groups of people in their aptitude for certain tasks: it is hard to imagine that anyone will wish to adhere to the very extreme position that no such differences exist. (Are we to say, for example, that there will be no differences in economic performance between a group whose ethic favours agricultural labour and one which considers it demeaning?) We might go even further and suggest that the Indian social system, with its self-perpetuating and self-regulating jatis, is peculiarly designed to ensure continuities in social attitudes.[11] Let us, then, postulate the existence of, say, 'good' cultivators. It is logically inescapable that equally 'good' cultivators will perform equally well in any given conditions; in such a theoretical case objective, physical factors will be the sole determinants of relative success. We must ask, however, not only whether all cultivators are equally good, but, given the social, political and economic structure of different regions, whether equally good performers are everywhere equally well-placed to perform. In Bihar, for example, it might be said that strategic agricultural decisions generally lay with those who were, culturally, least well-disposed to direct involvement with agriculture, and that therefore while a Bihari Kurmi, say, might be thoroughly a match for a Punjabi Jat, in industry, competence and enterprise, he was less able to increase his productivity and profit, and unable to effect improvements regionally. Thus I would not argue against the importance of objective factors, and might well accept that the social system and mores of dominant groups in Bihar and Bengal derive from long experience of surplus agriculture in a fertile region, or, now that population growth has removed this advantage, that the problems in the area are due as Brass suggests to the objective difficulty there of water-management.[12] But I would argue that receptivity to change does depend very much on attitude and aptitudes, and that these play a vital role in economic performance.

The importance of external linkages may be said

therefore to rest on their role in development, but more fundamentally on the extent to which they determine or define the character of all societies. They illustrate, what is more, the tendency for substitution or adaptation on the one hand, and the need for an appropriate match between input and receptivity on the other. To examine the nature and function of linkages is, indeed, to invite complex explanations. It was easy, for example, to characterize the impact of European rulers and traders on an India made up of self-sufficient communities: to open them up to the world was to introduce qualitative change. But what of the communities found in the pages of this volume, communities already bound up with the world, selecting among the influences which impinge from time to time and reacting with them? We are dealing with quantitative change perhaps, or with adjustments, matters difficult to interpret. This difficulty also is reflected in these pages. Kooiman is inclined to accept that 'indigenous agriculture' was at variance with and has submitted to the exigencies of imperial rule and the world market; but his account is open to a different interpretration at several points about which he seems wary. He shows that the mills were neither exactly capitalist nor wholly an enclave in a 'traditional' economy, and therefore approaches the conclusion that what has emerged today is a new amalgam and not the submergence of one system by another. He sees the jobber as a capitalist agent and as a form of labour organization continuous with unionization; but equally the conclusions might be drawn that the jobber was a means whereby villages distanced themselves from an industry in which they wished to partake; and that the unionization to which he gave his support was thereby different in character from unionization elsewhere. Kooiman sees the villages as being exploited by an industry which did not pay a family wage, though the example of wages in Ahmedabad, with its different pattern of labour, rightly makes him uneasy; Pandey too quantifies contributions to some villages by migrants: one might even try linking rural change to what millworkers remitted home. Finally he treats the workers' use of their wages and in particular their indebtedness to the jobbers as examples of their being disadvantaged by inclusion in an unfamiliar kind of economy; but the example of Bird's Naikens suggests that the use of debt as a currency may represent on the contrary the continuation of an economy that was familiar. Similarly Pandey, the other writer who deals explicitly

The External Dimension

with the question of imperial impact, is bound to be somewhat equivocal in his assessment. He has to prove not that weavers ceased to be independent and prosperous for he knows they had long been dependent and poor, but that they suffered a reduction in their circumstances. He is led to conclude that they were left producing coarser cloth and that this was less profitable to them; he does not have the space to expand this point but of course it is a difficult one to argue if we are talking about weavers who were already on a subsistence level, their profits being taken by intermediaries. Whether cheaper goods are less profitable therefore depends not just on establishing that they are produced with a smaller margin of profit, allowing for the different cost of materials and labour, or with a smaller quantity of profit, allowing for the different scale of production and consumption, but on establishing that the producers themselves are able to enjoy less of the margin than they did with the finer grades in the past. Profit is not the same as value, to be sure; but how much more difficult is our assessment when we know that the enjoyment of profit by the producer is largely a matter of status and politics because of the linkages within the community and beyond it. By the same token the judgment of any decline in an industry or in the economy as a whole is fraught with difficulty: can we say that imports or any of the other changes mentioned by Pandey - migration, subdivision or fragmentation of land, indebtedness - are necessarily net depressors of the economy? They are not as certainly as they were when we began with the image of a stable, sealed community.

Milton Singer, in summarizing a symposium on occupational cultures, has concluded that a 'traditional' system is not necessarily a major obstacle to modernization, though innovators may (only may) be deviants from their culture; that modernization does not require a 'modern' ethic; and that existing cultures may be displaced or adapted but not according to whether that culture is ascriptive or achievement-oriented, parochial or cosmopolitan.[13] If the analysis in the present volume does not make our way clearer through all questions, it does help, it seems to me, with some, and in particular perhaps the rather subtle, paradoxical and even ultimately verbal distinctions which Singer has made. His views certainly differ from ours, but what is more interesting perhaps is that he and his contributors also appear to accept that the nature of a culture, apparently in its specific features rather than in its normative aspects, does influence its reaction to change, and that modernization depends upon the pre-existence of 'functionally-appropriate' cultures or flexibility in inappropriate ones. Thus Richard Fox argues that India was not inherently unprepared for capitalism but was only thought to be so because, in the nineteenth century, the British reduced a wide range of commercial activity to the level of the lowly bania, and because of what Fox considers a false Weberian dichotomy between commercial and industrial capitalism: industrialization may, according to this account, be induced *within* a 'bazar' economy and mentality.[14] But Fox, it appears on closer examination, is not denying the importance of appropriate culture, merely denying the necessary instrumentality of one culture, that of the Protestant ethic. How far do we agree? Certainly we seem to accept that there is more than one road to change and more than one kind of development. We conclude indeed that all cultures are 'appropriate', in the sense described, and, by implication at least, that development depends on the availability or adoption of goals which favour it. On the other hand, Neale's arguments can hardly be matched with Fox's speculation that the bania was merely the debased survivor of a more vital commercial life, for he had long performed necessary functions from his particular niche, and for that matter traders and money-lenders certainly remained differentiated in the nineteenth century even if not precisely as in the past. And to me it is improbable that different sets of cultural characteristics may be appropriate to a single kind of development, as might seem to be implied in Singer's conclusions. If it is agreed for the sake of argument that the Protestant ethic helped produce European-style industrial capitalism, then it is hard to argue that another radically different ethic will produce it also. (It might of course be argued that the ethic is irrelevant but that was not the point being made.) Where we seem to be at one, is in asserting that, given (as said) that there is more than one kind of development, then certainly some ways of increasing productivity, providing industrial labour, coping with a market economy, and so on, will be more suitable to some societies than others.

The idea of historical movement at different rates is akin to but less static than Braudel's idea of time: identifying the movement with external forces is, to my mind, a consequence of that model. The present discussion leads, therefore, if its conclusions are true, to the replacement of history's dialectic with dialogue.

In place of the supposed co-existence of different cultures, or of 'great' and 'little' traditions, or of opposed modes of production, we are left with a continuum through which the manner of exchange is all-important: this, it seems, is an external dimension which may not be quite the one with which we began but which is worthy of investigation.

We return to the assertion that it has tended to be assumed that the isolated Asian village provides a tabula rasa in a certain sense, in terms of trade and the input of ideas and technology, whereas it is of course already within a web of social and economic linkages and interactions. In development terms this is a conclusion of hope rather than despair: marry the appropriate input to local culture and conditions and, as in some of Shah's examples, prosperity will increase. Less optimistic, on the other hand, is the emphasis in these pages on the preference for substitution over transformation. It seems to me that this is strong evidence for the conclusion that cultural features are subsequent to but more resilient than ecological ones (if one separates them out for the sake of theory); or, to put it another way, for the existence of yet another distinction between internal and external - the external world of activities and production against the internal world of attitudes, hopes and, by extension, social customs. The former seem to change quite readily, but not the latter: cultural lag seems the ultimate conservative. Thus it is that practices may change within the mould of custom, as seen repeatedly in this volume, while the mould itself is rarely broken. Rather it decays. By this token, development must often be a slow process of attrition whereby those social features appropriate to change wear away those which are not. In a perfect world there would be sufficient wisdom, knowledge and resources to create environmental upheavals wherever they were necessary to neutralize cultural or ecological constraints on improvement. In reality prosperity seems attainable, in the short run, only by those fortunate in their physical, social or political conditions; they will not of course be the same people or regions for ever.

The objection which I am making, in terms of recent studies of rural Asia, is not just to the idealistic tradition which sees the peasantry as embodying values which the urbanized, industrial, individualistic modern world has lost (a line stretching from Rousseau, through German romantics and British jurists and Russian populists, to some of today's anthropologists).[15] It is

equally to the alternative view of the peasants as
apathetic, fatalistic and predisposed against change
(by contrast, implicitly or explicitly, with self-maxi-
mising economic man in his Western habitat). The
suggestion is that it is an error to treat the peasants
as a distinctive category apart from the rest of humanity
until disturbed by 'modernity'. There *is* a trend, a
third approach, which sees the peasantry as rational
decision-makers: it tends to replace 'they are less
advanced than ourselves' with 'they are just as mean-
natured as we are', and often implies that the fault
is not in themselves but in their stars, in their feudal,
imperialist or capitalist overlords. The arguments in
this book suggest, however, that, once we look at the
context, at rural societies' links with a wider world,
the peasantry may be found to have a common share of the
rational and the irrational, and all societies may be
seen to differ in ways specific to themselves, resulting
from the mix of cultural and physical conditions in which
they exist. We leave behind, therefore, the supposedly
inevitable consequences of isolation or subsistence, the
disabilities or advantages peculiar to a single genus,
rural Asiatic society. In the same way, and indeed in
order to achieve this perspective, we leave behind some
of the assumptions of our Euro-centric sciences: it is no
accident that, for example, Brass in his essay decries
not just inept or ignorant cultural explanations but also
Malthusian arguments which are used to justify inappropriate development strategies.

NOTES

Robb, 'The external dimension in rural South Asia'

1. 1951; reprinted in Daniel Thorner, *The Shaping of Modern India* (Bombay etc. 1980).
2. Henry Maine, *Village-Communities in the East and West* (London 1871); also quoted in the third edition (1876) by Thorner, op.cit., p.263. It is true that Maine did argue that 'the stable part of our mental, moral and physical constitution is the larger part of it': see *Ancient Law* (London 1870), pp.116-17. I shall follow this line of argument below. But Maine also believed in a necessary evolution from joint to several property, from less to more 'civilized' societies, and it is to this belief that I refer here. See also Clive Dewey's Cambridge Ph.D. dissertation (1976).
3. Gilbert Etienne, 'Asia's Rural Development with special reference to India: the village and the outside world', paper presented to the conference on the external dimension in rural South Asia, SOAS 1980; see *Kurukshetra* (New Delhi, April 1979).
4. See Eric Stokes, *The Peasant and the Raj* (Cambridge 1978) pp.4-9.
5. Stokes; ibid., pp.265 ff.
6. See Peter Robb, 'British Rule and Indian "Improvement"', *Economic History Review* 2nd series, XXXIV, 4 (November 1981).
7. See for example H.C. Brookfield, *Colonialism, Development and Independence: the case of the Melanesian islands in the South Pacific* (Cambridge 1972).
8. J.S. Furnivall, *Netherlands India: a study of plural economy* (London 1939); J.H. Boeke,*Economics and Economic Policy of Dual Societies as exemplified by Indonesia* (New York 1953).
9. The argument here is not intended to be strictly functionalist and certainly not wholly quantitative. It is something of a compromise between the two extremes recently described by Lawrence Stone, between historical writing that is descriptive, focused on man and specifics, and that which is analytical, focussed on circumstances, collectivities and statistics. Stone suggests that many historians now believe the 'culture of the group, and even the will of the individual, are potentially at least as important causal agents of change as the impersonal forces of material output and demographic growth'. ('The Revival of Narrative', *Past and Present* 85, November 1979.) The conclusion

Notes to pages 14-19

is not apt, it seems to me, for peasant studies. I would argue that, for the changes which affect peasants, the will of a single individual (amongst the peasantry) is insignificant even 'potentially', whatever that means, while both the culture *and* the material conditions are crucial, and also interdependent. Feelings or states of mind matter, but not more than other factors, from which moreover they can hardly be divorced. Perhaps we seek to understand the *personal* forces of material output and so on - which is not far, surprisingly, from a dictum of Trevor-Roper's, quoted with approval by Stone, that we should study not circumstances (and, I would add, not man) but 'man in circumstances'.

10. These questions are discussed further in the companion volume (see the Preface, above), especially by Neil Charlesworth.

11. I am indebted for this remark to James Manor.

12. See Stokes, op.cit. pp.228-242. The point of course is that the answers (apathy, casteism) given repeatedly to explain Bihar's impoverishment are not really answers at all - they are repetitions of the question - whereas answers may lie in ecological factors, probably compounded by political ones. A possible British government role is discussed in a paper of mine in the companion volume and is generally suggested by the comparative neglect of the region, in terms of official expenditure; see Stephen Henningham, *Peasant Movements in Colonial India. North Bihar 1917-1942* (Canberra 1982), pp.16-35.

13. Milton Singer, ed., *Entrepreneurship and Modernization of Occupational Cultures in South Asia* (Duke University 1973), pp.13-15.

14. Richard G.Fox, 'Pariah Capitalism and Traditional Indian Merchants, Past and Present', in Singer, op.cit.

15. See James C.Scott, *The Moral Economy of the Peasant: rebellion and subsistence in Southeast Asia* (New Haven 1976), in comparison with Samuel L. Popkin, *The Rational Peasant: the political economy of rural society in Vietnam* (Berkeley 1979), and the review of both by Jonathan Lieberman in *New York Review of Books* XXVIII, 16 (22 October 1981). In the present volume only the paper by Pandey seems much influenced by such sentiments: they led him to celebrate the weavers' sense of 'community' (p.116) which he also described as lost (p.114), and to add a moral gloss to the change in the nature of migration which he discerns in his period.

THE PLANTATION SYSTEM AND VILLAGE STRUCTURE IN BRITISH CEYLON: INVOLUTION OR EVOLUTION?

Eric Meyer

A controversy has arisen in Ceylon since the 1930s regarding the impact of the plantation system upon the village ecology. The nationalist elite, with a view to attract the votes of the Kandyan peasantry enfranchised when the Donoughmore proposals were implemented in 1931, tried consistently to make out that the plantations had a very detrimental impact on the villages: the highlands were forcibly taken away after 1840 and the villages became hemmed in by the estates as a result; with the felling of forests, climatic changes occurred, water courses became irregular, paddy-fields silted up. At the same time, a foreign enslaved immigrant population (mainly low-caste Tamils) was forced into the midst of the native Kandyan population, a tool in the hands of the British imperialists.

The British tried their best to defend their policy, on the grounds of economic development which according to them benefited the whole population. Sir Hugh Clifford, the Governor in the late 1920s, argued the case in public, but the Land Commission nominated by him, though moderate in its conclusions, nevertheless blamed the plantations for the plight of the Kandyan peasantry and recommended that the spatial growth of the plantations be altogether stopped and that the trend be reversed, with a priority for peasant agriculture. Some of its recommendations were implemented before independence, with D.S. Senanayake as Agriculture Minister.

After independence, the controversy was revived in its academic and its political aspects as well. On the academic side, several reports in the 1950s tried to substantiate the thesis of a regression in the peasant section; but during the following decade, some Ceylonese historians (especially Michael Roberts and also Lal Jayawardene) exposed the weakness of the nationalist thesis and tried to minimize the extent of the ecological change in the subsistence economy; they insisted on the responsibility of population growth for stagnation, and suggested that in the alienation of the peasantry, the Ceylonese landed class played a major part.

The political issue was closely connected with the

twin question of the take-over by government of the foreign-owned estates, and of the fate of the Indian immigrant population. The Bandaranaikes' Sri Lanka Freedom Party favoured an immediate take-over which it eventually implemented in 1972 and 1975, in some measure to take up the challenge of some of the young rebels of 1971 who went so far as to advocate the suppression of the plantation sector and the expulsion of the immigrant labourers. The policy of the present Jayawardene government is to bridge the gap between the plantation and the village, but the problem is far from being solved, and the communal clashes of 1977 have rather clouded the issue.

The aim of the present research is to ascertain some historical facts at the local level. I have mainly relied on the colonial records of the districts and of the Land Settlement Department (in Ceylon, settlement meant the delimitation of Crown and private property and had nothing to do with taxation), and have supplemented the archival information with the study on the spot of some villages and plantations. I had to select a test-district: Kegalla, on the boundary of the rubber, tea and coconut areas, was found to be best suited for my purpose, but as the Land Settlement Department was set up too late to carry its activities there, I have extended the research to the Ratnapura and Kurunegala districts which were major fields for settlement work. The research is not completed and the following remarks must be taken as hypotheses in the process of being tested.[1]

The classic essay by Clifford Geertz on Indonesia has paved the way for the study of colonial impact in ecological terms.[2] But the relations between the plantation and the village in Sri Lanka are distinctly different from those prevailing in Indonesia. According to Geertz, two ecosystems existed side by side in this region. In Java, paddy cultivation was predominant, and the plantation system was forced into the paddy-cultivation cycles by the so-called culture system, which compelled the peasants to grow by rotation on a fraction of their lands a plantation crop, usually sugar, in lieu of a land tax. (The indigo plantations in north Bihar studied by J. Pouchepadass and by C.M. Fisher present an interesting variant of the Java case.)[3] In outer Indonesia, especially Sumatra, the dominant ecosystem was based on slash-and-burn cultivation of temporary fields, and there the plantation structure was inserted as a cyst in the available space without being integrated

The Plantation System and Village Structure

as a rule into the peasant structure. In short, in Java it was rather a matter of time-sharing or contest, in Sumatra of space-sharing or contest. According to Geertz, while the sugar economy forced the rice sector of Java into a process of intensification without modernization (called by him *involution*), the rubber and tobacco plantations in the outer islands brought about a development which extended by virtue of the spread effect to the smaller producers.

But in the wet zone of Sri Lanka there existed a single ecosystem combining the two types distinguished by Geertz. Every village was, more or less, a miniature Indonesia, with a rice-producing centre and a periphery of temporary fields. The plantation structure, though it encroached on the periphery alone, affected the system as a whole.

In fact, the typical pattern of land use in the hilly wet zone was tripartite. The valley bottoms were with few exceptions occupied by paddy-fields; they were surrounded by a belt of residential gardens permanently cultivated with fruit-trees; and the gardens were themselves surrounded by an area made up of temporary fields ('chena' in Anglo-Sinhalese), of secondary forest (sometimes called *landu*) and in the remotest or highest localities, of primeval forest (*mukulana*). The whole 'outfield' was included by the British in the ambiguous category of 'waste land', though it played various essential functions in the village ecology. The lands farther from the paddy-fields were used as hunting grounds, pastures, and for gathering wild fruit and other forest produce like jaggery (obtained from the *kitul* palm), creepers, fence sticks and the like. In the chenas two different kinds of crops used to be grown: after the first burn, the more fertile and wet tracts could be cultivated with hill paddy (*el-wi*) followed the second year with millets (*kurakkan*, *amu*), while the less favoured areas were planted with millets only; all were abandoned after two or three years for a period of rest of seven to fifteen years according to the local conditions.

The frontier between the garden belt and the chenas was constantly moving on; the villager was a micro-pioneer encroaching step by step, when required by population growth, on the temporary field area to convert it into more or less permanent gardens; most chenas and gardens bore the same name with a different suffix: for example: Kitulgahawatte / Kitulgahahena (the garden / the chena of the sugar palm tree). On the other hand the frontier between the gardens and the paddy-fields was much more rigid, the hill slopes being rather rarely converted into paddy fields as compared with the situation prevailing in South East Asia (except in Uva and along the main passes leading to the heart of the Kandyan country). [4]

The proportion between the outfield area and the infield area was extremely variable. In some districts, like Kurunegala, the colonial administration considered as normal a ratio of three (chena) to one (paddy) and settled high land on the villagers according to that rule. But ratios as high as ten to one could be found in poor villages, especially in the more hilly tracts of Sabaragamuwa and of the border between Kurunegala and Matale, where certain communities (notably the Vahumpura caste) lived mainly on chena culture and forest resources. [5]

The social perception of this geographical pattern was intense. The villagers viewed the paddy area as the sphere of stability, security and legality; everybody knew the limits, the ownership, the value of each plot. A family would not as a rule alienate its paddy-fields, but only mortgage them (*ukas*) or give them out to fellow villagers on a sharecropping basis (*ande*) - two forms of alienation of use without alienation of right which were basically identical. [6] By comparison, the highlands were considered as the realm of mobility, of imprecision, of casual activities, of enterprise, and also of illegality (from the point of view of the authorities). There the arbitrary powers of the local leading families (from which the headmen were drawn) had free play, with little interference from the kings or the colonial administration of the early days. One might argue that the headmen as a class derived their wealth from the paddy-fields and their authority from the control they exerted over the margins of the village territory.

In fact, chena cultivation was by no means a secondary element in the village economy; in the dry zone where paddy cultivation was highly unreliable it was clearly the basic element. But even in the wet zone, where the rains could be depended upon, it played a major role. Chenas provided the flexibility necessary for the survival of the ecosystem; they helped in some cases, to make good the loss of a poor paddy harvest; they could yield a surplus to provide for cere-

The Plantation System and Village Structure

monial expenses. Moreover they acted as a safety valve: they afforded means of subsistence to marginal individuals (such as young couples not yet settled in village life) or to marginal communities (such as hunters, food gatherers, sugar-palm tappers).[7]

The legal status of the villages had some bearing on the condition of access of the villagers to the highlands; during the Kandyan period, and up to the 1830s, there were three categories of villages. The *koralegam*, by far the most numerous, were also the smallest as a rule; most were inhabited by the Goyigama caste (numerically and hierarchically dominant). The villagers were recognized as having full ownership of their fields and gardens. But after 1840 the British Crown asserted, at least in principle, its rights over the highlands, including the new gardens. The villagers were supposed to pay a tithe when they cultivated their chenas with *el-wi* (hill paddy), receipts were issued and a register (*wattoru* register) was kept in the district office, and this came to be considered as a register of title deeds in highlands when the colonial administration began to check the claims of the villagers especially after 1870. But as no tax was paid on millets grown in chenas, the major part of the outfield was not covered by the *wattorus* and could be confiscated by the Crown.

The *gabadagam* (royal villages) disappeared as such during the 1830s, but the Crown tried up to the end of the century to assert its full ownership of the whole of the highlands, the paddy-fields and old gardens having been sold to villagers or headmen in the 1830s. These large and well-populated villages were quite often inhabited by peasants belonging to the Duraya castes who had a low status and were deprived of any control over the local power network which was entirely in the hands of the Goyigama headmen.

The third category was more composite: it included temple villages (*viharegam* and *devalegam*) and seigneurial villages (*nindagam*); their privileges were preserved in theory, but after 1850, the investigations of the Temple Land Commissioners and of the Service Tenure Commissioners resulted in the contraction of the extent of highland under the direct or indirect control of the feudal aristocracy; while the peasants who used to cultivate 'recognized' Temple or Ninda lands retained their access to unrestricted chena cultivation, subject to the goodwill of the landlord, those who used to chena 'rejected' Temple or Ninda lands (often Duraya or Berava villagers) lost their security because they had never paid any tax and could not establish any title over their chenas.[8]

Invasion of the village territories

During the first phase of the plantation growth (circa 1840-1855) land for coffee was alienated according to a process from which the Ceylonese were almost altogether excluded. The first areas to be absorbed were the upper slopes of the highlands occupied by primeval forest or pastures taken over by the Crown under the Waste Land Ordinance of 1840. The planters selected a tract suiting their needs; they filed an application, then bought the land from the Crown at depressed prices; quite often they occupied the land and felled the forest before the purchase actually took place. The villagers sometimes obstructed the surveyors or the planters, and during the 1848 rebellion, which was not unconnected with the off-hand behaviour of many up-country planters, some estate buildings were burnt down. But the headmen soon discovered that they could derive handsome profits by countenancing the spread of the plantations, owing to their position of middlemen between villagers, officials and planters and their traditional control over the highlands. However the headmen were not the only possible middlemen: at the same time, many low-country Sinhalese and Muslim traders, carters and carpenters came into the picture, and they gave a decisive impetus to the spread of native coffee plantations.[9]

Between 1855 and 1875, for want of sufficient forest land, coffee planters began to make inroads in the chena areas, and the roots of a conflict appeared between the Crown, the planters and the Kandyan families who retained authority at the village or district level. The appearance of a high land market heralded the second phase of the plantation invasion. In the Kandyan provinces, the grain tithe was often commuted long before the compulsory commutation system was established in 1878. The headmen were usually responsible for the assessment as well as the collection, so that when a peasant was penniless or on bad terms with the authorities, the headman combined to extort a mortgage or a highland transfer in his favour. As soon as these areas became valuable because of demand from the planters, these paper titles came to be eagerly sought after by middlemen who bought undefined amounts of chena land without at first taking possession.

Meanwhile the colonial administration began to

realize that in the areas still untouched by the plantations, the extent to which chena cultivation was carried on would impair the prospects of Crown land sales to planters - a sizeable source of revenue. The district Revenue Officers, especially in Kegalla, Kurunegala and Matara, tried to check chena cultivation, often in a ruthless manner: in the words of Fr. Saunders, then Agent at Kegalla, 'this form of cultivation must be put a stop to'. The new policy resulted in near-famine conditions, and after 1873 the authorities adopted a more conciliatory position in a test region, the Three Korales (i.e. the southern half of Kegalla). A settlement was first made according to the land registers (1873-1879), but the difficulties of the task and the dissatisfaction of many villagers led a new Agent, Ievers, to evolve a scheme of block settlements: the highlands of each village were partitioned in two blocks, one for the Crown, the other for the villagers.[10]

A decisive turning-point occurred between 1880 and 1890, when the collapse of coffee ruined the British planters and those villagers who had become more or less dependent on the new product, while at the same time the compulsory commutation of the grain tax (eventually abolished in 1892) made the need for ready cash all the more pressing. In Kegalla, the Crown lost no time in selling its compact blocks to planters in search of new land to experiment with tea, and the Three Korales became for a decade or two the scene of a dramatic speculative fever. The villagers were soon the prey of a host of land-grabbers and sold out for paltry sums the chena blocks shortly before settled on them; the planters, eager to extend their estates, hired the services of land-hunters such as traders and tavern keepers in the mushroom bazaars of the Kelani Valley, of low country carpenters employed to build the factories and lines, of headmen enticed by the prospect of bribes, and of petty lawyers of Kegalla and Avissawella, outdoor proctors who thrived on the land cases multiplied by the development of the land market and the boundary disputes to which the settlements gave rise. In spite of a fresh settlement made after 1890 to curb the massive alienation of private chenas, it was too late to check a process started by the government policy itself and countenanced by the chief headmen of the Three Korales, the Ratemahatmayas Ekneligoda and later Meedeniya.[11]

The same process of land-grabbing affected most of the wet zone. In the up-country, especially Matale and Uva, the land-grabbers were the European planters in search of tea or cocoa land; in Kurunegala, their example was followed by Ceylonese speculators anxious to invest in coconut land; in Ratnapura and Kalutara, the rubber boom created an extensive speculation after 1900; and in the Matara district of the Southern Province, trafficking in land became in the 1890s a prosperous local industry carried out by Ceylonese from the coast in collusion with the headmen of the interior. In the strategy of land-grabbing, the contest for the appropriation of the value created by the intrusion of the plantation system became especially eager when the rubber and coconut booms followed the tea boom at the turn of the century. Ceylonese planters as well as European planters tried to buy land as cheaply as possible, because an extensive capital of cheap land was, with the exploitation of cheap labour, the key to the maximization of profit, especially in rubber which could not pay within the first ten years of planting. On the other side the colonial government after years of laissez faire viewed with concern the near exhaustion of the Crown lands in the wet zone and the threatening pauperization of the local peasantry. The middlemen were amassing enough capital to open their own plantations and pose as respectable members of a growing middle-class. Many Kandyan aristocratic families were selling or leasing to planters their rights over the highlands, with less and less regard to the needs of their tenants and dependants.

The new Waste Lands Ordinance of 1897 and the subsequent establishment of a Land Settlement Department were an attempt on the part of the colonial authorities to check land speculation; the new policy took shape at a period when European land-grabbing was practically over and when Ceylonese land-grabbing was at its worst: it was easier for government to take the side of the poor peasant against the mischievous Ceylonese speculator than against the powerful British planter. By that time the rising Ceylonese elite had not a sufficient bargaining power to oppose the new policy. But after 1915 the nationalist movement made it the target of virulent attacks and the Ceylonese bourgeoisie pretended in its turn to take the side of the peasantry against the Land Settlement activities. The Land Commission reviewed the whole question, and according to its recommendations, the territorial extension of plantation agriculture was definitively stopped and all available land in the wet zone reserved for village expansion: but such a conversion could not have taken

place had the Settlement Officers not saved thousands of
acres from the clutches of land-grabbers, and had the
Great Depression not killed the speculative fever of the
1920s.[12]

The disruptive impact on the village ecology

Wherever the villages have been hemmed in by plantations,
the ancient agrarian regime has been shattered and a
kind of ecological revolution has taken place. It is not
yet possible, for want of local monographs, to assess
the phenomenon island-wide, and the following remarks
are limited to the Kegalla district.

The north of the district (the Four Korales) was
well provided with paddy lands, but the commercial
activity created by the Colombo-Kandy road and the
heavy density of population led to the early disappearance of the self-sufficiency in rice (probably circa
1860). The south (the Three Korales), where human
settlements were usually small and widely dispersed,
was largely dependent on chena cultivation (especially
hill paddy), but had small paddy fields as well; while
in the north chenas were also universal.

The more sparsely-populated parts of the district
were the first affected by the early settlements of the
1870s and '80s and by the subsequent development of the
large tea and later rubber plantations. Most of the
small villages of the Three Korales were taken in the
storm of the large-scale land speculation, and reduced
to their tiny paddy-fields and their narrow garden
belts. Their demographic growth was not however stopped
and very few cases of deserted villages are on record,
while many such cases are to be found in Kurunegala at
the northern fringe of the coconut areas; it appears
that their inhabitants found alternative resources
more or less related to the proximity of the plantations. In the more densely-populated parts, the growth
of the plantations which occurred later (after 1900)
did not affect the demographic growth, which continued
at a rapid pace, but the restriction of the areas open
to village expansion led to a dramatic overcrowding
after one or two generations and subsequent unemployment. The localities where the villagers were able to
take in their own hands their economic development were
those where the absence of large plantations left the
more enterprising free to convert their chenas into
commercial crops (instead of subsistence gardens): Kinigoda Korale (northern-most of the Four Korales) is a
typical case of such an evolution.[13]

The impact of the plantations on the village ecosystem is very complex. In the Kegalla district, the silting of paddy fields was very extensive during the first years of the opening of the plantations - tea in the 1880s and 1840s in the Three Korales, rubber in the 1910s in Beligal Korale (the most western of the Four Korales). Most of the small irrigation and drainage channels on the border between the lower slopes of the estates and the village paddy fields were temporarily choked up. The only benefit for the cultivators was the free provision of manure washed down with the silt. But while in the nearby Kalutara district extensive areas appear to have been abandoned, in Kegalla less than 50 acres went out of cultivation for good, and in most cases these were paddy-fields already irregularly cultivated. The alleged drying up of springs is rather difficult to prove; but so far as I have been able to ascertain the facts at the micro-level, it seems frequently to have occurred in the areas where tea plantations came into direct contact with paddy-fields, and to have been rarer where the villages kept their garden belt intact, and where rubber plantations replaced the chenas. (This consistent differentiation should be tested over a much larger sample than mine.) I have also met several cases of planters diverting water courses for their factories (especially before 1900). Another trouble frequently alluded to was the reduction in the number of buffaloes resulting from the restriction of the grazing grounds in the highlands. Michael Roberts has argued that for the coffee period no proof can be produced of the responsibility of plantation growth for the alleged retrogression of paddy techniques, and his main argument is that buffaloes were not generally used in the Kandyan provinces: this might be true of the terraced paddy-fields up-country, but does not seem to have been the case in the numerous fields in the bottom of the valleys in the Four Korales. In general, the relation between the number of buffaloes and the growth of plantations cannot be established on a statistical basis.[14]

The only clear feature is the very frequent occurrence of cattle trespass on estate land - a major cause of ill-feeling between peasants and planters, even if it had no serious consequences on paddy cultivation, which remains to be proved. The problems resulting from the contact between the territory of the village and that of the plantation were of a political as well as economic nature. The villagers used to fence their paddy-fields and to let their cattle graze freely over the rest of the village area. When forests and chenas were converted into estates, the animals continued to wander in their favourite areas which were not enclosed as a rule, and developed a taste for young tea leaves. Some plantation workers, especially beef-eater Paraiyars, used to hunt the animals in the estate or even to lift them in the villagers. These border incidents became the source of strained relations between village headmen and planters; the peasants blamed the planters for not enclosing their estates, while the planters, resting on their western notion of property and for some of them literally obsessed by agoraphobia, resented as intolerable any presence of 'native elements in British territory' (in the humourous words of W.E. Davidson, a Civil Servant of that time); most of them would not speak a word of Sinhalese (though they spoke Tamil), many considered the village as a strange land, the hotbed of lawlessness, where 'their' coolies were led astray, attracted by illicit arrack and toddy taverns and by gambling dens. Some of them got the idea that the development of small village plantations was in every case the result of the theft of seedlings in their nurseries, and the planting lobby obtained from the colonial authorities the right to make use of corporal punishment on the spot. Many superintendents refused to let the villagers use footpaths and cattle tracks across the estates, but they never scrupled to widen their access roads to the detriment of the village gardens; the peasants sometimes retaliated by closing to the plantation workers the paths across the fields.[15]

When they were blamed for all these troubles, the planters used to retort that the estates brought prosperity to the villagers, and that the traditional system of chenaing the highlands was no less damaging to the fields. (The argument is not borne out by the facts: chenas were almost never cultivated on the slopes just above paddy fields, the peasants being careful to reserve a garden or forest belt, and the very principle of chena cultivation was to allow the rapid growth of a secondary vegetal cover, while the practice of clean weeding by the plantations led to the unavoidable erosion of the slopes.) An Assistant Government Agent of the 1920s, Hobday, epitomized the argument: 'After all, it is the capitalist who makes good use of the land, and the peasant who spoils it; the best off is the man who supplements the small returns of his paddy land and chena with good pay from a neighbouring estate.'[16]

The major change in the village ecology lies in the almost complete disappearance of chena cultivation in the plantation areas between 1890 and 1930, while the pace of population growth accelerated: the traditional ecosystem lost its flexibility at the very moment when it became more necessary. The fact has been overlooked by most scholars who focused their attention on the paddy sector and did not take into account the vital part played by the highlands in the village economy (at least in Kegalla). But what is still more important is that such a revolution did not lead to a dramatic regression, nor to an involution on the Javanese lines. Some will argue that the chenas were not really essential after all. My own view is quite the opposite: the Kandyan villagers adapted themselves by looking for resources which provided flexibility similar to that of chena cultivation.[17]

Towards a new economic system

The opportunities were not the same everywhere. In some cases, the villagers were able to get full benefit from the change; in others they could not recoup their losses; but in most they had to build up a fragile equilibrium out of complementary resources.

In the areas where land sales by the Crown or the villagers themselves to outsiders had not been extensive, and where land speculation had not broken out, the more enterprising villagers converted their chenas into small plantations. The operations of land settlement were instrumental in this adaptation, provided that there was a ready market at hand for the sale of the products.

A detailed study of the peasant bidders at the 'sale and settlement' auctions at the beginning of this century would likely reveal that a process of 'kulakization' was on its way in such areas: only a fraction of the peasantry was able to seize the opportunity, and the difficulty of financing their purchase led these enterprising villagers to mortgage their lands to moneylenders, especially to Nattukottai Chettiars who were very active in the Kurunegala district (around Narammala, Kurunegala, in the hinterland of the coastal strip between Negombo and Madampe, and to a lesser extent in the Southern Province and the Kandyan highlands). This new class was not however strong enough to overcome economic crises: between 1880 and 1890, the great bulk of the village coffee gardens disappeared; and later thousands

The Plantation System and Village Structure

of small coconut and rubber plantations which had sprung up since 1910 were caught in the dramatic 1930s depression.[18]

Kinigoda Korale, in the Kegalla district, provides a typical case of such an evolution. One of the most backward and unhealthy areas of the district, with a high incidence of malaria, a majority of villagers belonging to the depressed Batagama and Vahumpura castes, a heavy rate of crime (especially cattle stealing on the border of the Kurunegala district, and homicide resulting from drunkenness), it was entirely transformed at the turn of the century as the result of an endogenous, indigenous development. External conditions were provided by the presence of the Colombo-Kandy railway: a large slice on both sides of the line was reserved for the fuel supply of the engines, so that the government abstained from selling Crown land till coal replaced wood; by that time, the new Land Settlement policy was well established, and most of the area, being free from the larger European plantations and from the devestating activities of the Ceylonese land-grabbers, could be settled on lesser Ceylonese entrepreneurs and on villagers around 1910. At the same time, the station at Rambukkana provided an excellent outlet for the local produce: a purely indigenous trade network sprang up around it, and Muslim traders and Sinhalese merchants from the Karawa and Batgama communities fought fierce battles for the control of the market. The villagers first converted their chenas into banana, then into coconut plantations, with no other incentive than the demand; some of them became rich enough to purchase at very high prices the land put up by government 'for sale and settlement'. But after 1910 the expansion of the small plantations slowed down because it met its physical limits, and banana cultivation was affected by the 'bunchy top' disease. A process of concentration appeared, and Kinigoda was a vulnerable area, with a heavy population pressure and signs of increasing landlessness, when the Great Depression brought coconut prices to an unremunerative level; several village colonies were established for the landless after 1931 on the initiative of the local M.P. But when on the top of the depression a severe drought took place in 1934, the area was the first and the worst affected by the deadly malaria epidemic of 1934-1935.[19]

In other areas, the chenas were planted up by the villagers with rubber (for example in the central part

of the Kegalla district) and even with tea (for example
in Kotmale, south of Kandy, and around Balangoda, east
of Ratnapura) when in the 1920s Ceylonese entrepreneurs
set up numerous bought-leaf factories. The extension
of these small-scale plantations can be gauged from the
returns of the Tea and Rubber Controller during the depression, and the diaries of the officials detailed for
the task.[20]

But in most cases, for want of space and of capital,
the loss of the chenas was not balanced by a sufficient
development of village-owned plantations, so that a complex economic system evolved, based on the diversification and the more or less casual nature of the resources
resulting from the presence of the plantation. The
village economy did not merge into the plantation economy, rather it borrowed from it what was necessary for
its survival, and this limited symbiosis came to be as
essential to the new village equilibrium as chena had
been in the ancient ecosystem. The system was and is
still based on three sources of income: paddy cultivation, in many cases involving the yearly rotation of a
plot between different members of the same lineage,
according to their position in the genealogy (*tattumaru*);
garden produce, quite often marketed, especially in those
areas where the Indian immigrant plantation workers were
numerous (the spectacular development of the Sunday markets after 1910 is largely the result of this tendency);
and last, casual or regular jobs directly or indirectly
provided by the estates, such as felling the jungle,
tapping rubber, weeding on contract, cutting timber,
even tea picking, and the whole range of activities
derived from coconut and its manifold uses.

The territorial extension of the rotation system
(Kalutara, Kegalle and Ratnapura are its main areas)
has never been satisfactorily explained. I venture to
suggest that this distribution has something to do with
that of hill paddy cultivation, and with that of rubber
which in most cases replaced hill paddy: lineal rotation
cannot be a workable proposition if there is no alternative resource for the coparcener who has access to the
paddy field only once in two, three or even more years.
Hill paddy was in the ancient system a good substitute
(much better than millets); imported rice purchased with
the earnings of casual labour replaced it in the new
system.[21]

The social impact

The social changes brought about in the villages by the

The Plantation System and Village Structure

intrusion of the plantations are quite difficult to ascertain, and the following remarks are an outline derived from the study of Kegalla; detailed studies of other areas are required before one can reach definite conclusions at the national level.

At the district level, the structure of power does not seem to have undergone such a radical transformation as is often assumed. It is true that many leading families in the Kandyan areas were wiped out during the nineteenth century, and that the control by the British of the highlands, through the 1840 Ordinance and the settlements effected by the Temple Land Commissioners, deprived them of one of their traditional sources of authority. In the Three Korales, the fate of the Eheliyagoda family is a case in point; the policy initiated by F. Saunders (see above) checked the extensive felling of forests by local villagers whence Eheliyagoda Dissawa, the local chief, used to derive handsome profits in the 1860s (the timber was sold to Moratuwa carpenters or to Colombo merchants). But if one leading family replaced another, the system remained basically the same: though a faithful servant of the British, and an outsider from the neighbouring Ratnapura district, the chief headman who succeeded Eheliyagoda, Ekneligoda, was eventually dismissed because he was involved in underhand dealings with the European planters and the Ceylonese landhunters during the speculative fever of the 1880s in the Three Korales. His successor, Meedeniya, who ended his career with full honours, was a man of more humble birth who owed his position to the protection of the local Revenue Officers, but though he was appointed in the Three Korales explicitly to clean up land matters, he was in his turn involved in land speculations in the very areas where the Eheliyagodas possessed villages. [22]

The immediate subordinates of these chief headmen, the korales, who were all local men, usually got their share of the spoils, because they had the knowledge of the local situation (an essential requirement for the success of the land-grabbing strategy). In spite of several casualties usually attributable to the vicious circle of drunkenness, indebtedness and crime, most families overcame the trial.

At the village headman level, however, the establishment of the planters' raj over the highlands had more serious consequences. Some of the headmen were employed as middlemen by the planters and pocketed commissions for each sale of land by villagers to estate owners; others recruited village labour for the plantations. But they were not powerful enough to haggle with the planters like the chief headmen, they could not speak English in most cases, and they were in the hands of their superiors who could and did report against them to the Revenue Officer with every chance of being believed. Study of a small area south of Kegalla reveals the contrasting fate of the two leading families of adjoining villages. One tried to rely on its traditional influence (it even possessed a small seigneurial estate) in order to act as intermediary between the villagers and the planter. It entirely collapsed during the 1930s and left the district to take up land in a dry zone colony intended for landless villagers. The other family, though of an inferior status, was able to reinforce its power and wealth. It began by planting coconut or rubber on small plots often bought at government sales, and then took over much other land, including the major part of the other family's paddy-fields. As a next stage the family's sons were educated in order to become clerks in the local administration; they have now reached a level sufficient to send their brightest son abroad. Another has become a successful local trader. Clearly it was more profitable to emulate the planters than to traffic with them.[23]

In the same village, the ordinary peasants seem to have reacted to the intrusion of the plantation in different ways. In 1862, this small locality was inhabited, apart from the leading family, by six lineages (four Goyigama, one Batgama, one Berava). One hundred years later, the same families are still there, with a few newcomers: a group of Goyigama families related by marriage to each other and to the original leading family which has left the village, and including a son of that family who came back a few years ago to live in the crumbling dwelling of his ancestors and earns a livelihood by cutting timber; a Goyigama lineage settled in the outskirts of the territory, entirely landless and dependent for work on the estate or outside the village; two very poor Batgama landless nuclear families with only casual employment as timber sawyers; and one well-to-do Batgama group from the neighbouring village, enriched by small plantations and minor jobs in the government service, who have started buying land in the village, including some originally belonging to the leading Goyigama family. When the tea and rubber plantation was established in the 1900s, most of the families sold their chenas through the leading family and also through a well-known town proctor. The Berava lineage sold its paddy-fields as well and became dependent on estate employment at an early stage: most of its members became full-time estate workers while continuing to reside in the village, and they have rather improved their lot. The original Batgama lineage on the contrary has stuck to its fields, which are not sufficient for its subsistance but still provide a sizeable proportion of its resources. Of the Goyigama lineages, the smallest in 1882 has not multiplied locally; the largest was already marginal one hundred years ago, with tiny paddy-fields and extensive chenas: it has certainly suffered from the growth of the plantation which has arrested its spatial expansion, and the main resource of its present ten households is provided by estate employment; except for one member who has succeeded in getting access to the university, the group is impoverished as a whole and has lost a large slice of its lands to outsiders. The two other lineages have kept their paddy-fields, which are held under the rotation system and are quite insufficient as a result of population growth; but they have reacted in two opposite ways to the presence of the plantation: while one of them makes a point of not working on the estate (caste pride is among its motives) and tries to find urban jobs for its sons, the other is fully engaged in estate work and insists on its children learning Tamil. In the particular case of this village, the peasant response to the growth of the plantation appears far more complex than one might assume. For example, caste is a factor which certainly has an impact, but I am not sure that a clear-cut pattern will appear at the national level. In Kegalla, Kurunegala and Ratnapura, the lower castes seem to have been in a weaker position to withstand the land speculation activities, when their members were tenants of feudal lords or temples; but in other cases, as in Kinigoda or around Kadugannawa, the enterprise of some of their members enabled them to make the best of the opportunities offered by the new system, while many of them, undeterred by caste pride, may have improved their lot by salaried work which meant freedom from feudal dependence. [24]

In any case, the main beneficiaries of the new system were the middlemen and the investors, and most of them were outsiders from the low-country who had come to try their luck up-country, some during the coffee period, others at the turn of the century. The decisive role played by up-country enterprises in the growth of a

Ceylonese elite of low-country origin (Sinhalese as well as Muslim) has been clearly demonstrated and need not be discussed here.[25] I may add however that at the local level similar tendencies were at work in the small towns and roadside bazaars, and I suggest that the present emergence of the trading class is somehow related to small-scale land speculation during the first half of this century.

The settlement of very numerous Indian immigrant communities in the neighbourhood of most Kandyan villages is a social fact of the first magnitude in the history of the island. The history of the contact or non-contact between the immigrant and the native community is still in a large measure an unexplored field, for want of documentary evidence and of local monographs, while the inside history of the coolies begins to be better known.[26]

The reasons for the import of Tamil labour by the British coffee planters have been discussed elsewhere. The function of immigration was not only to ensure a sufficient number of labourers, but also to provide an uprooted labour force easy to control. In fact, the only serious objection raised by the planters against the employment of local villagers was that they refused to live in the lines and left the estate to look after their own interests when the occasion required; what planters called instability or indiscipline was just the refusal to be drawn into the 'new system of slavery'. But soon after the beginning of the tea boom and also during the rubber boom, the planters found that Indian labour was becoming scarce, more expensive, and more difficult to control. By that time the recruiters-cum-overseers had accumulated capital and an authority which enabled them to haggle with the planters over the supply of labour, while the new administrative requirements in the matter of social provision (health, and housing) increased the cost of labour. As many villagers by that time were looking for complementary resources, estate labour, especially rubber-tapping, became more popular. After decades of rather limited contact, villagers and planters began to need each other. In the larger tea and rubber estates where Indians were employed, the percentage of Sinhalese rose to ten per cent around 1930, and almost twenty-five per cent fifteen years later. Up-country the estates retained an overwhelming majority of immigrants and in the low-country coconut plantations local villagers predominated, but most mid-country estates, where rubber is the main product, often in association with tea, evolved a socio-economic pattern combining immigrant and villagers. There would be a nucleus of resident immigrant labour, mainly Indian but with some low-country Sinhalese, mostly from the Matara district. At a periphery would be Kandyan Sinhalese commuting more or less regularly between the village and the plantation; among these commuters were more than the average of young people, of women, and of members of the lower Kandyan castes: marginal they were in village life, marginal they remained in the plantation structure. But I maintain that their activity was nevertheless essential to the equilibrium of the village, and in a growing number of cases to that of the estate.

As far as the Kegalla district is concerned, it appears that no serious social problem resulted from the presence of numerous Tamil-speaking Hindus, with a majority of Untouchables among them, in the middle of Sinhalese Buddhist villagers with a Goyigama majority. It might be argued that these relatively peaceful relations were in fact not relations at all, or that local incidents remained unnoticed. This last argument is hardly convincing: the Revenue Officers were quite sensitive in the matter, and a comprehensive perusal of their diaries (in the case of Kegalla) from the 1860s up to the 1930s yields only a few cases.[27] When supplemented with the meagre evidence collected from other diaries and published sources, they suggest that, up to the 1930s, there was a cerain amount of antipathy and sporadic incidents of very limited extent, but that the relations were far better than those between villagers and Sinhalese workers of the plumbago mines or Coast Moor merchants. The most common occurrences were of cattle lifting and shooting on the part of the Indians, while the coolies who had to pass through the villages (messengers, beef coolies and so on) were sometimes waylaid and robbed of their gold earrings, or otherwise harassed. In addition, the few Kandyans who came to reside in the lines were regarded by the villagers with a kind of joking contempt, so much so that to live in the plantation and to be a Tamil were considered as one and the same thing: some of these Kandyans actually lost their socio-cultural identity by conforming to the dominant model, adopting Tamil names, customs and language.[28]

But if Goyigama-Tamil relations did not reach a critical stage before the late 1930s, it was not because there was no contact between the communities before them. I have already mentioned the market relations soon established between estate workers and the small village producers ready to sell them fruits, vegetables and drinks: coolies were supplied only with rice by their masters (except in the larger estates where shops were opened and workers sometimes allowed a small garden plot), and they used to barter a portion of it against materials for curry. When 'bolting' became more common after 1900, many indebted fugitive coolies found shelter with the villagers or the shopkeepers of the roadside bazaars and became regularly employed on the small native plantations, where their skills were much appreciated.[29]

However, social relations remained limited, and intermarriage extremely rare, except in the province of Uva (this curious anomaly should be investigated in depth). But endogamy was in the nature of the prevailing caste system, and had never prevented caste groups from integrating themselves as a body in the Sinhalese social structure. It was not the first time that Indians had been established in the midst of the Sinhalese areas of the island; the case of the Karawa fishermen is well known, but two other examples are more relevant to our point. The Salagama caste, originally a South Indian community of weavers, was systematically employed by the Portuguese and the Dutch to peel cinnamon, then the major export product of Ceylon, under a system of compulsory delivery which amounted in fact to compulsory labour. And, in the Sinhalese kingdoms, numerous groups were attracted from India by the kings and landlords to serve as 'soldiers and husbandmen', with the status of bondsmen; these immigrants came to be known collectively under the name of Durayas, and even if they were placed at the bottom of the hierarchy, they were fully accommodated within Sinhalese society (many kings and landlords were themselves of more or less recent Tamil origin). But under British rule, for the first time in the history of Ceylon, the integration process was altogether arrested. As in other countries, the reason for segregation may be found in the plantation system itself, in which direct control of production was based on absolute control of the worker, which under British superintendents was much more effective than any control which had been exercised in the royal or feudal villages over low-caste bondsmen. The planters wanted a submissive, punctual, amenable labour force; they therefore tried consistently to shut it up in the estate and encouraged in every respect its traditionalism, according to the general pattern in force in most of the planting and mining areas of the colonies. It is for

The Plantation System and Village Structure

example symptomatic that, in spite of the facilities given to missionaries in the island, no large-scale attempt was made to convert the coolies. Another feature of plantation life helped to maintain the separateness of the immigrant community: when tea replaced coffee, women came to be employed in equal if not superior numbers to men, with the result that immigration became a family affair and that the sex-ratio of the community made endogamy a matter of course. A last significant factor lies in the suddenness and size of the migratory movement, which was quite different from the earlier small-scale immigration, and which led to the concentration of a critical mass preventing amalgamation with Sinhalese society.[30]

A turning-point in the relations between immigrants and villagers was reached between 1930 and 1940, the result of outside influences. Among them, the first place must be given to the general tendency to communalism (affecting caste relations as well) following the granting of universal franchise and limited self-rule under the Donoughmore constitution. Although only a fraction of the Indians was enfranchised, Sinhalese politicians began to view them as potential allies of the colonial power, and some found that they could make use of the age-long resentment of the Kandyans against the take-over of their highlands by the planters, and of the contempt in which they held the Tamils. Both aspects were merged into a queer image portraying immigrant coolies as the agents of British imperialism. But other less-known factors were at work, and three of them should be mentioned here. One is the role played by enriched Tamil overseers in some areas, notably Uva, where they began to lend money to Kandyans and to buy village land as well as existing estates; the trend should not be overestimated, but it was enough to arouse the bitterness of the Kandyans.[31] Another is the attempt on the part of government and of some planters to increase the intake of Sinhalese labourers on estates. Incidents worsened when, in the face of growing discontent among Tamil workers, linked with the unsettled conditions brought about by the Great Depression and the subsequent rise of trade unionism, certain superintendents tried to employ Sinhalese workers as black-legs. On the top of it, the stoppage by India, for political reasons, of the free migration between the two countries, precipitated strikes on an unprecedented scale in 1940.[32] Another cause of dispute was the purchase by the government of estate land on which to settle landless villagers, especially in Kegalla: it happened that the Tamil workers were ruthlessly evicted when they tried to resist.[33]

What happened next is well-known: after independence, most of the immigrants became stateless, and in 1964 a 'repatriation scheme' was set up; the nationalization of the larger estates in 1972 and 1975 accelerated the pace of emigration, and the bloody pogroms which occurred immediately before and after the 1977 elections on several estates created a panic, especially in mid and low-country estates. The resulting desertion of many plantations by the Tamils is perceived by some Kandyan villagers as a kind of social decolonization, while the official policy of integration betwen village and plantation provides a certain number of jobs, usually distributed on the basis of political recommendations. However, a nucleus of workers of Indian origin is likely to remain in the larger estates, and they are to be given Ceylonese citizenship. How these will merge into Ceylonese society is another question, the issue being clouded by the increasingly tense relations between the Jaffna Tamils and the Sinhalese. But at the local level, in the particular area where I have carried out my observations, anti-Indian feeling appears to be a product imported from the towns and bazaars, whence came the rowdies who killed and burnt in 1977. The local Kandyan villagers and Tamil estate workers get on rather well in the estate or the shops.[34]

Involution or evolution?

The impact of the plantation system on village structure in British Ceylon cannot be characterized as an involution on the Javanese lines. The paddy sector never revealed the labour-absorbing capacity ascribed to it by Geertz, nor have the two sectors operated like watertight compartments as assumed by the champions of the dualistic theories first developed by Boeke in his analysis of the Javanese economy.[35]

After a traumatic phase which revolutionized the ancient ecological regime, the village sector and the plantation sector came to depend upon each other. The absence of duality was revealed during the depression years of the 1880s and the 1930s, when the so-called village sector was affected by the drying-up of the whole range of marginal resources drawn from the plantation sector. One might even argue that the very elasticity of the village economic structure was ensured by what the village could borrow from the plantation system.

The Plantation System and Village Structure

The difference between Ceylon and Java may be explained by the fact that in the ancient regime, elasticity was already marginally ensured by the peripheral extension of chena cultivation and not by the intensification of paddy cultivation at the centre. When space ran short as a result of the simultaneous growth of the plantation-controlled areas and of village population, the peasants did not rely on the intensification of paddy cultivation to make good the loss of their lebensraum. At this crucial stage, several other factors may have operated. Paddy cultivation was certainly depressed by the plantation system: ecologically (through silting for example) and moreover economically. On the labour side, the attraction of wages in cash diverted a substantial number of peasants, especially the young, from paddy cultivation usually paid for in kind. On the income side, the massive imports of Indian and Burmese rice by the planters to keep down their labour costs, depressed the price of local paddy and made it unremunerative for the Ceylonese peasants. They were altogether kept out of the market, which was entirely controlled by Indian traders. The dispersion of ownership in paddy land and the large extension of the sharecropping system may have been contributing factors: the only two districts which exported a notable rice surplus, Hambantota and Batticaloa, were quite outside the plantation area; but they were also those where property was more concentrated. While in other respects the village economy experienced an evolution, a fragile development jeopardized during each depression, in the paddy sector there was stagnation; but not 'involution'. The only similarity with the Java case lies in the complication of the system of land tenure so as to preserve the access of almost every villager to paddy cultivation, often viewed as a criterion of village citizenship; but Geertz may well be wrong when he consistently associates in his concept of involution complication and intensification.

The case of Burma as analysed by Michael Adas presents some similarities with that of Ceylon, in so far as in both countries there was an indigenous development in the commercial sector, which was ultimately jeopardized by the impact of the Great Depression and the collapse of the British imperial economic system.[36] But the great difference between Ceylon and Burma lies in the fact that the rice frontier in the Irrawaddy delta could progress unhindered by a foreign body; and also that paddy technology was familiar to the Burmese peasant and that this export commodity was at the same time a food staple. In Ceylon on the contrary, out of the three main agricultural exports, only coconut was a traditional food product, and it was coconut indeed which represented the main field for indigenous expansion. As regards rubber and tea, village expansion was in competition with estate expansion, the latter being better equipped to overcome market depressions. In these respects, the external constraints prevailing in the wet zone of Ceylon appeared less favourable to indigenous development than in Burma. I cannot follow N. Shanmugaratnam, the author of a recent paper on the subject, when he describes 'the peasant cultivating tea or rubber [as] an anachronism, a relic in the new world of estates'. Such a peasant was a product of this new world and was able, during the periods of prosperity and where the larger estates left him room for expansion, to make the most of his situation. Between 1922 and 1934, the acreage of rubber holdings of less then ten acres doubled; they accounted for 21.6 per cent of the planted area in 1934 against 13.8 per cent in 1922. The growth of the largest estates (those of more than fifty acres) was much slower (twelve per cent) and their share of the total area actually diminished from 67 to 57 per cent.[37] But, as in other countries, the small producer in Ceylon was wholly dependent on a structure and on a market over which he had no control: in the 1920s, the expansion of small-scale production progressed out of proportion with demand in all the Asian producing countries, and became a powerful if not decisive factor in the subsequent depression. At the same time, at the local level the non-peasant owners of small estates were growing in numbers and left little chance to the genuine kulak. In that historical context, I agree with Shanmugaratnam that it was impossible even for the peasant cultivating tea or rubber to become a 'dynamic small-scale capitalist' farmer, because, all things considered 'the plantation system did not permit the evolution' of such a class 'from the ranks of the peasantry'.[38]

NOTES

Meyer, 'The plantation system and village structure in British Ceylon: involution or evolution?'

Abbreviations

AGA Ke	Diary of the Assistant Government Agent Kegalla (SNLA lot 30)
ASO	Diary of the Assistant Settlement Officer (LSDR)
CO	Colonial Office Records
LSDR	Land Settlement Department Records, Colombo
SLNA	Sri Lanka National Archives
SO	Diary of the Settlement Officer (LSDR)

The paper is based on research in the SNLA and LSDR, with some information derived from the British colonial archives, Public Record Office, series CO54. A small portion of the local records is still retained in the district offices; I have explored those of Kegalla. I have also carried out a study of a small area in that district, especially a village that we shall call 'Hallinda'. The section of this paper concerning the period 1925-39 is developed in Eric Meyer, 'Dépression et malaria à Sri Lanka, 1925-1939: l'impact de la crise économique des années 1930 sur une société rurale dépendante', Doctorat Ecole des Hautes Etudes en Sciences Sociales, Paris 1980.

    1. For the historical background, see K.M. De Silva ed., *History of Ceylon*, vol III (Peradeniya, Sri Lanka 1973) especially pp.89-164. I. van den Driesen, 'Plantation Agriculture and Land Sales Policy in Ceylon, the first phase, 1836-1886', *University of Ceylon Review* XIV (1956) pp.6-25 and XV (1957) pp.36-52 inclines towards the nationalist thesis, which is assumed in the *Report of the Kandyan Peasantry Commission* (Ceylon Sessional Paper 18 of 1951) and in N.K. Sarkar and L. Tambiah, *The Disintegrating Village* (Peradeniya, U. of Ceylon 1957). L.R.U. Jayawardena, 'The Supply of Sinhalese Labour to Ceylon Plantations, 1830-1930 (Cambridge Ph.D. 1963), Michael Roberts, 'Some Aspects of Social and Economic Policy in Ceylon 1840-1871' (Oxford, D.Phil 1965) and 'The Impact of the Waste Lands Legislation and the Growth of Plantations on the Techniques of Paddy

Cultivation in British Ceylon, a critique', *Modern Ceylon Studies* I (1970) pp.157-98, are strongly critical of the nationalist point of view. The colonial policy is defended in Sir H.Clifford 'Some Reflections on the Ceylon Land Question', *Tropical Agriculturist* LXVIII (1927) pp.283-307. N. Shanmugaratnam, 'Impact of Plantation Economy and Colonial Policy on Sri Lanka Peasantry', *Economic and Political Weekly*, XVI, 3 (Bombay, 17 January 1981) is interesting for its systematic Marxist approach, but from the historical point of view, it lacks first-hand data. See also note 38 below.

2. Clifford Geertz, *Agricultural Involution: The process of ecological change in Indonesia* (Berkeley and Los Angeles 1963).

3. J. Pouchepadass, 'Planteurs et paysans du Bihar, 1860-1920' (Paris, Doctorat Ecole des Hautes Etudes en Sciences Sociales 1978), and Colin M.Fisher, 'Planters and Peasants: The ecological context of agrarian unrest on the indigo plantations of North Bihar' in Clive Dewey and A.G. Hopkins, *The Imperial Impact* (London 1978) pp. 114-31.

4. On the ancient village ecology in Ceylon wet zone, see R.Pieris, *Sinhalese Social Organization, the Kandyan period* (Colombo 1956) and H.W. Codrington, *Ancient Land Tenure and Revenue in Ceylon* (Colombo 1938). On chena cultivation, there is a very extensive documentation in the colonial records, which cannot be cited here in full; its techniques are best described for Kegalla in the Diaries and Administration Reports of the Assistant Government Agents (see especially AGA KE 14 August 1884) and its importance can be measured by the recourse to the original findings of the AGAs and Forest Settlement Officers (especially Ievers and L.W. Booth) kept in the Kegalla office, which I am exploiting village by village. At the island level, there is a wealth of information in the P.R.O. (especially CO 54/345, for 1859 and previous years), in the Administration Reports of the Central Provinces and of Kegalla, Ratnapura and Kurunegala districts before 1880 (those for the years before 1868 are among the most interesting, for example Sabaragamuwa 1864, but are not printed as such: they may be found as appendices to the Reports on the Blue Books sent to London and printed as British Parliamentary Papers, or in a manuscript form in the CO 54 series). See also the Ceylon Sessional Paper XV of 1873. The diaries and final village reports of the Land Settlement Officers, after 1898, are also very suggestive; among countless references see for example SO 21 November

1900 and 20 November 1901, concerning the Morawak korale of Matara district.

5. On the proportion between 'infield' and 'outfield' see Pieris, op.cit. p.48; AGA Ke February 1884; Administration Report Kegalla 1868, p.32 ff. Jaggery making was widely practised by the Vahumpura caste but not only by them; see CO 54/746, enclosure to despatch 756, 21 December 1911; ASO Rasaretnam, January 1933 (Kurunegala district); AGA Ke, January 1861, 16 June 1892. For Ratnapura district (a very large village, Bambarabotuwa, surveyed at the end of the 19th century) see Frederic Lewis, *Sixty Four Years in Ceylon* (Colombo 1926).

6. The sociology of paddy versus chena cultivation in the dry zone has been recently analysed by James Brow, *Vedda Villages of Anuradhapura* (Seattle 1978), p.104ff. On *ande-ukas* systems of land tenure, see G. Obeyesekere, *Land Tenure in Village Ceylon* (Cambridge 1967). My view is mainly based on Kegalla settlement village cases, and the Certificates of Quiet Possession files of Kegalla (SLNA lot 30); see also note 22 below.

7. Most authors hold that chena cultivation, at least in the wet zone, is marginal and unessential (Jayawardena, op.cit.; Roberts 1970, op.cit.). I maintain that in the wet zone (1) many hilly villages were mainly dependent on chena, and (2) in the valley it was marginal, but still essential. Most villages in the Three Korales fall in category (1), and most in the Four Korales in category (2). See AGA Ke 15 December 1864, SLNA 30/449 and 59/1352 (C.Q.P. Wattagedara file), 59/958 (Kelani Forest Reserve File), CO54/635 (Stanmore to Selbourne, 16 January 1897), and references in note 4 above.

8. On the legal status of Kandyan villages, see R. Pieris, op.cit., and Sir J D'Oyly, *A Sketch of the Constitution of the Kandyan Kingdom* (Colombo 1929): this text is perhaps based on documents collected by Molligoda Adigar ca. 1820, see CO54/137 folio 367-9. On *gabadagam* lands, see findings of the Forest Settlement Officer (L.W. Booth), on village Dorawaka, Kegalla district records (another copy in LSDR). On chena cultivation in feudal villages, see Administration Report of the Service Tenures Commissioner 1870, p.286 (J.F. Dickson). Many cases of exploitative relations are recorded (in Kegalla, the case of Ratwatte Basnayake Nilame: AGA Ke 20 June 1895 ff.). The bonded community here called Duraya is in fact a very complex group of castes (Padu/Batgam, Panna, Velli), never appropriately described by anthropologists; Bryce Ryan's classic *Caste in Modern*

Notes to pages 28-31

Ceylon (New Brunswick 1953) is very defective about them. J. Jiggins, *Caste and Family in the Politics of the Sinhalese* (Cambridge 1979) emphasizes their importance, but often uses imprecise or unverifiable and unfortunately not historical data. A.C. Lawrie, *A Gazetteer of the Central Province of Ceylon* (Colombo 1897) is useful. Much historical evidence is scattered in district records or local lore.

9. Van den Driesen, op.cit.; A.C.L. Ameer Ali, 'Peasant Coffee in Ceylon during the XIXth century', *Ceylon Journal of Historical and Social Studies* n.s. II (1972) pp.50-9. The earliest case of village land sale is in Gampola (G. Bird's estate); see CO 416/3 (A.22). For villagers' attitudes see CO 54/261 (despatch of 5 December 1849), CO 54/196 (desp. 18 April 1842); P.D. Millie, *Thirty Years Ago, or Reminiscences of the early days of coffee planting in Ceylon* (Colombo 1878) ch.XX; and British Parliamentary Papers, Reports from the Committees, vol.XII (1850) 5 June 1849 s.3185 (evidence of George Ackland on the 1848 rebellion). The headmen's role is clear in CO 54/282 (despatch of 5 December 1851 no.191, enclosure no.4, G.A., Kandy, to Colonial Secretary, 16 November 1951); also CO 54/237 (despatch no.54 of 17 July 1847), and in several instances in Kegalla: AGA Ke 2 November 1854, 2 October 1859, 8 January 1860, 7 September 1861.

10. For Saunders see AGA Ke 1 October 1864, and also AGA Ke for 1864 and 1865. On famine see Administration Report, Matara district, 1868, p.233; for the restriction of chena cultivation: Administration Report, Ratnapura district, 1868, pp.18-22. See K.M. De Silva (ed.), op.cit., p.130, on early chena settlements in Kegalla. A detailed study of my own is forthcoming.

11. See note 10, and SLNA 59/178 (land sales by villagers) and Certificate of Quiet Possession files in Kegalla (SLNA lot 30, especially the cases of Udabage 30/574 and Padugama 30/495 which show the conflict of interest between the Crown, the planters, the speculators and the peasants.) Also SLNA 45/1867.

12. On land speculation and land policy up to 1930, see the very stimulating analysis of L.R.U. Jayawardena, op.cit.; LSDR, partially exploited in ibid. and mainly on Matara, Kurunegala and Ratnapura; and SLNA 59/178 (for Kegalla, Uva, Matale and Kurunegala). The last areas to to 'opened' for rubber, and where land-grabbing reached phenomenal proportions, were the Kukul korale of the Ratnapura district and the Kelerata (S.E. corner of Kegalla).

13. On deserted villages in the North Western Province, see Administration Report, Puttalam district, 1928, p. F.16; ASO Fox 3 March 1906; ASO Bassett 12 June 1929; ASO Seneviratne 4 January 1933. In Kegalla, there are several cases of villages encircled by estates as early as the 1880s (for example AGA Ke 9 April 1884, 18 March 1885), but only one blatant case of a plantation destroying a village (Dabar Estate in the Kelerata): AGA Ke 10 April 1931, SO 18 January 1930, and Land Commissioner Department Records, Colombo, file L.212).

14. On the ecological impact, see Michael Roberts, op.cit. 1970, which I cannot discuss in detail here. He argues that the effects of the contraction of pasture have been exaggerated, but this is not supported by many statements he cites himself (see also AGA Ke 13 May 1854); the idea *was* a contemporary common-place and cannot be proved. Nor can the climatic changes brought about by deforestation (see Millie, op.cit, ch.II, and J.E. Tennent, *Ceylon*,II, p.206). But the silting of paddy fields is too often reported to be easily dismissed. There are repeated references (I have at least 80 between November 1872 and July 1938) in AGA Ke, and others may be found elsewhere, for example in Administration Reports: Matara 1927, p.C.23('a whole valley permanently ruined in Morawak'), Ratnapura 1926, p.I.9, and 1933, p.I.7, Kandy 1926. See also Ceylon Sessional Papers IV and XIV, 1890 (Kalutara district seems to have been the worst affected); SO October 1933, ASO Hunter, March 1928, ASO Egan 11 April 1927, ASO Rajasingham October 1933. In these cases rubber was planted on paddy-fields; in other cases, notably near Dandagamuwa, Kurunegala district, it was coconut: ASO Luddington, February 1927. For a general view of the question, Ceylon Sessional Paper III of 1931 (Soil Erosion Committee). In AGA Ke, the most numerous cases gather round the dates of tea and rubber estate opening, and round 1930 when the problem attracted public attention.

15. On cattle trespass, see J. Capper, *Old Ceylon* (London 1878), p.143; *Days of Old, or the Commencement of the Coffee Enterprise in Ceylon, by an Old Planter* (Colombo 1878), p.14; Report of the Committee on Cattle Trespass (Colombo 1853), CO 54/309. Among references from Kegalla are AGA Ke 21 February and 11 November 1885, 21 February 1886, 20 August 1890, 4 February 1900, 10 March 1902, 15 November 1914, 14 September 1916 and SLNA 6/10990 (Petition included in G.A. Sabaragamuwa to Colonial Secretary, 18 October 1897. W.E. Davidson (AGA Ke 16 March 1891) was certainly the most perceptive and

Notes to pages 34-5

able Agent in Kegalla; he later became Governor of the Seychelles, Newfoundland and New South Wales. On border incidents, right-of-way problems and tense planter-villager relations see AGA Ke July and August 1884, 3 July 1885, 11 July 1891, 10 September and 8 December 1892, 2 May 1898, 29 October 1910, 30 July 1914, 1 June 1916, 17 February 1917, 28 September 1931; concerning more precisely 'Hallinda' estate, AGA Ke 8 June 1925, 20 June 1929 and 27 October 1936, confirmed by local tradition (1979). In Kegalla, the anti-Muslim riots of 1915 were followed by the shooting of low-country Sinhalese shopkeepers and a Kandyan headman by the European militia which included many planters: the violence seems related to the earlier tension.

16. SLNA L 62/1928 (Reports of the Revenue Officers on the third interim report of the Land Commission - Report by the AGA for Kegalla, Hobday). For a similar analysis, see Administration Report, Matara, 1928, p. C. 34, S.157, and SLNA 59/1074 (J. Malcolmson to the Governor of Ceylon, 10 August 1904).

17. Here I agree with Michael Roberts, op.cit. (1970), pp.181-2, on the 'modification in the economy' but I am sceptical that diversification 'may even be considered an improvement'.

18. On villagers' purchases of Crown land, LSDR are very full (and as yet unexploited). Patrick Peebles, 'The Transformation of a Colonial Elite, the Mudaliyars of XIXth century Ceylon' (Ph.D. Chicago 1973) is very interesting on the low country headmen. On kulaks and land settlement see SO October 1903 and 20 December 1904, SLNA 59/1684A (Report by SO Fox, 1 July 1906). Land for plantain and coconut was purchased by some villagers at more than 200 rupees an acre (AGA Ke 20 May 1899, 8 May 1903, 24 July 1906, 9 August 1907, 8 May 1908 etc.). But indebtedness and the sources of money are easier to imagine than to study; SOs in 1930s show that peasants could not purchase Crown land even at reduced prices (cf. ASO Sandys June 1930, ASO Rasaretnam December 1932), and numerous judicial sales especially in Kurunegala district. It is hard to distinguish between peasant and non-resident small owners among debtors, but I conclude that the Nattukottai Chettiar are responsible for a very large proportion of sales in the North-Western and Central provinces, especially early in the depression; their role in expropriation should not be overestimated in spite of contemporary anti-Indian propaganda. Later, and also in areas where the Chettiars were not numerous, small sums were almost invariable lent by well-to-do

Notes to pages 35-9

Sinhalese: the expropriation of the peasantry probably benefited the new petite bourgeoisie from which the present *mudalai* (trading) class is partly drawn. For a fuller discussion see my thesis, and its appendices, especially the interview with N.H. Keerthiratne of Rambukkana (1978).

19. On Kinigoda korale, see the Final Village Reports of the area settled along the railway (LS R), diaries of F. Lewis and L.D.C. Hugues (ASOs in the 1910s and 1920s), AGA Ke, especially 17 November 1904, 21 September 1905, 21 April 1907, 24 August 1910. For peasant settlement schemes of Wijeyeratne, see AGA Ke 5 September to 30 May 1931, interviews with Tissa Wijeyeratne (1977-8) and N.H. Keerthiratne, whose father was one of the most successful entrepreneurs of Kinigoda (1978). On malaria, see my thesis, part III.

20. Administration Reports of the Rubber Controller and Administration Reports of the Tea Controller, especially 1938. See also Administration Report of the eee Registrar of Cooperative Societies 1933, ASO, Aluvihare 4 April 1930, Administration Report, Nuwara Eliya, 1925, p.B.27-8.

21. Obeyesekere, op.cit.; M.P. Moore and G. Wickremasinghe, *Thattumaru, Kattimaru, Systems of Land Tenure* (Colombo 1978).

22. For Eheliyagoda see AGA Ke 5 May 1857, 3 August 1863, 5 October 1864 ff; for Ekneligoda, AGA Ke 3 June 1893, 17 April 1894, and SLNA 30/572 and 573 (cases of underhand dealings); for Meedeniya, AGA Ke 17 January 1904, 4 June 1923, 15 September 1925, 19 November 1925, 11 January 1927, 22 February 1927, and interviews in the Kegalla district and Colombo, with an ex-korala of Uduwe and with Dr N.M. Perera (1978).

23. Interviews, Kegalla district, 1978 and 1979. For 'Hallinda' and its neighbouring estate, see also SLNA 30/540 (C.Q.P. case), 33/7291 (Grain tax register for 1882) and the private archives of the estate.

24. See notes 5 and 8 above, and interview of N.H. Keerthiratne (1978): 'The depressed classes were not given any responsible position in the country. Their job was planting: for that there is no objection. We had lands all over - jungle lands. We started cultivating.' (See my thesis, vol.2, pp.79-81.) On caste and salaried labour, there is scattered evidence in Administration Reports, Sabaragamuwa, (for example 1868 app.A, p.25). In the Kolonna and Atakalan korales, where the Vahumpura are especially numerous, estates employed Sinhalese labourers from an early date.

25. See Michael Roberts' very useful 'Elite Formation and Elites, 1832-1931', in K.M. De Silva, op. cit., pp.263-84.

26. D. Wesumperuma, 'The Migration and Conditions of Immigrant Labour in Ceylon, 1880-1910' (Ph.D. London 1974) and 'Unindentured Indian Labour Overseas: Plantation Labour in British Ceylon' in *Asie du Sud, traditions et changements* (Paris, Colloques internationaux du Centre National de la Recherche Scientifique 1979) pp. 469-76; E.Meyer, 'Between Village and Plantation: Sinhalese estate labour in British Ceylon', ibid., p.459-68.

27. In Kegalla, the only recorded clashes are AGA Ke 24 June 1873 (Pelampitiya), 18 March 1885 (Gangwarily), 19 December 1891 (Dolosbage), 16 August 1893 (Walagam), 25 May 1917 (Mapitigama: but involving low-country Sinhalese coolies and *not* Kandyan villagers), 10 September 1925 (Debatgama: the only serious case). However on 5 October 1914, the AGA wrote: 'The Kandyan villagers are rather fond of having a little sport (*sic*) with the T mil coolies, and it is a matter of great difficulty to bring home offences in such cases, since the headmen never fail to support their fellow villagers.' See also Mary Steuart, *Everyday Life on a Ceylon Cocoa Estate* (London 1906) p.79.

28. E. Meyer, op.cit. (1979); and see N.Shanmugaratnam, op.cit., p.79.

29. On economic relations between immigrants and villagers: Frederick Lewis,op.cit., p.192, Administration Report, Sabaragamuwa, 1881, Ceylon Sessional Paper II of 1893, p.4 (evidence of the planter Young), *Report and Proceedings of the Labour Commission* (Colombo 1908) pp. 7, 34, 38, 329, 361, 458, 465, 597; SLNA 59/2693 (half-starved fugitive Mahratti coolies from a Ratnapura estate obtaining work and shelter in the villages on their way down to Colombo); *India*: Report of the Agent of the Government of India in Ceylon for 1934, p.19; AGA Ke 3 January 1935 ('Tamil is understood by a large majority of Sinhalese villagers'); interview with Dr N.M. Perera (1978).

30. See B.H. Farmer, *Ceylon, a Divided Nation* (London 1963); M. Roberts, 'Indian Estate Labour in Ceylon during the Coffee Period 1830-1880', *Indian Economic and Social History Review* III, 1 and 2 (March and June 1966).

31. On Tamil overseers and land see SLNA L 615/1929 (Petition of A.M.N. Banda about Idamegama in Udukinda and subsequent inquiry); SO 20 August 1928 (Maliyadda); ASO Abeyakoon 25-27 April 1934 (Diyabokadare: 'There

Notes to pages 43-6

appears to be plenty of bad feeling in the village over these land matters. The villagers complain that as a result of their protesting against the encroachments by the estate Tamils they are not given work on the estates. The Tamils complain that the villagers are threatening to do them bodily harm and are generally behaving in a manner calculated to disturb the hitherto peaceful character of these villages'; ASO Seneviratna, August 1933.) The lists of estate owners in the *Ceylon Ferguson Directories* of the 1930s are also very suggestive. For particular cases see for example Ceylon Government Gazette 13 September 1929, p.912, and 20 August 1937, p.891.

32. CO 54/974 and 975 (very voluminous reports by the Controller of Labour, F.C. Gimson, 1940-1).

33. One such case is that of Knavesmire estate: see CO 54/988 and interview with Dr N.M. Parera (1978). On the history of these early take-overs, see Gerald Peiris, 'The Current Land Reform and Peasant Agriculture in Sri Lanka', *South Asia*, 5 (December 1975). The Kegalla district office holds very detailed files on each of these estates (Village expansion files, series LK).

34. On the riots, see 'Race Relations in Sri Lanka', *Logos* (Colombo) vol.16 (April 1978). In 'Hallinda', some villagers went so far as to give shelter to the Indians to help them escape the killings.

35. Clifford Geertz, op.cit.; J.H. Boeke, *Economics and Economic Policy of Dual Societies* (Amsterdam 1953).

36. Michael Adas, *The Burma Delta: Economic Development and Social Change on an Asian Rice Frontier* (Madison 1974). Stagnation in the paddy sector was explained thus by a Ceylonese official: 'The yield is poor where the fields adjoin cart roads; the labour spent in producing and marketing is not sufficiently rewarded. When the price of commodities rose, paddy retained its original value and the agriculturist was never well-to-do' (ASO Rasaretnam, February 1934).

37. N. Shanmugaratnam, op.cit., p.73; Administration Report of the Rubber Controller for 1938, appendix A p.T8.

38. N. Shanmugaratnam, op.cit., and see my thesis, conclusions. L.A. Wickremeratne, 'The Establishment of the Tea Industry in Ceylon, the first phase (c.1870-1900)', *Ceylon Journal of Historical and Social Studies* n.s. II, 2 (1972) especially pp.138-51, is quite useful on Ceylonese small holdings, Sinhalese labour on estates, and land sales by villagers before 1900; it uses only printed sources. See also V. Samaraweera, 'Land, Labour, Capital and Sectional Interests in the

Notes to page 46

National Politics of Sri Lanka', *Modern Asian Studies* 15, 1 (1981) was published after this essay was written, and discusses many of the same issues. I agree on the whole, but, first, I would give more emphasis to the indigenous development of small-scale plantations before 1930, and secondly, I would add, on the inherent contradiction in the position of the nationalists about land, that there were numerous cases of politicians involved in land-grabbing activities, either personally or through their family. SOs in the 1920s are full of such stories: among others, G.E.Madawela, Victor Corea and Ch. Batuwantudawe are called 'notorious land-grabbers' (by officers undoubtedly anxious that the colonial land policy would be upset). One, though I would not go so far, even claimed that the land-grabbing class and the political class were synonymous. Many politicians were not involved - in Kegalla, E.A.P. Wijeyeratne for example - while some of the closest collaborators of the colonial regime were: in Kegalla, Meedeniya Adigar was implicated in very extensive dealings with one of the most prominent speculators of the time, A.J. Vanderpoorten. A third point: the hostility shown by many Kandyans towards immigrant Indians was not only the reflection of political attitudes at the national level; it was also, and perhaps mainly, the reaction to extensive land purchases by enriched overseers, which are mentioned in the local monographs included in the Kandyan Peasantry Commission Report. One such case in LSDR is that of the villages of north Udukinda (Uva Province), just below the extensive tea estates of the Kirklees.

WAGE-GATHERING: SOCIO-ECONOMIC CHANGES AND THE CASE OF THE FOOD-GATHERER NAIKENS OF SOUTH INDIA

Nurit Bird

In his 1976 Malinowski lecture Bloch critically considers the approaches to the theoretical explanation of social change of both the Structural Functional school of thought,[1] and the French Marxist work (mentioning Meillassoux, Terray and Godelier). The former follows the Durkheimian notion of the social determination of concepts and is therefore faced with the problem that 'this leaves the actors with no language to talk *about* their society, and so change it, since they can only talk *within* it'.[2] The latter follows Marx's notion of the infrastructure which is considered as 'totally external to either rules or concepts'; changes are said to take place at the level of the infrastructure, but for the infrastructure 'to be a source of criticism of the social order it means that people must apprehend it in terms available to them and which are different from and incompatible with those of the dominant social theory'.[3] To an extent, and as Bloch presents it, the Structural Functional and the French Marxist schools follow opposite directions - 'either they see the social process in terms used by the actors and so are unable to explain how it is that actors can change these terms, or they see the mechanism of change as occurring in terms totally alien to the actors and so are unable to explain how these mechanisms can be transformed into meaningful action'.[4] Common to both approaches, however, seems to be the underlying problematic issue of how external changes, whether outside or already in the infrastructure of the society, are transmitted into people's thought and action or, in short, how the external changes are internalized.

This paper is centred on a particular case study,[5] the features of which make it suitable both for the demonstration of the explanatory relevance of the above approaches, and for the consideration of the problem underlying them. The case is that of the food-gatherer Naikens and their interaction with the plantation opened in their locality. It is a suitable case or 'experiment' as it were, for four reasons. First, it offers a manageable scale: as is typical of a certain type of hunter-gatherer society, the society in question is characterized by both a very small population and a simple culture. Second, it gives a clear-cut identifiable reaction - the range of changes undergone by this society is outstanding: from the most primitive hunter-gatherer economy at one end of the scale of economic development, to the modern cash economy. Third, there are minimal interfering restrictions - there are favourable circumstances in that the people have had their traditional means of livelihood relatively intact and their habitat not overcrowded, and have therefore had a certain choice in their response to the external developments. Consequently, fourth, there is a control group - while some of the people have undergone changes, part of the society has maintained to a significant extent the traditional mode of life and can act as a control group. It is impossible here to explore the response to the external changes in the manifold aspects of the culture in question.[6] The economic domain, and in particular the social relations embedded in it, is the aspect discussed here as it is most susceptible to changes resulting from the new economic possibilities, and is of particular relevance to the discussion above in view of the French Marxist explanation. The scope of the paper dictates that the main focus is laid upon this ethnographic aspect of the case itself, and only in conclusion are its general implications drawn.

The Naikens are a food-gathering group of about 1000 people, inhabiting forested areas in the Nilgiri - Wynad region of South India. (In the literature on the Nilgriris tribes they have often been referred to as Jenu Kurumbas, but Naiken is the name used by themselves and their immediate neighbours.) During 1979 fieldwork was conducted among one local community of about 70 people distributed in five hamlets spread throughout an area of approximately 5000 acres. During the latter part of the nineteenth century, a Scottish company cleared 500 acres in this area for a rubber plantation, here referred to as the Gir plantation. The plantation was surrounded by forest and was only accessible by a steep and narrow forest path. At first the Naikens were hardly affected. Labour was brought in during the dry season to tap and process the latex. Naikens were occasionally engaged to clear jungle tracks and weed between the rubber trees, but only during the rainy season. Significant changes took place in the 1950s. Coffee bushes, fruit trees and spices were planted, and a need was created for weeding work throughout the year. The cost of bringing outside labour increased as a result of the 1951 Labour Act, and the demand for weeding labour was therefore directed towards the local Naiken population. The latter were in any case better than the migrant workers at unskilled tasks in the jungle terrain. A mud track, usable only in the dry season but nevertheless jeep-worthy, was opened, and the seasonal workers moved in permanently with their families. From the 1960s to the 1970s some clearing and felling operations took place in the 4500 acres of forest surrounding the plantation, but the changes were limited in extent and imposed only relatively minor obstacles to the viable execution of the traditional Naiken forest-based subsistence. Over the last 30 years Naikens therefore had the choice of either working in the plantation and/or maintaining their traditional means of livelihood. Indeed only some have been involved with plantation employment throughout this period. At present (that is, from September 1978 to September 1979) about two-thirds of the adult Naikens studied are involved with regular plantation work, while the remaining third still live by the traditional mode of subsistence. The former still occasionally practise the traditional foraging and collecting for trade - often during weekends, holidays and the high season for tradable forest produce. But by and large they are integrated into the plantation world and its wage employment; are members of trade unions; are entitled to pension schemes etc. They can therefore be considered as belonging to the world of wage employment, the cash economy, and bureaucratic industrial organization.

   This analysis is concerned with the socio-economic developments which have followed these occupational changes in the period 1950 to 1979. Discussion is focused on those Naikens who took up plantation employment (in the paper referred to simply as Naikens). The changes, or lack thereof, are measured against the traditional economy still practised to a considerable extent by their present food-gatherer counterparts. Both sub-groups profess an economy 30 years ago similar to that of present food-gathering Naikens. This verbal evidence is further supported by a short investigateion conducted among an intact Naiken community in a neighbouring locality. Furthermore, the picture portrayed by the life of the present food-gatherer sub-group, and which is conjured up from all Naikens' accounts of the past, accords in its broad lines with that which is depicted both in the work of Morris, Gardner and

Ehrenfels on other food-gatherer tribes in South India, and in the literature of other hunter-gatherer societies especially in the work of Woodburn.[7] For brevity (and with no other implications) the past tense and the adjectives 'traditional' and sometimes 'pre-existing' are used in referring to the food-gathering mode of life, while the present tense is reserved for the wage-labourer Naikens.

The essence of the traditional food-gatherer Naikens can best be conveyed by using three important characterizations of hunter-gatherer societies. The Naikens unquestionably belong to a type of hunter-gatherer societies which has been categorized in the literature, by Woodburn as an 'immediate return system',[8] by Gardner as 'extreme individualism',[9] and by Sahlins as the 'Zen road to affluence'.[10] Woodburn refers by his term, among other features, to an immediate return for labour and immediate consumption, both contrasting with the intrinsic delay in return for labour and delayed consumption which characterize the agricultural system; a lack of investment in capital or storage facilities; and the general lack of concern about the past and the future.[11] Woodburn describes the way of life which is tied up with 'an immediate return' system as follows:

> Individuals and groups go out for part of most days to obtain their food and other requirements which are then consumed for the most part on that particular day or casually over the days that follow. Members of such societies avoid long-term commitments in using their labour, and they are not concerned to develop stores of food or other possessions; even their tools and weapons and other technical items used in obtaining food and other requirements are, in general, of types which do not involve a substantial involvement of time.[12]

Gardner covers by his term, among other features, the lack of cooperation and competition between individuals; 'a very strong expectation for autonomy',[13] and a reluctance to be controlled by others. Sahlins contrasts the 'Zen strategy' which departs from the premises that 'Human material wants are finite and few, and technical means unchanging but on the whole adequate', or crudely speaking the minimalization of needs to meet available means, with the 'Galbraithian way' of the West, which assumed that 'man's wants are great, not to say infinite, whereas his means are limited, although improvable', or

Wage-gathering

crudely speaking the maximization of material means in an attempt to satisfy ever-growing needs.

The change from a primitive hunting-and-gathering economy into a modern cash economy seems a fundamental one. But viewed away from the plantation, in their hamlets, one cannot distinguish between those Naikens who are plantation workers and those who are still by and large hunter-gatherers. Close familiarity with the group also reveals that the social cohesiveness of the community as a whole has indeed been retained in almost every respect. Through the separate discussion and closely magnified analysis of three areas of the present economy - I. Production, II. Consumption and III. Distribution (money and exchange) - this statement is explored, and the proposition argued that the changes are not as fundamental as they seem.

Production

Naikens work in the plantation in one of two categories: permanent employment and casual employment. The distinction between these two categories was defined in 1964 in order to protect what were then called the 'non-act' employees, that is, those employees who were not covered under the 1951 Labour Act with its detailed regulations concerning work conditions and the rights of employees. While a permanent worker was simply defined as one who is engaged in work on a permanent basis, an important distinction was made between the temporary and the casual labourer. The temporary worker was defined as one who is engaged temporarily for a specific period or for work of a temporary nature not exceeding six months; while the casual worker was defined as one who works regularly on the estate, but not exceeding fifteen consecutive days, and with no obligation to report for work daily. Under regulations, both the permanent and the casual labourers have the right to a minimum of 54 and 40 hours of work per week respectively for adults and adolescents, one rest day each week and national holidays, sickness allowance and medical facilities. In addition, on certain plantations (including the one studied) workers are entitled to an annual bonus calculated as a percentage of the annual earned salary of each worker - the percentage negotiated between planters and trade unions according to the former's profit. Unlike the casual worker, only the permanent workers are entitled to a provident fund (created by a monthly contribution of worker and employer), and to a gratuity which is paid to employees on retirement in accordance with the number of years of service. Similarly, only the permanent workers have the right to be provided with accommodation, supplied with drinking water and latrines; and only the permanent female worker has the right to a paid maternity leave of twelve weeks.

Table A shows the distribution (percentages) of employable Naikens by category of employment for all employables; for female employables alone; and for male employables alone. At present there are 69 Naikens in the five hamlets within walking distance of the plantation. Old people and children excluded, there are 33 adults who can potentially work. Of these employable Naikens 36 per cent are not connected at all with wage work in the plantation; the remaining 64 per cent are the subject of this paper. The majority of then (72 per cent) are casual workers, while only 28 per cent (or 18 per cent of all employables) are permanent workers. It is noteworthy that while 75 per cent of the men work in the plantation, almost all of them (92 per cent) are casual labourers, whereas only about half of the women work (53 per cent), but more than half of these (54 per cent) are permanent workers.[14]

To explain the general predominance of the casual status, yet at the same time to account for the different patterns which are reflected in the employment of men and women, it is necessary to pinpoint other indicators of involvement in work. Categories of employment only reflect an annual registration of workers in the plantation. They do not reflect the regularity of, or fluctuation in, attendance at work. Tables B and C provide the actual number of workers and the average number of days each of them worked in a month, for February and July. These months represent two extremes in the seasonal cycle of forest subsistence. In the dry month of February forest produce is abundant. Soap nut can be collected for trade; wild yam is available; and the honey season is just about to start. During the wet month of July forest subsistence is least viable. Tubers and berries are hard to find; walking in the leech infested and muddy forest is to be avoided. Tables B and C clearly show that attendance during February is only about half that of July. Table C further confirms the findings of Table A, that is, not only with regard to categories of employment, but also when it comes to actual attendance at work - half of the women who worked during these two months were permanent, whereas the majority of men (94 per cent) were casual labourers. A second peculiar feature however appears. Against the expectation that the permanent workers work on average more days in a month than the casual ones, Table B shows that for both male and female, for February and July, casual workers on average worked more days than the permanent workers (for example, permanent female workers worked on average nine days in February while their casual workmates worked fifteen).

The distribution of Naikens' categories of employment is not merely a certain phase in the often presumed progress from a non-employed to a temporary, to a casual and, finally, to a 'permanent' status. A different pattern is revealed by the data. Until 1958 no Naiken was in the permanent position. From 1958 to date 27 Naikens have all been employed at one time or another as permanent; at present only six still are. Table D shows the distribution of workers according to length of permanent employment, that is Naikens who ceased their permanent term. The mean is five years; the mode is only one year. It is also significant that five of the six present permanent employees entered employment only in January 1979, while the remaining one (a woman) has been a permanent worker for the last seventeen years. It is important to look at what alternative occupations people moved to when their permanent employment ceased. Unfortunately, at present, of the 21 Naikens, seven are either dead or no longer in the area. Table E shows the present position of the remaining fourteen: four are too old to be employed; eight out of the ten employable people have moved to casual employment, while the other two ceased their employment completely. It is noteworthy that the average period of permanent employment for those moving from the permanent position into a casual one was seven years, and that they all chose to resign from their permanent status. It would appear then that over time there is a tendency among employable Naikens to move away from the permanent position, showing a preference for the casual position.

Four features thus stand out in the analysis of Naikens' involvement in plantation work, and pose queries which are to be explained. First, the majority are involved with casual labour. Second, there is a greater popularity of permanent employment among women than among men. Third, the permanent worker on average works fewer days in a month than a casual one (although over a year he works more). Fourth, there has been a tendency over time to move from permanent to casual employment. It can be suggested that the explanation for this syndrome of features lies with the management's strategy; that is, that the management favours employing the Naikens as casual labourers rather than as permanent workers; that if they give Naikens a permanent status their preference is shown to women; and that when possible they dismiss the permanent Naiken employees. The combined examination of the development of labour organization and work conditions in South Indian plantations in general, and the development of the structure of tasks required in the plantation in question, would appear to cast doubt upon this hypothesis.

During the first half of the twentieth century a significant majority of South Indian plantation workers were immigrants to the plantation areas from other regions. They were recruited by, worked under, and were paid by 'maistries', having no direct contact with the management. In the Gir Rubber Estate they worked only during the dry season, and when the rains started went back to their villages. Only very temporary and rudimentary accommodation was offered in the plantation area and most, if not all, workers left their families behind. With the 1951 Plantation Labour Act the 'maistries' system was abolished. Plantation managements were invested with the direct responsibility for their employees, and were subjected to detailed regulations including giving daily regular work, and hence permanent employment, and providing and maintaining adequate housing accommodation supplied with drinking water and latrines for all immigrant workers. From the management's point of view therefore it has become more economic to employ local workers. Only Naikens were local to the Gir Plantation Estate.

There are generally three categories of tasks in the Gir Rubber Estate: tapping; smoking and packing the latex; and weeding. While the latter is a blanket term for a variety of unskilled tasks, the first two are specialized tasks. Tapping is a skill which until recently, and still by and large today, is handed down from father to son. Smoking and packing the latex - locally and here referred to as 'factory' work - is a semi-skilled task which can be taught through work but requires regular attendance. Most of the non-Naiken male workers are employed as tappers or factory workers. Some Naikens were encouraged to take up factory work but avoided it. Non-Naiken female workers tend to work as weeders, but the majority of weeding work is done by both male and female Naikens. Over the last 30 years the proportional position of the different categories of tasks within the overall plantation work has undergone changes. Essentially, until 1948-9, there was a major need for tapping and factory work, and only occasionally was weeding required. In the 1950s, with the introduction of coffee and fruit (at the expense of ageing rubber trees), came a greater need for diversified non-skilled jobs and less need for tapping and factory work. Table G shows tapping and factory work in 1948-9 as about two-thirds and weeding about one-third of the range of work required; in 1978-9 the former occupied less than a third and the latter more than two-thirds of the work performed in the plantation. It is the Naikens who are both better than the other workers in the performance of these increasing tasks, and locally available to be called upon, since the majority of the non-Naiken workers are tappers and factory workers.

The administrative personnel are well aware of a certain dependence upon Naiken labour, and express it by and large by an explicit willingness, and in many cases direct encouragement, for Naikens to take up responsible tasks and permanent positions in the plantation. Thus it is the supply of labour rather than the demand for labour which influences the actual involvement of Naikens in the work of the plantation, and Naikens themselves indeed give an explicit expression of their preferences. To understand Naikens' perception of the world of the plantation and their approach to employment within it, it is necessary to look at their traditional socio-economic structure, and within its framework to consider aspects of work in the plantation. The possible usefulness of such an examination is suggested by the above but is also hinted at by the fact that whereas other food-gatherers in South India have responded negatively to government attempts to settle them into agricultural life - attempts which were accompanied by explanations and clear material incentives —[15] Naikens who have never been approached by welfare officers happily moved into plantation work. Furthermore, as pointed out, it seems that no social gulf has opened between the plantation worker Naiken and his food-gatherer counterpart who maintains more or less the traditional way of life. In considering Naikens' work in the plantation from the perspectives of the traditional socio-economic organization it is perhaps useful to centre the discussion around six simple questions: what? how much? when? how? what for? and by whom work in the plantation is done?

With respect to the first question - what? -

traditional subsistence work included these tasks: digging and cutting vegetal material such as roots, bamboos and wood to be used for accommodation and other requirements; picking fruits and berries, and digging wild yam for sustenance; constructing huts and making baskets from bamboo, grass and wood; and, of less importance for the present argument, collecting honey and other minor forest produce for trade; fishing and, to a limited extent, hunting. It has been mentioned above that in addition to the specialized tasks of tapping and factory work the plantation requires a variety of unskilled tasks referred to as 'weeding'. These include tasks which can be grouped under five headings. First there is weeding itself, including weeding in the plantation area, clearing paths of shrubs and mud after the rainy season, clearing a fire belt in the forest around the borders of the estate, cutting the branches of jungle trees in the plantation to regulate shade over plants (shade lopping), and pruning coffee bushes. All these tasks involve clearing the 'wild' - mostly vegetal material - away from the 'tame' - the plantation. Secondly there is picking, denoting picking coffee berries, fruits and spices grown in the plantation, and thirdly traditional construction, including construction of temporary sheds from bamboo; thatching with grass; construction and maintenance of bamboo conduits; making bamboo fences and baskets to protect young plants etc. This group of tasks involves simple traditional technology, drawing upon raw material from the surrounding forest. Fourthly there is 'lines' work, the maintenance of, and unskilled labour in assistance to the building of, workers' accommodation (locally referred to as 'lines') and latrines. Fifth and last, there is cultivation, which includes manuring, spraying and planting. From Table G it can be seen that the first three categories expanded from 25 per cent in 1948-9 to more than 50 per cent in 1978-9 of the total labour required, and that they constitute the majority of the unskilled tasks performed in the plantation. The tasks included in these three categories, however, are in essence similar to the tasks performed in the traditional Naiken mode of subsistence, and are indeed the ones mostly performed by the plantation-worker Naikens.

With respect to the second question - how much? - it is certain that traditionally Naikens did not need to go daily to collect food. Quantitative information regarding the amount of work required is not available, but an gratuity and provident fund considerable sums ranging from Rs.700 to Rs.1500. Some of them were over 60 years of age. But invariably they stayed in their huts over a period of several months and spent the money on foodstuffs and drinks. When the money was exhausted they took up casual employment. With respect to the fifth question - what for? - it can therefore be proposed that the underlying rationale of both traditional subsistence activities and work in the plantation is the same: immediate consumption. It has been mentioned before that most Naikens tend not to work on Monday and Tuesday. The reason may well be that the money which they receive on a Saturday often lasts until Tuesday or even Wednesday, and only when they need more for immediate consumption do they go back to work.

Finally, with respect to the question - by whom? - although traditionally most subsistence activities were pursued by both men and women, only men collected certain types of honey and hunted certain types of game, while women were more associated with the regular task of digging wild yam which was the staple food. Similarly in the plantation both men and women work, but women are regularly involved with the tasks of weeding and picking, while men are also allocated to perform tasks such as manuring and planting. As a result, partly because they avoid the tasks which they do not like, and partly because they take time off to pursue traditional collecting of honey and other minor forest produce for trade, the fluctuation in the number of male workers is significantly higher than that of women. In the plantation therefore, as in the traditional mode of subsistence, women attend more regularly at work, and are there associated more than men with the regular provision of the new, purchased staple food.

It would appear then that a significant parallel can be drawn between the food-gathering pattern of production and certain aspects of the plantation work. This similarity also extends to account for the four features (above) which emerge from the analysis of data relevant to the involvement of Naikens with plantation work. The tendency towards casual employment appears to be linked with the resemblance between this type of employment and the traditional mode of production. The casual work consists of tasks involving traditional construction, clearing the 'wild' and collecting vegetal produce, which are similar to those of the traditional activities. The labourer can work independently and by and large autonomously, and is least subject to control and supervision.

He can work as much as and when he wants, in direct response to his immediate needs. Unlike the permanent worker, his return from labour is maximized in the present. The greater popularity of permanent employment among women (second, above) clearly relates to the traditional association of women with the role of the regular provider of staple food. The higher average of working days per month of the casual labourer in comparison with the permanent one (third, above) can well be explained by Naikens' customary tendency to avoid pressure and authority. Finally, the trend over time from permanent to casual labour (fourth, above) reflects the enrolment of Naikens for permanent labour by the management and the Naikens' consequent resignation, further enhanced with the 1964 establishment of the casual status. In conclusion then it can be argued that Naiken involvement with plantation work, or in other words, their new pattern of production, has to a great extent been shaped by their traditional economic structure. The question raised is therefore how the new items of consumption, and the purchase rather than the gathering of commodities, affect the traditional patterns of consumption.

Consumption

Like other food-gatherers in South India, Naikens had access to commodities from the outside through the trade in minor forest produce even before they started to work in the plantation. But they used only a limited range of such commodities, mainly salt, cloths, tobacco and billhooks. From the 1950s onwards - with the regular involvement with plantation work, the resulting cash income, the intensified and constant contact with the other workers, the opening of a forest track to the neighbouring village markets, and the establishment of a tea shop in their habitat - major changes in Naikens' durable and non-durable consumption could have been expected. However, while there have been clear changes of the latter there has been little apparent alteration in the former. It is impossible even at present to distinguish by their material possessions between many individuals who are engaged in plantation work and those who still maintain the traditional way of life. They all live in similar huts constructed of bamboo walls and grass thatched roof, next to each other. The possessions of all resemble the following inventory: a few metal pots; metal plates; empty bottles; a cloth which they wear and a few old clothes and rugs which also serve

Wage-gathering

when necessary as sleeping mats and carrying bundles; a billhook; a home-made bamboo basket; possibly a metal digging stick; occasionally an axe; beads and other odds and ends such as wooden boxes, a broken mirror, empty tins.

Not only do the possessions look significantly alike, but the attitude towards them has also remained much the same. There is little concern with the accumulation of material possessions, as the inventory well manifests, nor any consideration for the maintenance of things already possessed, even if only recently bought. For example, a few cases were observed where, while working in the plantation Naikens cut themselves, and with no hesitation tore a strip of their new cloth to bandage the cuts. It is important to note that in a few cases transistors and watches entered the Naiken huts but did not remain there long. In one example a transistor was sold only two weeks after it was purchased, when the purchaser discovered that it was necessary to spend money on new batteries.

In the area of non-durable consumption, especially in their diet, clear changes have taken place. Naikens traditionally subsisted on foraging in the forest. Staple food consisted of nine varieties of wild yam, which were usually cooked and eaten in the evening. During the months of March and April jackfruit replaced the wild yam. Leafy material and figs were occasionally made into a spicy paste which was added to the staple food. Honey and fruits, berries and nuts were collected in their respective seasons, and consumed where and when they were gathered, or sporadically throughout the day. Very occasionally, fish and game were caught, and on such occasions eaten at the evening meal, substituting for the wild yam or the jackfruit. At present *ganji* (rice porridge) is the main staple food, and is eaten at the evening meal. Leafy material and figs are still occasionally collected around the huts, but now accompany the ganji. Other customary forest produce is still occasionally consumed, especially when people happen to notice it, for example on their way back home from work in the plantation, and sometimes even during work when they gather building material for the plantation. Tea and pastries are now frequently purchased from a tea shop opened in the plantation area (tea shop referring to a shack in which tea, pastries, tobacco produce and a few other items of provisions are sold). Naikens frequent the tea shop almost daily - often more than once - to consume these commodities.

The change from consumption which centred on the wild yam, to the new one in which rice and items from the tea shop occupy a prominent place, could be assessed as fundamental. Furthermore, those who are familiar with South India would perhaps suggest that the present Naikens' pattern of consumption basically resembles the consumption of other poor low-caste people, and that consequently the change observed is in emulation of the latter as a result of an increasing integration into South India society. To further qualify the discussion of Naikens' new pattern of non-durable consumption it is useful to contrast it with that of their work mates in the plantation who earn the same daily wage. The majority of these are Moppala, and this name is therefore used to refer to all the non-Naiken workers, among whom Hindu and Christians are also included.

The staple food of Moppalas is rice, but they eat it dry with curry and other side dishes. Porridge rice, which the Naikens eat, is considered by them the least esteemed form of cooked grain, and they rarely eat it. Moppalas take their main meal at lunch, but they also eat in the morning and evening. For Naikens the main, and often the only meal, is eaten in the evening. Moppalas prepare their pastries and tea. Naikens, who are particularly fond of them, never prepare pastries. They can buy tea powder in the shop, but even tea they rarely prepare themselves, and prefer bringing the ready-made tea in old glass bottles from the tea shop to their hut. There is also a difference in the sexual division of domestic labour between Naikens and Moppalas. In the Moppala family only the wife cooks, whereas in the Naiken family both the wife and her husband can cook. Both Moppalas and Naikens frequent the tea shop, but not wholly for the same reasons. For the Moppalas the tea shop is mainly a social institution, where only men can go and where they stay for relatively long periods; they buy each other tea, exchange gossip, and sometimes play cards. For the Naikens, the tea shop is by and large simply a place from which tea, pastries and tobacco produce can be obtained. Both male and female Naikens visit the tea shop. Often the whole nuclear family goes there. They either take back their purchases, or sit separately in a corner of the tea shop to consume them. Naikens and Moppalas also differ with respect to expenditure in the tea shop. Table H provides comparative details of the daily expenditure of two Naiken and one Moppala families during one representative week. The Naiken families spent respectively six

Wage-gathering

and four times more than the Moppala family. In general, the daily expenditure of Moppalas is almost always between Rs.$\frac{1}{2}$ and Rs.$2\frac{1}{2}$. In contrast the daily expenditure of Naikens would appear to vary in direct relation to the money available to them, and in inverse relation to the number of members of the nuclear family.

The difference in pattern of non-durable consumption between Naikens and Moppalas, in spite of the similarity of the main items consumed, suggests that it may be useful to follow what has been done in the analysis of change in production patterns, and examine changes from the perspectives of the traditional socio-economic structure. It further suggests that it is necessary to conduct such an examination with reference to the fabric of culture surrounding these items as well as to the items themselves. It is useful here to centre such an examination on six related aspects of food consumption which reflect the relations between the three parameters of raw food, cooked food, and people.

The first point to be looked at is cooking equipment. The traditional cooking vessels Naikens used would appear to have been made of bamboo. These lasted only for one occasion and were prepared just before use. Raw food was put into a split of bamboo which was then placed on the fire. The external layer of bamboo caught fire at once, but the food was ready before the internal layer started to burn. For some considerable time, however, Naikens also used earthen pots and, when available, metal pots. At present Naikens only use earthen and cheap metal pots; splits of bamboo are used only for carrying water and sometimes as crockery. Every family has one or two good pots in which the ganji is cooked. The pots are left near the fireplace after the evening meal, and only the following morning one of the family (often an adolescent girl or boy) goes to the river to wash them and then place them out of the way in a corner of the hut. Furthermore it has been observed that when people move from one hamlet to another they leave their pots behind and use those available in the hamlet they move to. Thus it can be suggested that the present attitude towards cooking equipment is linked with the past attitude in its casual and temporary aspect.

The storage of provisions is the second point to be discussed. Traditionally, Naikens did not store provisions for very long, and at most kept food for only a few days. The situation at present is very similar. Even when provisions (rice and a few chillies) bought on pay day last for a few days, there is no attempt to store them properly. They are simply put in a corner of the hut, still wrapped in the newspaper or leaf in which they were bought, until they are exhausted. This tendency partly explains why Naikens do not prepare their own tea - it requires the storage of provisions.

The third relevant point is the method of cooking. In the past, staple food was prepared by simply boiling the wild yam in water. Occasionally the wild yam was also roasted on fire, but boiling was the predominant method, and both the seasonal substitute for wild yam - the jack fruit - and the leafy material sometimes eaten with it, were boiled. Significantly the only form of grain which the Naikens consume, and which their neighbours least esteem, is simply raw food boiled in an unspecified amount of water. Naikens do not prepare the complicated cooked pastries such as idli and dossa which they so much like. The traditional simplicity of cooking thus appears to have been retained.

The maintenance of this simplicity partly contributes to the preservation of the customary division of labour in preparing the food (point four). As with the traditional staple food, both men and women, and even children, can prepare the ganji. The division of labour in obtaining the food has also been retained. In the past both man and woman could collect the food, or occasionally obtain it in exchange for minor forest produce. At present, both can obtain it in exchange for money earned. The traditional independence has also been implemented with regard to the new dietary items of tea and pastries, since whereas Moppala women customarily cannot go to the tea shop, Naiken women can.

Fifth is the aspect of the storage of cooked food. Both now and in the past, the pot is normally emptied during the evening meal. Leftovers, if any, remain in the pot somewhere in the cooking area and can occasionally be consumed the following morning. Finally, with regard to time and manner of eating, traditionally a main or only meal was taken by the nuclear family together, or by its individual members, each serving himself from the pot in his own time. Today the situation is exactly the same, except that ganji and not wild yam constitutes the meal.

A certain resemblance appears between the traditional and the present pattern of non-durable consumption. To assess the nature of the changes it is useful to distinguish between two analytical levels - that of the pattern of cultural parameters and the network of ties connecting them, and that of the content assigned

Wage-gathering

to these parameters. In the case of the Naikens it can be suggested that ganji has replaced the wild yam as the content of the parameter of staple food but with no overall change in the 'pre-existing pattern'. The first part of this proposition, namely the interchangeability between ganji and the wild yam, already emerges from the discussion above. It can be further supported by looking at the elements of 'food-gathering' in the society. At present even the food-gatherer Naikens increase their consumption of rice whenever they can obtain it through trade in minor forest produce. As often as not, when any Naiken goes to the forest, for example on a traditional expedition of honey collection, he is likely, instead of following the traditional pattern by collecting wild yam as and where he finds it, to take a small bundle of rice.

The second part of the proposition, namely that there was no overall change in the 'pre-existing pattern' concerning food consumption, can be demonstrated by examining Naikens' organization of food. Four clear categories of food are distinguishable by their place within the Naiken diet: staple food, seasonal substitutes for staple food, items supplementary to the staple food, and others which are consumed sporadically throughout the day (Table I). These we may picture as concentric circles at the core of which is the first category and surrounding it, the second, the third, and the fourth. In the past these four categories included respectively: the wild yam; jack fruit and occasionally game and fish; leafy material and figs; and, lastly, honey and fruits, berries and nuts. At present these four categories include respectively: ganji; wild yam, jackfruit and occasionally game and fish; leafy material and figs; and, finally, tea and pastries, honey and occasionally certain fruits, berries and nuts. Thus it seems that through the contact with wage employment, ganji moved into the core of the food categories, wild yam moved into the second category, and the 'tea shop produce' entered the fourth category together with the other 'forestry produce', but there was no overall change in the organization of categories of food and their properties. Thus while there has been no significant change in the durable consumption, the changes in the non-durable consumption are a matter of change in the content of a few parameters while the 'pre-existing pattern' as a whole has hardly been affected. But if it is argued that changes in consumption and production are limited, the question is raised where has the money disappeared to? How is cash integrated into the Naiken culture?

Distribution (Exchange and Money)

There is no ground to assume that Naikens had not known of money before they started to be regularly involved with plantation work, but it is certain that only after that event did they have to deal with it constantly and to find a place for it in their economy. In the examination of contexts in which money is presently used it is necessary to distinguish between coins and cash in general, since coins sometimes seem to stand as a separate category of money and are regarded as a kind of durable property. For example, when a Naiken dies, his coins as well as his knife and pots are buried with him. Alternatively, they are taken by friends and relatives who wish to remember the deceased. In the most important of Naiken rituals, the souls of people who have died during the year previous to the ritual, and who are still free and harmful in the forest, are brought home into the 'hut of the spirits'. During the ritual, beads, and nowadays also coins, of the deceased are put in the place of death, and the shaman in a trance envelops them in a cloth and carries them to the 'hut of the spirits'. Coins in these contexts are therefore taken into the Naiken culture without the monetary properties given to them in the industrial economy, and are associated with their owner, as is the case with other Naiken possessions.

To consider the contexts in whch cash money is used it is useful to refer to three criteria often used in the literature to define money. They are, first, a medium of exchange, second, a store of value, and third, a measure of value. It would appear that Naikens rarely, if at all, use money as a store of value or as a measure of value. They rarely possess money - when they do earn some they immediately exchange it. They do not see the intrinsic value of a commodity, only what money they paid for it. They do not say, for example, that the knife is worth Rs.15, but that they paid Rs.15 for the knife. Naikens use money as a medium of exchange, but the way in which they do so needs to be carefully examined. In the capitalist system money, as a medium of exchange, facilitates 'barter' over time and 'barter' of any one commodity for another, irrespective of the related requirements of those who provide the commodities and the relative values of the goods. Naikens use money as a medium of exchange, but not for these purposes. They immediately exchange whatever cash money they earn.

They never save up in order to buy a durable commodity, which they only get by an immediate exchange when they obtain a suitable sum of money. In general they prefer to be paid with commodities. For example, when occasionally Moppalas want to employ Naikens for work such as clearing land and building huts, they generally find it difficult to get Naikens to work, but have a better response if they offer them a low daily wage, supplemented by tea and pastries during the working day, than if they offer the same wage plus an extra sum of money which even exceeds the value of the tea and pastries provided. (This is another example to show that Naikens do not see the intrinsic monetary value of these commodities.) For Naikens cash money is almost entirely a token which they are given, and is immediately substituted for commodities.

It is possible to suggest that it is not so much 'cash money' but its counterpart 'debt' which is the instrumental currency for the Naikens. According to an arrangement between them, the local rice dealer gives Naikens rice on credit, and the plantation clerk deducts the debt from their wages and gives it directly to the rice dealer. The dealer only extends credit facilities to those Naikens who attend work. Consequently it is the need for credit facilities which directly motivates Naikens to work and by which they are practically paid. Naikens' purchases from the tea shop are a more revealing case. They only buy from the tea shop on credit. The shop owner tries to extract a partial payment weekly, but with little success. The account is settled when Naikens get their annual leave wage and bonus, usually sometime between July and September. A sort of seasonal cycle in the availability of provisions is thus created. During the period which immediately follows the 'settlement day' (as it is called locally), Naikens intensively purchase provisions by credit. As the debts gradually grow, the shopkeeper both increases his pressure for partial payments and restricts further credit facilities; so that, as the year goes on, Naikens have gradually fewer and fewer provisions available to them. Towards the day of settlement they get little, if any, credit; and on the day they pay their debt, the cycle begins again.

It is possible to relate the predominant use of debt or credit to the long established traditional practice of trade in minor forest produce. From Morris's work on the food-gathering Mallapantaram of Kerala,[17] who are very similar to the Naikens, it can indeed be seen that most of the traditional barter was regulated by debt. The contractor gave some provisions to the Mallapantaram who later supplied him with minor forest produce, but immediately took some more provisions so that the debt was kept open and called for further transactions. Only a simple historical continuity is established by this explanation, which is partial because it is not interwoven with the explanation so far provided of changes in the patterns of production and consumption, and also because it accounts only for the fact that debt is used, overlooking its new predominant place which is not comparable with that of the past. A more comprehensive and structural explanation can perhaps be offered if, following the approach employed in the above discussion of production and consumption, the use of debt is viewed from the perspectives of the traditional food-gathering socio-economic structure. Furthermore, it could then be suggested that such an explanation also accounts for the changes, back in the past, when food-gatherers in South India entered into a relationship of trade in minor forest produce with the surrounding developed society, and the fact that in spite of this contact and trade they have for centuries retained their food-gathering way of life.

The foraging mode of subsistence meant that traditionally, like most other hunter-gatherer societies, each individual Naiken could be self-sufficient. Transfer of goods - even trivial commodities which could be easily collected in the forest - was rarely practised even between those closely related to each other. An incident observed during fieldwork may bring home the extreme to which this point can be taken. Maran's family did not collect firewood during the day. That night they sat cold in the dark, and I sat with them. Maran's younger brother, who lives only five metres away, sat near a bright fire, with a big stack of firewood which could have lasted for several days. When asked why he did not borrow from his brother some wood which he could return the very next day Maran answered that if he did so people would laugh at him, saying he was not a 'person' if he could not collect his own firewood. Thus only collecting commodities from the environment would appear to have been acceptable, while getting them from other people was socially disapproved of. In contrast to goods, services were occasionally exchanged between Naikens, but were followed by an instantaneous repayment. For example, a young man who helped an older one to collect honey would get a share of the honey. It can be said that this 'instantaneous repayment' in itself only served to prevent the creation of a chain of obligation and the consequent exchange of goods.

The notion and practice of sharing would appear in the literature to be a predominant characteristic of hunting-gathering people, and is even claimed by some scholars to be the very principle which makes the foraging economy viable.[18] Since it is one form of material exchange, it is necessary briefly to examine the practice of sharing among Naikens. Sharing was not in general obligatory. Cases were often observed when members of a food-gathering Naiken family ate their food, making no offer to share it with visitors sitting with them. While for some hunting-gathering people the notion of sharing is extended to non-edible items (European clothes in the case of the Bushmen),[19] Naikens only shared edible food, mostly game, which could not be immediately consumed by one nuclear family. But it was only rarely that big game was caught, and even then, unlike cases where particular parts are distributed to particular categories of kin (for example, Hadza), and perhaps to prevent the perpetuation of exchange, there was a strictly equal distribution, both in terms of the meat's quality and quantity, to all the families in the hamlet. In the traditional Naiken society, therefore, even the sharing of commodities was minimal.

It is possible to show that to some extent buying on credit is not identified by Naikens as an exchange of commodities. A debt is not tangibly comprehended since money in itself is not used as a store of value or as a measure of value, and since the future is disregarded. Obtaining the commodities, and the later need to repay the debt, are considered two separate actions; obtaining commodities on credit therefore is conceived of as a one-way transfer of goods. A striking example, observed during fieldwork, can illustrate this point. Jackfruit, which often substitues for ganji during March and April, can be cultivated and is sold in shops. Towards the end of the season wild jackfruit was exhausted in the immediate surroundings of the hamlet, and to obtain it Naikens would have needed to go far into the forest. Instead they were happy to buy jackfruit on credit for Rs.2 a piece.

The two transactions are considered separate but, in addition, getting commodities on credit from shops would not appear to be considered by Naikens as an interpersonal transfer of goods; rather it is as if they obtain them from the extended environment, so to speak.

This point is clearly illustrated by contrasting the Naiken attitude towards, first, services rendered by non-Naikens and, second, goods obtained from the shops. When they are rendered services by non-Naikens, still as traditionally practised among themselves, Naikens immediately make a repayment. For example, while at work Mathen felt ill, and the supervisor took him back to his hut. The very next day Mathen sent the supervisor seven eggs of wild chickens. In contrast, Naikens continuously take commodities from the shop, with no bother about the shopkeeper and their relations with him. It can therefore be suggested that, in its structural place within the culture, purchase by credit for the Naikens is not so much buying but rather something analogous to the collection of food resources in the forest. Indeed, there is a neat analogy between the seasonal availability of credit and that of forest foods. Both reach their lowest point in about the same period between July and September. Furthermore, while wages are principally paid weekly, by using 'credit' Naikens can collect food from the shops daily.

Through the selective use of debt, money would appear to have fitted in with the traditional 'pre-existing pattern', and its introduction did not disturb the web of relations within the society. There are several features which can, and often do, accompany the introduction of cash into a tribal society. First, there can follow stratification in wealth. But since Naikens have not changed their patterns of consumption - neither accumulating durable commodities nor greatly altering their attitude towards non-durable commodities - a material equality has been retained. Second, there can follow changes in the sexual division of labour. But both women and men could work in the plantation, and could buy from the shop, so that the sexes' equality and independence has been maintained. Furthermore, traditional division of labour was even reinforced, since women more than men tend to work as permanent workers, to earn money regularly, to have shop accounts in their names and therefore to be, as in the past, more responsible for the supply of the staple food. Third, there can follow differentiation in social status - either by different access to new means of production, or by changes in patterns of consumption. But neither did the latter occur (as just mentioned above), nor were there changes with regard to the former, since all Naikens could work, and since most of those who did so, chose to get only partially involved with the new means of livelihood (casual employment). Lastly, there can follow changes in relations between people, when traditional material exchanges which can symbolically tie the society together are swept away by money. The Naikens traditionally had minimal material exchanges, and money could even be useful for the instantaneous reciprocation of a service (for example, often today the helper in honey collection may be paid in money). Together, the structural similarity for the Naikens between their present transaction by credit and their traditional collection of requirements from the environment, and the related fact that introduction of money did not disturb the relations with other cultural parameters may well explain how it was that, in contact with a cash economy, debt (or credit) has been the one form of money which has been taken into the Naiken economy, without much disturbance to the 'pre-existing pattern' of the Naiken socio-economic structure as a whole.

Conclusion

It is argued in this paper that in spite of 30 years' contact with, and some integration into, a money and national economy, the Naiken economy as a whole - production, consumption and distribution - and the social relations embedded in it, have retained their traditional 'pre-existing pattern'. There have been changes which could have been considered far-reaching ones, in the areas of production (wage labour), consumption (rice) and distribution (money), but these are shown to amount to changes in the content of pre-existing cultural parameters and not in the traditional pattern of cultural parameters and the network of ties connecting them. The explanation for this development cannot be provided within the scope of this paper. It can only be observed that these developments could take place partly because the traditional base of livelihood was not destroyed and at the same time the Naikens were needed by the plantation; partly because of the important place of trade in minor forest produce within the traditional base of livelihood;[20] and partly due to a sufficiently close fit between the traditional Naiken social structure and that of the western capitalist one.[21] In a nutshell, it can be concluded: new items were incorporated into the Naiken economy but were treated as traditional forest resources; Naikens clearly took to shops and the purchase of rice, tea and pastries, but through credit 'collected' these from the environment, extended as it were to include the shops; Naikens positively responded to the possibilities of wage employment, but went to 'gather' wage in the plantation.

The notion of 'wage gathering' encapsulates the very argument which the case raises; and it therefore appears appropriate to link the brief discussion of the case's implications to it; that is to each component separately and to both combined.

'Wage' focuses attention upon the external changes themselves, the new items which are introduced to the culture in question from the outside. The Naiken case shows that wages and money entered into the economy, but have been taken without the economic properties attributed to them in the modern world, and are merely used as a token which is given instead of, and immediately substituted for, commodities. That is to say, the presence and certain use of new items may, but need not, indicate profound changes and modernization; or, in general, external changes cannot be assessed simply by reading into them the meaning ascribed by the new encroaching system (most often the western world).

'Gathering' directs attention to the importance of the traditional system in the interpretation of the external changes. The Naiken case shows that the traditional system influences the adjustment to external changes - an adjustment which is partial, and more important, even selective. This selectiveness is explicit, quite clearly articulated, and certainly acted out. Hence it could be said that the traditional system is influential not only in the actual adjustment to external changes, but first of all and at a deeper level, in seeing and evaluating the possibilities opened up by the new surrounding conditions. That is, to use the terminological framework within which Bloch writes, the actors see the process occurring around them in terms of their own traditional, pre-existing culture, and accordingly act. Or it could be even better expressed by reading Durkheim's own statement as if it had been written for the Naikens: 'In a word, society substitutes for the world revealed to us by our senses a different world that is the projection of the ideals created by society itself'.[22] But how then is the new input to the traditional structure dealt with, or how are the external changes internalized?

What the notion of 'wage-gathering' implies is that the Naikens manage to interpret their new experiences in traditional terms. Their case demonstrates that it is useful to distinguish between changes at two analytical levels: first, the 'pre-existing pattern' - the cultural parameters and the network of ties connecting them - and second, the content of these parameters. The Naikens show that it is possible for changes to occur at the latter level alone. For example, rice was brought into the diet but in replacement for the traditional wild yam, taking on its role and not altering the ways matters to do with food were organized. Again, wage income which is almost completely and immediately exchanged for rice has been perceived as analogous to rice, and thence to wild yam. Thus because they 'gather' wages, rather than earn them, the Naikens have internalized the new input which wages represent. What they have done is to alter the content of an aspect of the traditional culture, while the aspect itself and its function are still defined in terms of the 'pre-existing pattern', the way that the one parameter relates to all the others. In Bloch's terms, this is to say that the actors talk *within* their society, but that, through and in accordance with the grammar of their language, they can make meaningful statements of external changes and act accordingly. From the notion of 'wage gathering', therefore, a formula for the process of change can be derived. It follows Durkheim's premise in seeing social process in terms used by the actors; but at the same time it is able to suggest how it is that the actors change these terms.

TABLES

A. DISTRIBUTION OF EMPLOYABLE NAIKENS BY CATEGORY OF
   EMPLOYMENT 1978-9

	Male and Female	*Female*	*Male*
Hamlet 1	XXXXX■■OO	■■■■■■■OOO	XXXXXXXXXO
2	XXXXXXXX■■	XXXXXXX■■■	XXXXXXXXXX
3	OOOOOOOOOO	OOOOOOOOOO	OOOOOOOOOO
4	XXXXXXOOOO	XXXXXXOOOO	XXXOOOOOOO
5	XX■■OOOOOO	OOOOOOOOOO	XXX■■■■■■■
All hamlets	XXXX■■OOOO	XX■■■OOOOO	XXXXXXX■OO
Percentage	46 18 36	24 29 47	69 6 25

Key: XX Casual worker   ■■ Permanent worker
        OO Non-worker

B. NAIKENS' ATTENDANCE AT WORK: AVERAGE WORKING DAYS
   PER WORKER PER MONTH (1979)

	Male and Female		*Female*		*Male*	
	February	July	Feb.	Jly.	Feb.	Jly.
Casual	12	23	15	22	10	22
Permanent	9	18	9	17	0	21
Total	11	21	12	19	10	22

C. NAIKENS' ATTENDANCE AT WORK: NUMBER OF WORKERS
   PER MONTH (1979)

	Male and Female		*Female*		*Male*	
	February	July	Feb.	Jly.	Feb.	Jly.
Casual	10	15	4	4	6	11
Permanent	3	6	3	5	0	1
Total	13	21	7	9	6	12

D. DISTRIBUTION OF NAIKENS' PERIOD OF PERMANENT
   EMPLOYMENT

Number of workers	6	5	1	2	1	1	3	1	1
Years of employment	1*	2	6	7	9	10	12	14	16

*The probationary period was not completed.

Wage-gathering

E. PRESENT POSITION OF NAIKENS WHO WERE PERMANENT
   EMPLOYEES

	Unknown	Unemployable Old	Employable Non-workers	Casual
Number	7	4	2	8

F. DETAILS OF EMPLOYEES, 1958-78

	Male	Female
Permanent employees, 1958-78	13	14
Permanent employees at present	1	5
Employables who resigned from permanent employment	7	3
Ex-permanent employees who now work as casual workers	7	1
Ex-permanent employees who do not work at present	0	2

G. DISTRIBUTION OF TASKS REQUIRED BY THE PLANTATION,
   BY RELATIVE PROPORTIONS OF TOTAL TASKS

	1949-50	1978-9
Tapping	XXXXXXXXXXXXXXXXXXXXXXXXX	XXXXXXXXXXXX
Weeding	XXXXXXXXXXXX	XXXXXXXXXXXXXX
Factory	XXXXXXX	XXXX
Picking		XXXXXX
Trad.Cn.*	XX	XXXXX
Cultivn.	X	XXX
Lines	X	XXX

*Traditional construction work

H. COMPARATIVE DAILY EXPENDITURE IN THE LOCAL TEA SHOP
   FOR NAIKENS AND MOPPALA FAMILIES, 1979, IN RUPEES

Date:	29.4	30.4	1.5	2.5	3.5	4.5	Total
Family 1	1.30	4.20	4.10	3.75	4.75	5.25	23.35
Family 2	12.90	6.15	6.55	7.00	4.70	10.35	47.65
Family 3	.80	1.02	2.20	1.70	1.17	.90	7.79

Notes: Family 1. Naiken, 2 working parents, 2 children
       Family 2. Naiken, 2 working parents, 1 child
       Family 3. Moppala, 2 working parents, 2 children

Nurit Bird

I. CHANGES IN CATEGORIES OF FOOD

	Past	*Present*
Staple	Wild yam	Ganji
Seasonal substitutes	Jackfruit, meat, fish	Wild yam, jackfruit, meat, fish
Supplementary	Leafy material	Leafy material
Others	Fruits, berries, nuts	Pastries, tea, fruits, berries, nuts

Sources: For tables A to G, Records of the Gir Plantation (daily registration of attendance; task-allocation).
For table H, Accounts of the tea shop.

NOTES

Bird, 'Wage-gathering: socio-economic changes and the case of the food-gatherer Naikens of South India'

This paper is a version of part of a thesis to be submitted for the Ph.D. degree to the Department of Social Anthropology, Cambridge.

1. Particular reference is to A.R. Radcliffe-Browne, *Structure and Function in Primitive Society: essays and addresses* (London 1957), R. Firth, *Essays on Social Organization and Values* (London 1964) and E.R. Leach, *Political Systems of Highland Burma* (London 1954).
2. M. Bloch, 'The Past and the Present in the Present', *Man* 12 (1977), pp.278-92.
3. Ibid. In the same paper Bloch puts forward his own theoretical scheme, which for lack of space cannot be dealt with here.
4. Ibid., p.279.
5. Fieldwork was carried out from September 1978 to September 1979 supported by a College Bursary from Trinity College, Cambridge, the 1978 A. Wilkin Studentship, the 1979 H.M. Chadwick Studentship, and a research grant from the Smuts Memorial Fund. I am indebted to the above for this support. I am grateful to my supervisor, Dr Alan Macfarlane, to Mr Phillip for access to the records of the plantation, and to Mr Lakshmanan, my assistant during fieldwork.
6. This task is being undertaken in the forthcoming doctoral thesis.
7. J. Woodburn, 'An Introduction to Hadza Ecology' in R.B. Lee and I. De Vore, eds., *Man the Hunter* (New York 1968); 'Minimal Politics: the political organization of the Hadza of North Tanzania' in W.A. Shack and P.S. Cohen, eds., *Politics in Leadership: A comparative perspective* (Oxford 1979) and 'Hunters and Gatherers Today and Reconstruction of the Past' in E. Gellner, ed., *Soviet and Western Anthropology* (London 1980).
8. Woodburn, 'Minimal Politics'. In a footnote Woodburn points out that immediate return systems are not only restricted to hunter-gatherer societies but also found 'in a few highly restricted and specialized contexts in industrial societies' ('Hunters and Gatherers', p.115).
9. P.M. Gardner, 'Symetric Respect and Memorate Knowledge: the structure and ecology of individualistic

culture', *Southern Journal of Anthropology* 22, (1966) pp.389-415, and 'The Paliyans' in M.G. Bicchieri, ed., *Hunters and Gatherers Today* (New York 1972).
    10. M. Sahlins, *Stone Age Economics* (London 1972).
    11. Woodburn, 'Hadza Ecology', p.91.
    12. Woodburn, 'Hunters and Gatherers', p.98.
    13. Gardner, 'Symetric Respect', p.394.
    14. The fact that more men work in the plantation than women is not dealt with in this paper. It can be explained in line with the general argument but the explanation involves idiosyncratic factors relating to particular circumstances.
    15. See B. Morris, 'Settlement and Social Change among the Hill Pandaram', *Man in India* 56, 2 (1976); P.K. Misra, 'Social Transformation among Food Gatherers: a case study' in M.N. Srinivas and others, eds., *Dimension of Social Change in India* (Bombay 1977); and P.R.G. Mathur, 'Forest Based Economy for Tribal Communities in Kerala', paper given at the tenth International Congress of Anthropological and Ethnological Sciences, Delhi 1978.
    16. See the summary of these studies in Sahlins, op. cit., pp.14-21.
    17. B. Morris, 'Tappers, Trappers and the Hill Pandaram (South India)', *Anthropos* 72 (1977).
    18. R.B. Lee, *The King San, Men, Women and Work in a Foraging Society* (Cambridge 1979).
    19. Ibid.
    20. See Morris, 'Tappers', and 'The Economy and Social Organization of the Malapantaram', Ph.D. thesis, London 1975. This topic will also be treated in my forthcoming thesis.
    21. See A. Macfarlane, 'Modes of Reproduction', *Journal of Development Studies* 14,4 (1978) and 'Demographic Structures and Cultural Regions in Europe', *Cambridge Anthropology* 6, 1 and 2 (1980). I draw upon this in my thesis and an article (*Journal of Cambridge Anthropology*, forthcoming).
    22. E. Durkheim, *Sociology and Philosophy* (New York 1911; reprint 1974). The point may be developed in two ways: further stages in the process of change (for example when new content enters a close cluster of cultural parameters, new linkages can be formed between them, and a new substructure established conflicting with, paralleling, supplementing or even replacing the original) and more complicated cases, where the operation of parts of the traditional system is restricted (see Meyer's paper above).

ECONOMIC DISLOCATION IN NINETEENTH-CENTURY
EASTERN UTTAR PRADESH: SOME IMPLICATIONS OF
THE DECLINE OF ARTISANAL INDUSTRY IN COLONIAL
INDIA

Gyan Pandey

Recent studies of 'de-industrialization' in the Indian
sub-continent have helped to clarify some major questions regarding the overall impact of colonialism,
although the debate on the fate of India's traditional
industries begun in the late nineteenth century will not
easily be closed. [1] What the nineteenth-century participants in the debate missed out, and more recent scholarship too has not been directly concerned with, is the
differential impact of colonial developments on different sections of the local handicraftsmen, and the sharp
fluctuations that accompanied the process of tying up
India's regional economies with the metropolitan economy
of Britain. It is these features that I seek to highlight in this paper, using for the purpose the nineteenth-century evidence relating to the most important
artisanal class of pre-colonial India, the cloth-manufacturers, in Azamgarh and some of its neighbouring
districts in eastern Uttar Pradesh. In addition, I hope
to be able to indicate some of the social and cultural
implications of the massive economic dislocation that
came with colonialism, by reference to the more neglected
aspects of the cloth-manufacturers' history and
struggles: their organization and consciousness, their
periodic if short-lived demonstrations of solidarity,
and their resistance to various developments of the
colonial period.

2

Historians writing about India in the seventeenth and
eighteenth centuries have pointed to the various 'levels'
of production that existed in the traditional textile
industry, the regional and functional specialization in
the manufacture of cloth, and the complex organization
for production and marketing that had developed. A hierarchy of intermediaries, advancing loans and exercising
various types of controls had evidently come to mark
different stages of the enterprise (from the procurement of raw material through the preparation of yarn

and the weaving and dressing of the cloth to the stage
of transfer to a prospective consumer). By the eighteenth century the growing demands of the European
companies had added much to the complexity of the Indian
clothing business, and further separated the makers of
quality cloth both from their raw materials (cotton,
silk, mixtures of silk and cotton, or wool) and from the
market for their products. The European traders were
particularly concerned to promote productivity, standardization and variation of product, and sought to
extend their hold not only (as the Mughals had done) in
the small urban *karkhanas*, or workshops, but indeed into
rural units. [2]

Alongside the centres of fine textile production,
meant for the nobility or for sale in the distant markets, there existed all along more humble units of production, turning out coarse or medium-quality cloth for
use locally or by consumers in nearby towns and villages.
At the lower levels, it has been suggested, cloth production (from the cultivation of cotton to the stage of
weaving) was sometimes carried out within the family
unit of specific caste groups, such as the Jogis and
Julahas of Bengal. But there is some evidence of the
intervention of middlemen even in these humbler spheres.[3]

Taking as his touchstone 'the degree of division of
labour and specialisation, and the extent of capitalists'
participation in and control over marketing and production', Sabyasachi Bhattacharya has distinguished three
different levels of organization in the industry. The
first was typical of rural handicrafts: production was
dispersed, artisans worked at home often aided by family
members, and marketing was often unmediated by any trader. Here, spinning and weaving might be combined in
the weaver's household, or the weavers might use thread
already spun in the cultivator's household to produce
cloth needed by the latter. However, a good deal even
of the coarse cloth produced at this level was marketed
through middlemen. At the second level of development,
the middleman sought to ensure a regular supply of goods
of a specified standard by advancing cash (*dadan*) to the
artisan. He also invested in raw-material purchase beyond the means of the artisan in industries involving
high-value inputs, including silk textiles. The third
level saw the expansion of the work group beyond the
family unit, the intervention of one or more middlemen
in the procuring of raw material and marketing of produce, and in certain cases even the emergence of protocapitalist 'factories'. Bhattacharya notes that the

Economic Dislocation

traditional cloth industry had units located at all these levels, though the majority of weavers were in the second level; but the levels of course only represent 'some points on a continuum along which the denizens of the artisanal production system travelled (sometimes sliding back ...)'.[4]

The work of these scholars has established, then, the existence of intermediaries and the penetration of money-lenders down even to the lower levels of the textile industry. One inference that follows may be noted at once: while India's foreign trade grew and the external demand for her cloth expanded, and huge fortunes were made by entrepreneurs in different parts of the sub-continent at different times in the seventeenth and eighteenth centuries, it is almost certain that all but a small minority of the cloth-manufacturers - spinners and dyers, weavers and bleachers - shared but little in the profits.[5] Together with this it should be borne in mind that the textile trade (as of that in a number of other commodities), based as it was more and more at this time on an expanding foreign demand, remained extremely vulnerable.

The relatively rapid rise and decline of trade in a particular area, like the rise and fall of medieval towns and cities, may not have been a new phenomenon. Babar's observation that 'in Hindustan hamlets and villages, towns indeed, are depopulated and set up in a moment!'[6] deserves consideration, for all the prejudices of the conqueror, and this conqueror's deep nostalgia for the land he had left behind. Nevertheless, what Chris Bayly calls the 'forced' town growth of the late eighteenth and early nineteenth centuries in northern India was the product of a different situation - more 'settled', yet perhaps altogether more volatile. Political uncertainty and turbulence were marked in eastern Uttar Pradesh at least until the 1810s or 1820s: neighbouring areas, in Awadh, central India and the Punjab, remained unpacified for even longer. At the local level this was reflected in the establishment and decay of many small towns and *qasbas* in the latter half of the eighteenth century, the extended jostling for power in the countryside (which of course continued until much later), and often violent revolt against new authorities, British and Indian: the great uprising of 1857-59 appears, from one perspective, as the culminating point of these extended struggles.

But there was, in addition to the problem of political and social instability, another major factor of uncertainty. Traders, even far inland, were now deeply sensitive to changing demands from Europe, about which, however, they did not always have very direct or up-to-date information, and over which they had absolutely no control. Indeed, in a situation when war, famine and an admittedly harsh assessment, in succession, had ravaged much of the land, we may expect that those who lived in the line of 'prosperity' established along the riverine route to Calcutta, looked ever more anxiously 'outward'. Any shift in the nature or quantum of the foreign demand had repercussions that spread far into the interior of the Indian sub-continent.[7] The shock-waves from Europe spread in an expanding circle as the British consolidated their position in India. It was somewhere on the periphery of this circle that the cloth-manufacturers of eastern Uttar Pradesh stood at the beginning of the nineteenth century, when Gorakhpur district (then including Azamgarh) and other parts of the region were ceded by the Nawab of Awadh and brought under the administration of the English East India Company.

3

In terms of the sheer scale of its cloth-manufacturing industry Azamgarh was, at this time, one of the leading districts of the area that came to be known as U.P. The cloth produced here had long enjoyed a certain regional renown: the district is mentioned in the *Ain-i-Akbari*, along with Banaras and Jalalabad, as a cloth-manufacturing centre of distinction. Mubarakpur, the largest weaving town in the district when the East India Company took over, was known for its compound cotton and silk, *tassar* (wild silk) and wool cloths; Maunath Bhanjan (or Mau) had been famous from before the days of the Nawabs of Awadh for its fine muslins, in the weaving of which counts as high as 150s were used. Kopaganj, six miles from Mau, had developed since the middle of the eighteenth century into another major centre of textile production. Nearby, in other districts, there were other centres renowned for the particular kinds of cloth that they produced. Much of what follows in this paper is based on reports relating to the experience of the spinners and weavers of these specialised centres. But there are some important pieces of evidence, from the second half of the nineteenth century, regarding their less well-known brethren in other small towns and villages.

Economic Dislocation

Any account of the fortunes of the textile industry in eastern U.P. in the course of the nineteenth century must begin with the famous, if mistitled, Company 'investments'. In Gorakhpur and Padrauna towns, major weaving centres of Gorakhpur district just north of Azamgarh, there were, as the commercial representatives of the East India Company reported on arrival there in 1803, numerous weavers 'desirous of entering into the Hon'ble Company's employ'.[8] Numbers of them had evidently migrated from the district in the preceding 30 or 40 years, and gone to live in the Nawab Wazir's dominions in Awadh: there were 49 houses of weavers that had settled in Tanda (Faizabad district) in this way. The Company's Commercial Resident at Gorakhpur and its Reporter-General on External Commerce based at Patna, not unique in this respect (see Sleeman on Awadh in 1849-50, and the comments on Mau-Azamgarh referred to below), found in this clear evidence of the misrule and rapine that Gorakhpur had fallen prey to before the coming of the English. But in passing, the Reporter-General noticed another factor of significance in the migration of the weavers. The 49 households were induced to move to Tanda, it transpires, by 'the liberal encouragement' of a private English merchant, J.P. Scott, who gave each weaver 'a bounty of four rupees, and advanced money to enable them to purchase their looms and thread'.[9] This was said to have occurred 'about 1780': could it have been in 1782-83, the year of the great famine, or *chalisa*, in which many among the poorer classes died from starvation and which people still remembered in the eastern districts of U.P. a hundred years later?[10]

At any rate, the Company's representatives were confident that given the right encouragement, including a suitable 'investment' at Gorakhpur, such weavers could be induced to return to what were now the Company's dominions. Indeed their hopes for the future soared much higher: 'nothing appears to be wanting', as the Reporter-General put it in pleading the case for Gorakhpur, in order 'to secure to Great Britain annually' from 20,000-30,000 and, later, even 100,000 tons of hemp, sugar, saltpetre, cotton piece-goods and other articles - the produce of the Ceded Provinces, to be transported on ships built from timber provided by the forests of Gorakhpur:[11] it was an age of confidence and ambition.

The commercial residency (or factory) at Gorakhpur in fact proved to be a disappointment. In the year of its establishment, 1803, it was allowed 100,000 Calcutta sicca rupees for 'investment', of which it could use only s.Rs.15,000 by the end of March 1804. For this sum, only 280 piece-goods, valued at s.Rs.2359 had been delivered to the export warehouse by that date.[12] In 1805, the Gorakhpur residency was closed.

The Mau-Azamgarh factory, established at the same time, fared far better. Of the sanctioned sum of Rs. 500,000 (s.Rs.478,487/8/0), the residency had used well over half (s.Rs.258,356/4/0) by March 1804. Of this sum, s.Rs.50,306/4/7 was used for 'investment' in sugar, leaving s.Rs.208,049/15/5 for 'investment' in cloth. For this, the export warehouse keeper had received by 29 March 1804, 21,679 pieces valued at s.Rs.149,266/8/11; and the reports on the 10,025 pieces that had by then been 'prized' were 'very favourable'.[13]

Given the numerous difficulties that were bound to arise on 'the establishment of so very extensive a provision under the system of advances', this was without doubt a good start. The Commercial Resident for Mau-Azamgarh noted in August 1803 that the average monthly deliveries by weavers had reached a number that would provide 57,000 pieces annually. He calculated that with a little tender care, this figure could soon be raised to 78,000 pieces per annum, equivalent at a medium of Rs. 7/8 per piece, to Rs.585,000 (or s.Rs.560,000) excluding commission.[14]

Independent of the Company's investments, a large private trade flourished. The value of piece-goods annually exported by private traders from the areas under the Mau-Azamgarh and Gorakhpur Factories was thought to be about Rs.8 lakhs (800,000).[15] This consisted chiefly of very narrow cloths, said to be in great demand inland and quite unsuitable for the Company's foreign markets, but there was no reason to believe that part of this industry and trade could not be diverted to the Company's purposes. In 1804, then, while the amount sanctioned for 'investment' in Gorakhpur piece-goods, saltpetre and hemp remained at s.Rs.100,000 that for the Mau-Azamgarh residency was raised to s.Rs.600,000.[16]

In 1818 the commercial residency at Azamgarh was wound up and amalgamated with the one at Banaras. The tract continued to figure prominently in the Company's 'investments', but the allotment for piece-goods had declined considerably relative to that for other commodities, most notably sugar.[17] In spite of its reduced importance however the external demand for the region's cloth was, at the time of the termination of the East

Economic Dislocation

India Company's trading position in 1833, yet to run dry. In the mid-1830s, R. Montgomery, Collector of Azamgarh, estimated that there were 13,682 looms at work in the district, 10,561 for cotton and 3,121 for silk and *tassar*. The probable produce, he thought, was ten lakhs of pieces per annum, at a total value of perhaps Rs.23 lakhs. Of this, cloth worth Rs.10 lakhs was exported, leaving Rs.13 lakhs' worth to clothe the district's (estimated) eight million people.[18]

The statement of exports and imports contained in the Report on the Settlement of Chuklah Azimgurh prepared by J. Thomason in 1837 is instructive.[19] The exports were:

Cotton and silk piece-goods (handled entirely by Indian traders)	Rs.1,000,000
Opium	509,700
Indigo	270,000
Sugar (exported by Europeans)	1,900,000
Sugar (exported by Indians)	350,000
Total:	Rs.4,029,700

The imports were:

Raw cotton	Rs. 215,000
Miscellaneous, spices, etc	90,000
Grain	940,000
Total:	Rs.1,245,000

The Settlement Officer noted that sugar-cane (all of it refined within the district for export), indigo and opium were the chief 'natural products' of Azamgarh. Comparatively little grain was grown, and grain had to be imported from Gorakhpur, Bihar or districts in the west of U.P. to feed the local population. The river Ghaghra was the main channel for these imports:

> Golahs, or grain markets, are established all along the course of this stream, and the supplies

are thence poured in, as necessary, to *all the manufacturing towns in the district*.[20]

Forty years later, when J.R. Reid undertook the next settlement (or revenue assessment) of the district, a significant change had occurred. The chief exports of the district were still sugar and molasses, indigo, opium and cloth. But important additions had been made to the list of imports. After grain, the major items now were English cloth and yarn, cotton, silk, dried tobacco (*surti*), salt, metals and hardware, drugs, and leather goods.[21] British manufactures had entered this distant market.

4

By the beginning of the 1830s, as we know from other evidence, there had been a reversal in the direction of flow of textile products between the British metropolis and its Indian colony. What the consequences of this reversal were for the cloth-manufacturers of eastern U.P. it is difficult to compute with any exactness. Not only are statistics for the earlier years unavailable, the available statistics are also difficult to use. Thus J.R. Reid, a painstaking official who has left us a very detailed and valuable account of the results of his survey and settlement operations in Azamgarh district in 1877, declared it impossible, on the basis of the very imperfect returns he had, to reach a conclusion as regards the quantity and value of cloth manufactured in the district or the commodities imported into it.[22]

With all the limitations of the data, however, certain long-term trends are discernible. The traditional cloth industry was, from the 1830s, subjected to powerful new pressures which it had no way of combating. For several reasons, which I hope will become clear in the course of this paper, we must be careful not to assume that the impact of these pressures was necessarily, or primarily, reflected in the numbers involved in the textile trade. Nevertheless, some statistical tendencies might be noted.

All reports from the middle and later decades of the nineteenth century seem to agree that the spinning industry suffered a secular decline over this period. In Azamgarh, the decline of traditional spinners, like the Katuas of Mau and other specialized manufacturing towns and villages, was rapid and unchecked. More and

Economic Dislocation

more, as the nineteenth century progressed, English thread came to be used instead of local yarn even in the manufacture of cloth for local markets. While 'none but the more wealthy classes' appear to have worn any other than the manufactures of the district in the 1830s, it was observed at the same time that English twist had even at that early date begun to replace local thread. By the 1870s it was being noted that anyone who wished to dress 'with a certain degree of gloss' (without doubt a growing number) used English cloth or local cloth made from English yarn.[23] Filing his report on the new Settlement of Azamgarh district at the latter date, J.R. Reid observed that in Mau, where earlier thread had been spun of such fine quality that it sold for its own weight in silver, quality spinning was 'finished': the Katuas of the town now lived chiefly by shop-keeping and petty trading.[24] 'The spinning of cotton', wrote William Hoey from Lucknow just a few years later, 'has dwindled to almost nothing for it has been found cheaper to import European twist and yarn for weaving purposes.'[25]

While the reports are direct and unambigous as regards the fate of the specialized spinners of prominent centres like Mau, they have less to say about the substantial amount of spinning that was carried on, as a full or part-time occupation (especially by women), in widely dispersed households. Yet here too there are indications that the trend was similar. By the end of the century spinning was described as no more than the spare-time pursuit of those primarily occupied in other tasks and those (especially old women) who were incapable of doing any other work.[26] In the areas of cotton cultivation spinning certainly continued - in the households of the cotton-growers themselves, skilled neighbours or local weavers. So did it in many traditional cloth manufacturing districts like Azamgarh, from where Reid reported in 1877 that many of the looms were employed in the manufacture of coarse cloths from yarn 'which is spun by women of all castes in all parts of the district'.[27]

Yet the scales, even at this humbler level, were weighted against traditional spinning. Mill yarn was cheaper, finer and more even, and therefore easier to handle; and its attractiveness to weavers increased as Indian mills entered the fray to supply the yarn at still lower rates. In addition changing local tastes strengthened the case for the use of mill-made yarn. We have mentioned Reid's reference to the desire of men of 'status' to dress in English cloth or, at least, cloth made from English yarn. Reid observed, besides, that most of the low-caste labourers, 'a fair share of the lower ranks of the other classes [that is, 'castes']', and the majority of the women of the middle and lower classes still wore local cloth made from local thread. But, even for them, 'holiday attire' was an exception: festivals and other special occasions had begun to require 'a certain degree of gloss'.[28] Finally, hand-spinning was to be put under greater pressure as agents of foreign traders, and later Indian mills, extended their reach into the cotton-growing tracts and the controllers of cotton lands themselves saw a greater profit in the export of their produce.

The indigenous hand-spinning industry, then, was early on the slide. For most of the nineteenth century it was in the sphere of weaving that the real competition occurred. Here the traditional sector put up a stiffer resistance. The records show that the cheaper, coarser (and more durable) varieties supplied by the handloom weavers, as well as some of the finer cloths and unusual mixtures which could not easily be matched in conditions of factory production, for long held their own against the challenge of mill-made cloth. At the beginning of the twentieth century, at least one-third of the cloth worn in U.P. was woven by handloom weavers, and perhaps a million people (out of a provincial population of 48 million) were dependent for their livelihood on the proceeds of weaving.[29]

'A third' is, for all that, two-thirds down. Certainly, there remains the theoretical possibility that an expanding demand allowed mill cloth (foreign and Indian) to skim off the surface leaving undisturbed the market for the handloom sector.[30] Yet this suggestion fails to consider the timing of different historical events, besides taking a rather too sanguine view of the growing consumption of cloth in colonial India. The collapse of the export market, and much of the domestic one, from the 1820s or 1830s surely entailed a real loss, which was not made good until the end of the century - if then. From all the reports of the period, one gets the impression of a trade in deep trouble, uncertain of its future, surviving - but in altogether reduced circumstances.

'The weavers of Lucknow have been ruined by the import of English goods': Hoey's words written in 1880 echo the kind of report coming in from so many different parts of northern and central India towards the end of

Economic Dislocation

the nineteenth century. 'The Jolahas of Lucknow are fast leaving the city ... and seeking a livelihood in service.' East of Lucknow, the Jamdani or figured muslin weaving of Tanda and other places in Faizabad district was under severe pressure. The town of Tanda had approximately 1125 looms at work in 1862. The 'cotton famine' that then struck hastened certain processes already at work. Many weavers left their trade (and their homes): at the end of the 1870s there were estimated to be no more than 875 looms working in the town. And whereas before the annexation of Awadh in 1856 Tanda had exported more than Rs.$1\frac{1}{2}$ lakhs worth of cloth to Nepal, it was now said to send less than 'half that quantity'. Jais and Rae Bareli, in Rae Bareli district, where very similar work was done, suffered a similar fate. In the town of Jais there were, in the 1840s, 600 Julaha families, all of whom supported themselves by weaving. By the 1890s, no more than 200 of these remained and only a score or so of them lived by their traditional occupation. In Rae Bareli town too, by the latter date, no more than one in ten of the 150 resident Julaha families worked their looms.[31] Just over three decades later, in 1931, the Census Commissioner of U.P. recorded that 'the fine muslim (muslin?) weaving of Jais, Nasirabad and other places [in Rae Bareli district] is now ... extinct'.[32]

Lucknow, Faizabad and Rae Bareli districts were all part of the truncated kingdom of Awadh which was taken over by the British only in 1856. It might be supposed, therefore, that the end of the Nawabi administration automatically spelt the doom of the indigenous cloth manufacturers. However, the abolition of the court was altogether too narrow a reason to account for the decline even of the superior fabrics.[33] In Awadh the taluqdars and the taluqdari style remained, and indeed prospered. In Nepal, the only Hindu kingdom in the world lives on to this day. It was the massive influx of Manchester goods that caused the downfall of the traditional industry.

In Azamgarh, where English 'investments' gave a distinct fillip to handloom production at the beginning of the nineteenth century, we are evidently faced by a somewhat different example. Yet here, too, the impact of Manchester was felt before long. The fortunes of Mau illustrate this clearly. When C.R. Crommelin, the East India Company's Commercial Resident for Mau and Azamgarh, first visited the pargana of Mau in February 1803, he found that it had been 'desolated by the Zemindars' warning one against the other under the Nawab's dominion. 'As the City of Mow was generally an object for plunder to the most powerful party, it soon became a heap of ruins.'[34]

The Resident drew the inevitable distinction between the light and shade of Company administration and native rule: 'On entering the district of Mow from this Province [of Banaras], the contrast struck me most forcibly, the latter in luxuriant cultivation, the former a desert-waste as far as the eye could reach; indeed I travelled nearly two hours in my Palankeen without seeing a hut or scarcely a vestige of cultivation, until I arrived at the ruins of Mow'.[35] Such blanket condemnation one must take with a pinch of salt. There is some independent evidence of armed struggle for control of land in the region of Mau in the years before the arrival of the British.[36] But the more significant reasons for the decline of Mau before the coming of the British would appear to lie elsewhere.

For one thing, the adjacent weaving centre of Kopaganj was established and given special support in the second half of the eighteenth century. Though Kopa was an old village, the new town of Kopaganj (initially, Iradatganj) was founded there in 1745 by Iradat Khan, the Raja of Azamgarh. Weavers were brought over from Mau, we are told, and merchants, chiefly Agrawals, were 'attracted' by Iradat Khan from various places. In 1774 the French traveller, Comte de Modave, described Kopaganj as 'a large place', with houses that had 'a better look than those of other villages' he had passed on his route from Calcutta and a bazar that seemed to be 'very well filled' with printed and white cloths, pottery and grain.[37] Then, in the great famine of 1782-83, the population of Mau suffered greatly and 'deaths from starvation' were recorded. If the experience of later famines is anything to go by, weavers are likely to have been among the principal victims. 'But the general population did not die from starvation, and wheat sold in the Kopaganj market at 14 sers (80 tolas) for the rupee - an unprecendented rate for those days doubtless, but not indicative of absolute dearth.'[38] Kopaganj, still receiving the special favour of the authorities, indeed became the centre for relief operations: the construction of a mosque and several wells was taken up under the orders of Mirza Ata Beg, then *chakladar* of Azamgarh, in order to provide employment to the poor. We may expect that many of the weavers and spinners of Mau trudged across the distance of six miles in order to

Economic Dislocation

avail themselves of this charity.

In 1803, then, the *aurung* of Mau was found by Crommelin to be 'in its infancy, there being very few weavers settled in it'. The Resident was informed that somewhere between 450 and 500 looms were at work; and judging from the piece-goods that he received from the local weavers between February and July 1803, he felt that he could get no more than 1000 pieces a month from Mau by the close of that year. At the same time, he anticipated that he would obtain 1500 pieces per month from the Kopa aurung ('this aurung is ... firmly settled. There are many weavers residing in it, and a greater increase may probably be effected hereafter'); 1500 pieces from the Maharajganj aurung, which lay on the borders of Awadh (Tanda, Nawabganj and other places in Awadh were 'full of weavers', many of whom might be expected to migrate to the Maharajganj aurung once the value of the Company's protection became clear); and 2500 pieces from the Azamgarh aurung, which had been the most productive up to July, and in which presumably lay Mubarakpur - 'a flourishing place' at the time of cession to the Company, with an estimated population of 10,000 to 12,000, perhaps a quarter of whom were weavers.[39]

Contrary to Crommelin's expectations, Mau appears to have recovered quickly from the devastations of the late eighteenth century. It was aided of course by the restoration of the regional trade, but very distinctly too by the establishment locally of a Commercial Residency and by the East India Company's 'investment' in its cloth manufacturers, especially in the long cloth known as *sahan*. Yet, it was a fragile base for a meaningful recovery. Before long the market for Mau (and other indigenous) produce was adversely affected by the emergence of the entirely new factor of the competition from English mill-manufacturers.

By the 1830s, Thomason was already observing that the demand for the local cloth was 'much diminished' on account of this competition. The decades that followed hastened the decline. Reid remarked on the cloth trade of Azamgarh district, that, while still important, it was 'much less than it used to be'. Of the industry in Mau, he could only say that it was 'not quite dead'. His summary statement on the manufactures of the town might be said to stand for the traditional cloth industry in eastern U.P. as a whole:

> Private enterprise for a time kept up the trade of
> Mau after the abolition of the [East India] Company's

monopoly, but the introduction of English-made thread and cloth into this country has given a great blow to it. The place is now in a state of comparative decadence, and many of the weavers are said to seek a livelihood elsewhere.[40]

To what extent the number of weavers at work in the region declined over this period is probably impossible to establish. J.R. Reid provides a figure of 13,058 looms at work in Azamgarh district in 1877, a fall of 624 from Montgomery's estimate of 1837. But we cannot say whether the decline from the 1837 level, when the cloth industry of Azamgarh was already feeling the effects of English competition, was greater or less than this difference; we do not know the basis of Montgomery's 'estimate' or how rigorous he was.

One point may be made with certainty, however. There were very major fluctuations in the numbers involved in the handloom industry, periods of a sharp downturn followed by not insignificant revival. We have noticed this already for Mau at the turn of the nineteenth century. Another well-documented example comes from the early 1860s, when weavers all over Azamgarh suffered a serious set-back. The disturbed years of 1857-59 were followed in 1860-61 by famine and by general inflation. The great increase in the price of raw cotton, as the external demand for the commodity shot up with the outbreak of the American Civil War, together with the reduced demand for their products resulting from famine and inflation, hit the weavers hard. The number of looms at work in Azamgarh district fell from 12,500 in 1860 to 8,680 in 1863. The falling-off in the quantity of work actually done was no doubt greater than these figures indicate; and the Azamgarh experience was paralleled elsewhere.[41]

However, for Azamgarh and its major cloth manufacturing centres - Mubarakpur, Mau, Kopaganj and so on - the reversal proved to be a temporary one. Barely a decade after the American Civil War, Reid made his calculation of 13,058 looms being worked in the district: roughly 1700, 1200 and 500 in Mubarakpur, Mau and Kopaganj respectively, and between 100 and 300 in ten other villages, apart from smaller numbers scattered all over.[42]

The ebb and flow of fortune continued on a lesser scale in the succeeding years. At the end of the century, we learn from a survey conducted in the 1890s, the handloom industry of Azamgarh district was certainly 'on the decline', but it was 'still moderately flourishing' and

Economic Dislocation

'a fair export trade' in cloth was being carried on.[43] The plague took its toll: here and in other districts, it was migrant weavers who carried the disease back with them from Bombay and other industrial centres, and the weaving community suffered 'terribly'.[44] But the opening of a railway line through the district (and through the town of Mau) in 1898 occasioned some 'revival' of trade; fewer weavers now left Mau, the District Gazetteer of 1911 noted, 'to seek employment in the mills of Bombay, Cawnpore and Calcutta.'[45]

The population of Mau, like that of Mubarakpur, was said to have increased steadily in the latter part of the nineteenth century. For Mau the census gave 11,315 inhabitants in 1872, 14,945 in 1881, 15,547 in 1891 and 17,696 in 1901.[46] Whatever the reliability of these various enumerations, Mau appears to have survived up to that time as a trading and manufacturing centre,[47] and even registered some growth in the last decades of the century: the opening of the railway and the establishment here of a fairly important railway junction helped in the process. One might even argue, on the basis of this evidence, that the number of workers engaged in the local handloom enterprise probably held up fairly well throughout the nineteenth century, though the early nineteenth century evidence of progressive erosion after a short and sharp increase in the trade would suggest a somewhat different conclusion. But even if we suppose for a moment that the above inference was valid, we surely cannot equate the maintenance of steady numbers with 'prosperity', or for that matter unchanging conditions in the industry.[48] There is striking evidence to the contrary from Mau.

By the middle of the nineteenth century, the fine cloth manufacturers of Mau were facing a near total collapse of their market. Their history for the next three-quarters of a century is the history of an anxious search for alternatives. New kinds of goods came to be produced. Already by the 1860s, the *dakhini pagri* (literally 'southern turban', meant for sale in central and western India) had become an important product in Mau. In the 1870s, Reid observed that coarse cloths of country-spun thread, some better cotton cloths, and some of the silk and *tassar* cloths for which Mubarakpur was better known, were 'still' made at Mau. At the end of the century, while the weaving of muslins requiring yarn from 60s to a 100 counts or more continued, with silk being used for the weft in some cases, the *dakhini pagri* had become Mau's 'staple product'. Many varieties of red and white turbans were manufactured, but 'in the majority of them the texture is loose and the cotton used is of low counts, the quality of the finished article being considerably inferior to that manufactured in Bulandshahr', in western U.P.[49] Subsequent developments in western India, most notably the opening-up of mills for cloth production, appear to have forced the weavers of Mau to experiment in other directions; and since about the 1920s the local weaving community has been employed primarily in the production of coarse cotton saris, with simple single- or multiple- line borders, for sale in nearby markets.[50] Here was a 'sliding back' indeed. The industry of Mau had come a long way from the flowered muslins once sought by merchants from many parts of India and the quality *sahan* demanded by the agents of the East India Company. For the weavers it was without doubt a much less lucrative business.

5

The decline of the indigenous cloth manufacturing industry in the middle and later nineteenth century is reflected most dramatically in the reports from the old established centres of quality production. This is understandable. But some of the forces that threatened the existence of some of these places as industrial centres also seriously affected the lower reaches of the cloth industry. We have noticed this already in the case of hand-spinning. A closer examination of the circumstances in which a part of the handloom weaving industry survived indicates some of the adjustments that weavers at all levels had to make in the face of the challenges thrown up by the nineteenth century.

Among the factors traditionally held responsible for the survival of local cloth manufactures, one of obvious importance was the inaccessibility of many areas - untouched for long by railways and other modern means of communication. Yet, as the fate of the hand-spinning industry and of a good deal of weaving even before the coming of the railways suggests, this was perhaps not as critical an obstacle as it is sometimes made out to be.[51] Banjaras and other wandering traders had, after all, carried exotic and luxury items, as well as low-value commodities such as salt, into distant regions for some time before this: if there was a profit in it, we may expect that the entrepreneurs would be available to carry the cheap yarn and piece-goods produced by the mills into the deep countryside.

Another factor of significance was that the mill-made products coming from England tended to be cloth (and yarn) of middle and high quality. The production of coarser cloth using low counts of yarn remained primarily the concern of the Indian manufacturers. Most of the cheaper materials required by the rural poor continued, then, to be provided by the handloom weavers, whose products were preferred besides on account of their greater durability. This last advantage was lost to some extent as the finer, more even, but less durable machine-made yarn came to be used by the weavers; but the local cloths intended for poorer consumers appear to have maintained their position fairly well through the nineteenth century - although, here too, there was probably some displacement of part-time weavers by the more specialized handicraftsmen who were forced into the production of coarser cloth.

To these factors we may add the survival of old tastes for particular mixtures, traditional patterns and so on,[52] plus the cheapness of handloom products for those who could provide their own raw material. And while the importance of the first of these declined as tastes changed rapidly in the latter half of the nineteenth century, the second, it seems to me, proved to be of great significance even as the century wore on.

At the time of the American Civil War, European cloth interests expressed concern that the shortfall in the Indian demand for their products might have been 'occasioned by increased indigenous manufacture'. The official enquiry in what was then the North-Western Provinces (later, the Agra province of the United Provinces) revealed, however, that these very years had seen

> a marked and distressing contraction of local manufacture. This ... is less observable in the western districts, where perhaps from a sixth to a fourth of the looms in the cities and towns (though not in the outlying villages) have stopped working. But in the eastern districts the trade has altogether decayed, and within the last two or three years [i.e. 1860-61 to 1863] the falling-off is shown to have reached a third, and in some districts a half, of the looms; and even of the remainder a large portion are only worked occasionally.[53]

The different consequences in the 'eastern' and 'western' districts of U.P. flowed, according to officials, from the fact that the 'eastern districts' (including all of Banaras and Gorakhpur Divisions, and Awadh) grew little cotton, whereas the crop was grown on a large scale in the 'western districts' (including, in this classification, Allahabad district and Bundelkhand). Of the cotton they produced the cultivators of the 'western districts' were reported to be retaining for domestic use a quarter to a sixth, even in this period of inflated demand and soaring prices for the raw material. From this, then, the women spun the thread, and weavers were hired to make specified kinds of cloth. 'It seems to be in this way', the government report noted, 'that a large proportion of the population in the western districts are supplied with clothing'.[54]

What this enquiry brings home is that handloom production survived in these years of crisis, not in the tracts that were away from the railroads but in the areas where cotton was grown and where it was, consequently, still available to men with meagre resources. Thus, in a period of marked inflation, it was not so much the lack of penetration of wider market forces and, with them, of European manufacturers, but the availability of the raw material at an accessible price that ensured the continuation of the traditional industry.[55] In districts such as Azamgarh and Ghazipur, Gorakhpur and Banaras in eastern U.P., too, any cotton grown for local consumption may be expected to have helped the weavers survive. Yet here, even in the pockets where cotton was cultivated on a significant scale, the weaker position of the tenant-cultivators vis à vis the landowners and other exploiting classes would have rendered more difficult the possibility of retaining much of the produce for local use.[56] Consequently the contraction in handloom production was 'marked and distressing'. And all over U.P., even in the western region, weavers in the larger towns, 'unable to provide the capital required to purchase material for their trade', forsook their looms.[57]

Those that survived in the trade appear to have done so by a further reduction in their margin of profit. It was found in 1863 that the imports of foreign yarn had contracted sharply from the position of a decade earlier. Many weavers reverted in this era of rising prices to the use of local yarn (of low counts) and the production of cheaper, coarser cloths.[58] It was a sitaution evidently loaded with contradictions. The weavers of Mau told the Commissioner of Banaras in 1863 that 'they would make the finest quality [cloth] cheaper than the coarser, as the latter required more cotton thread.'[59] The scarcity of the raw material reduced the value of their labours; and weavers in Mau and elsewhere were forced to accept work on much less advantageous terms than before. Indeed, many who had so far succeeded in retaining a measure of independence were now brought under the closer control of the moneylender.

Thus H.D. Robertson, Collector of Saharanpur, wrote of the 'rather remarkable change' that had occurred in the weavers' social position as a result of the rise in cotton prices at the beginning of the 1860s.

> Formerly the weavers in this district generally purchased the thread on their own account, ultimately realizing the profits from the sale of the manufactured article. Since the rise in the price of the raw material, it appears that the weavers have, as a general rule, been unable to do this, and that they have consequently now assumed the position of daily labourers, employed by shopkeepers and merchants who supply the thread and make their own profits on the cloth. The zamindars and even cultivators are also turning their attention to this new source of profit by engaging the weavers as labourers for the manufacture into cloth of a portion at any rate of their cotton crops. The weavers naturally feel this change has rendered their position by no means so independent as was formerly the case.[60]

There had been periods of heavy demand and high prices for raw cotton earlier in the century, such as the phase after the end of the Napoleonic wars in Europe when prices reached a peak in 1818-19;[61] but the exceptional circumstances of the early 1860s were not to be repeated in the decades that followed. Indeed, while the prices of foodgrains and most industrial crops appear to have risen in the late nineteenth century, the price of raw cotton seems to have been relatively stagnant - in part, no doubt, because of the sharp increase somewhat earlier and the generally expanded area under the crop. From time to time, however, there were wide fluctuations.

> The trade in cotton and its price have been subject to wide fluctuations owing to variations in the supply and demand, [commented J.A. Robertson in a

summary statement published in 1908]. In the third year of the American War the index [of cotton prices; 1873 = 100] rose as high as 229, and in 1899, when the crop was a failure [sic] and American cotton was extremely cheap, it fell to 59. The latest rise ... [followed] on the gigantic speculation in American cotton; ... the price of January 1904, gives an index of 103, and during the same month the figures for yarn and cloth are 74 and 85 respectively.[62]

Whatever the prevailing price at a particular moment, there are indications of an increasing centralization and control over the disposal of the cotton produce, as mill agents and agents for exporters penetrated further into the cotton growing tracts and improved the mechanism for the extraction of the raw material in the latter half of the nineteenth century.[63] Thus, while the lower price of yarn would certainly have benefited many weavers, other weavers (as well as spinners) would presumably have been deprived of the customary access to their raw materials. Seasonal fluctuations in supply and demand could scarcely alter this situation: they probably contributed only to the prevailing sense of instability.

With all this, the generally inflationary trend of the period and the increasing severity of the competition they faced in the urban and rural markets tended to drive the handloom weavers more and more to the wall. Certainly by the end of the century their poverty and their dependence were being widely remarked on. As one participant in an industrial conference held at Naini Tal in 1907 put it,

> In the majority of cases the weaver at present lives a hand-to-mouth existence; his method of working, the appliances used by him, and the amount he has to pay to the money-lender to obtain money to purchase his materials, cut down his earnings to such a narrow limit that they are barely sufficient to supply his daily wants.[64]

'With the decline of the weaving industry', to quote another report of the same period 'and the natural growth of population' - a popular but simplistic explanation - 'the struggle for existence is severe'.[65]

It was an index of the extremely depressed condition of the weavers that time and again in the nineteenth century, when a region was struck by famine or some other calamity, they were among the classes found to be most in need of special relief or charity.[66] The weavers had been forced 'to give up their looms and take to the pick-axe and the shovel', wrote an official from Lalitpur district in Jhansi Division during the crisis years of the American Civil War. In this sparsely populated tract, where it had earlier been difficult to obtain labourers for works of any kind, it was now found that whole families of weavers 'flock to get work, and ... many have left the district'.[67]

We have other kinds of evidence, too, pointing to the deteriorating condition of the weaving community as the nineteenth century wore on. 'Fifty years ago he was far better off than he is now'. This was the view expressed in 1888 by Raza Julaha of village Usia in Ghazipur district, when the Government of India ordered a country-wide enquiry to establish whether or not the poorer classes suffered from a 'daily insufficiency' of food. Raza was about seventy. His family consisted of his wife, two married sons, their three wives and three small children. Like many other weaving households, this one possessed no land. Raza and his wife were now too old to weave. The older son had left for Calcutta a few months earlier in search of employment and 'since his departure had not been heard of'. The second son could weave no more than five yards of cloth a day: in any case, as Raza observed, the consumption of country cloth had greatly diminished on account of the import of European piece-goods. The income of this son was supplemented a little by the earnings of the women when they got work at harvest time.

> I question [wrote the Collector of Ghazipur] whether such a family as this does not often know what the meaning of a fast is, and whether their daily meal is so regular and sufficient as it should be. A few such families could undoubtedly be found in every populous village.[68]

The profits to be obtained from spinning and weaving at any time in the nineteenth century are hard to establish. 'It may be said with certainty, however', C.A. Silberrad wrote at the close of the period, 'that it is rare to earn more than 1 anna a day by spinning or $2\frac{1}{2}$ annas by weaving, while in many cases the earnings are much less'.[69] Raza's son appears to have been paid an anna for weaving five yards of cloth, that is, a day's work.[70] In Allahabad district, a decade later, Silberrad found that rural weavers earned on average three pies per yard and $4\frac{1}{2}$ pies per yard (that is, one quarter of an anna and just over one third of an anna) respectively for weaving yarn into coarse fabrics known as *gazi* and *garha*, and six pies ($\frac{1}{2}$ anna) per yard for weaving a dhoti.[71] These rates compared very poorly indeed with the $1\frac{1}{2}$ to 2 annas daily that a casual labourer could earn about the same time.[72] The weaver's problem was that he was a poor competitor for agricultural labour where so many sturdier men from the untouchable or other cultivating castes were available for the job. Hence, although in severely straitened circumstances, many handloom weavers carried on; looms were sometimes 'kept up merely in order that the children may not forget how to weave'.[73]

6

It is perhaps necessary to reiterate that the mass of spinners and weavers had probably never shared in the prosperity derived from the textile trade. Their dependance, too, was often of long standing. It will not do to exaggerate the changes that the late eighteenth or the nineteenth century brought in these respects. Yet while survival at subsistence, or slightly above subsistence level may not have been a novel experience for many artisans, the decline of spinning and weaving and other artisanal crafts in our period removed important sources of supplementary income from the villages at a time when supplementary incomes were direly needed. The significance of the decline of traditional industry might be better appreciated if the industry is situated within the context of the rural economy as a whole.

An idea of the importance of spinning and weaving and other traditional crafts in the economy of the rural poor can perhaps be gleaned from George Grierson's Notes on the district of Gaya in Bihar. In the 1880s, Grierson conducted a detailed inquiry into the economic condition of cultivators in Gaya, recording statistics of area, outturn, rent, cost of production of different crops, and so on, for over 3500 holdings. He wrote after the conclusion of his survey: 'One of the most remarkable facts about cultivation in Gaya is that it does not, as a rule, pay for its expenses.'[74] Having quoted the relevant figures regarding size of holding and average income and expenditure, he went on:

If we exclude other sources of income, 70 per cent

of the holdings of the district do not support their cultivators. Those of them who have sufficient clothing and two meals a day must, in addition to cultivation, have other sources of livelihood.[75]

As regards the sources of supplementary income, Grierson collected information from 163 families, comprising 1210 persons, in four villages. Their net income from agriculture, he found, was Rs.9,298, from other sources another Rs.5,810. Of the latter, the largest individual items were cattle-farming (Rs.1,027), 'service' (Rs.859) and artisanal work (Rs.814). It is likely that the positions of 'service' and artisanal work would earlier have been reversed. But now, about Rs.600 was brought home as wages by men working as chaukidars, peons, etc. within the district of Gaya, whether in the village or elsewhere. The remaining Rs.259 under 'service' was the amount remitted by men serving in Calcutta, Hooghly and other places outside the district, as *darwans*, peons, domestic servants or weavers in jute mills. 'The Howrah mills', commented Grierson, 'are full of Gaya Jolahas.'[76]

Conditions in Gaya were not markedly different from those that obtained in the nearby districts of eastern U.P., and villagers here may be expected to have relied in a similar way on a number of other occupations to supplement their income from agriculture. The tract as a whole was quite densely populated and, well before the close of the nineteenth century, aided by the rigorous land revenue administration and legal system established by the British, the problems of sub-division and fragmentation of holdings and rural indebtedness were already becoming evident. In this situation large numbers of the rural poor turned to the only avenue of alternative employment open to them, migrating, with their Gaya counterparts, to the industrial belt of eastern India, the tea gardens of Assam and, as indentured labourers, to plantations abroad. An official report on Azamgarh noted that during the decade 1891-1900 emigrants from the district had remitted an average of Rs.1,300,000 per annum to their relatives at home: it was probable, the report went on, that 'but for this addition to their earnings, it would be impossible for the people to support themselves by agriculture alone.'[77]

In 1881, the number of people living in the four districts of the Calcutta metropolitan area who came from outside Bengal was found to be 279,621 or seven per cent of the total number of inhabitants. In the twenty years, 1891 to 1911, the number of immigrants from Bihar, Orissa and U.P. swelled by over 100 per cent, to 695,855. U.P. alone provided about a third of the total number of migrants throughout this period: 95,346 in 1891, 188,543 in 1901, and 235,487 in 1911. Of the U.P. migrants, by far the largest number came from a handful of districts in the east of the province, notably Ghazipur which contributed nearly 29,000 migrants in 1901, Azamgarh and Ballia (nearly 25,000 each in the same year), Banaras (over 20,000) and Jaunpur (over 17,000).[78]

Nor may this be read as a simple case of changing one occupation for another. The point has been argued forcefully that the migrants from these areas had no choice in the matter.[79] The nature of this migration was quite without precedent in the history of the subcontinent, and the personal crises that it created - though we know precious little about all this yet - were entirely new.

7

'The history of the weavers in the nineteenth century is haunted by the legend of better days.'[80] E.P. Thompson's observation on English weavers is equally applicable to the weavers of eastern U.P. 'Fifty years ago ...': Raza's statement echoes a nostalgia found in many of the reports coming in from northern and central India in the later nineteenth century.[81] We know that Raza's comment was accurate in a quite specific sense: the conditions of trade in handloom products were distinctly more favourable in the 1830s than half a century later. Yet Raza's lament was the result not only of the decline of his particular craft, but of a more extensive dislocation that affected all sections of the society in which he lived. The growing trend of migration was one indication of this barely comprehended change all around.

Migration had in earlier times been an emergency remedy during famines and other situations of crisis. Frequently, it had been used by weaving communities and other oppressed classes as a weapon of protest. As Ranajit Guha says of eighteenth-century Bengal, 'The primitive or one might say natural method - the only method in fact - yet known to the ryot for enforcing [a] bargain was migration'.[82] It had been a collective action that not only succeeded occasionally in winning for peasants

Economic Dislocation

and artisans the concessions that they sought, but also emphasized their identity of interests and sense of community. By the latter decades of the nineteenth century, much of this was being eroded, the wholesale migration of a community either to escape from oppression or to look for greener pastures was no longer possible,[83] and a collective act of protest had been transformed into an individual act of desperation. The folklore of the Bhojpuri region (eastern U.P. and western Bihar) captures some of the hopes and travails that arose out of this transformation:

> *Poorab ke deshwa men kailee nokaria*
> *Te karee sonwan ke rojigar jania ho.*
>
> [One who gets a job in the East
> can fill his house with gold.]

But also:

> *Railia na bairee*
> *Jahajia na bairee*
> *Nokaria bairee na.*[84]
>
> [Railways are not our enemy,
> Nor are the steamships:
> Our real enemy is *naukri* [service]).

At the same time, the resistance of the lower classes in the region tended towards a new extremism and violence. The history of the weavers illustrates the point well. The Julahas (or Muslim weavers) were described repeatedly in the nineteenth century as a particularly 'bigoted' and 'fanatical' community who time and again took the lead in communal rioting. Weavers were singled out in contemporary reports from various parts of northern India as being among the most militant elements in the rising of 1857-59. They were prominent in other kinds of mass violence too - such as grain riots. An observer in central India wrote:

> It is significant of the hand-to-mouth existence of the weaving community, that at the time of the riots which in September 1896 followed in the Nagpur Division close on the sudden rise in prices that heralded the famine, the weavers were prominent among the ringleaders.[85]

The new elements in these outbursts perhaps need

emphasis: 'bigotry' and 'fanaticism', sectarian strife and (here, as in grain riots) hatred of the bania and the moneylender. This last appears, contrary to one's expectations, to have been a quite novel phenomenon. In medieval north India, the bhakti saints had extolled the services of the moneylender, and even likened the relationship between peasant and moneylender to that between a *bhakt* (devotee) and *bhagwan* (object of worship, god).[86] By the latter half of the eighteenth century, and more clearly in the century that followed, the popular perception of this relationship changed radically. Thus the term *mahajan* (substantial trader, moneylender) had come to be used in U.P. in the later nineteenth century as the Kahars' slang for human excrement. And a folk-ditty recorded in the region at the time, ran as follows:

> Sāt sunārā nau thaggā;
> Sau that Baniya ēk;
> Sau baniye ko mārke,
> Garho mahajan ēk.

[Seven Sunars, goldsmiths, equal nine thugs, a hundred thus one Bania. But you need to kill one hundred Banias to create one Mahajan.][87]

The fact that the bigger traders and moneylenders in the weaving centres of eastern U.P. tended to be Hindus, and that members of the hard-pressed communities of Muslim weavers were among their chief clients, certainly contributed to the atmosphere of communal animosity. It comes as small surprise to find, for instance, in the weaving town of Mubarakpur, which was the scene of extended friction between Hindus and Muslims in the earlier decades of the nineteenth century and of two major outbursts of rioting in 1813 and 1842, that Julahas were among the chief protagonists and Hindu moneylenders among their primary targets: in 1813 the houses of two moneylenders were attacked and a merchant moneylender called Rikhei Sahu killed; in 1842 some five moneylenders' households were plundered and relatives and servants found inside two of these houses were killed.[88] But growing communal feelings were probably as much a reflection of the loss of earlier community, of a search for identity in a world that appeared to be crumbling. The community of groups like the Julahas, grounded in a common heritage, in common occupations and actions in the past, was now severely threatened.

Economic Dislocation

Many individuals broke away in order to seek a better fortune for themselves and their families. But there is evidence, from the same period, of a community struggle to prevent the obliteration of their culture and way of life. One aspect of this struggle was the Julahas' underlining of their Islamic identity. Another, about which we know less, was an extended battle against the factory system.

8

At the turn of the present century a Kayasth entrepreneur set up a factory for the production of cloth in Mau. Immediately, however, he came up against a serious obstacle. The Mau Julaha refused to take up employment in his factory 'even for double the wage that he earns outside'.[89] Rai Bahadur Goshain Bhawanipuri had encountered exactly the same difficulty a little earlier in Banaras.[90]

Behind this resistance, and their sense of isolation and loss, lay not only the straitened material circumstances of the weavers and spinners but also the memories and self-consciousness and pride of living people. The cloth-manufacturers of Azamgarh district serve as a good example.

The handicraftsmen of Mau could trace the beginnings of their position as an important manufacturing class back to the reign of Shah Jahan. The pargana of Maunath Bhanjan was at the time assigned to the Emperor's daughters, Jahanara and Chimunee Begum, 'for their supply with cloth and sugar, the two great staples of the place', and its chief town (Mau) appears to have been named Jahanabad. Under the patronage of the two princesses, the town flourished.

> Substantial buildings were erected, a large market place built, and every means employed to induce persons to resort to the town and take up their abode there.

The town quickly grew to have 84 mohallas (residential areas) and 360 mosques. Julahas (Muslim weavers), Katuas (Hindu spinners) and traders constituted a large proportion of its population. An important cotton-cloth manufacturing industry developed, and the subsequent establishment of an imperial customs post at Mau indicates the volume of traffic that passed through it.[91]

It is scarcely surprising that Mau's skilled cloth-producers, thus promoted to a place of honour by the orders of the Imperial Court, should display deep pride and a strong sense of brotherhood. Communities of skilled artisans have everywhere tended to be proud of their independence and their skills. The Julahas of northern India have made a determined effort, over a long period, to overthrow the derisive, even contemptuous, view that other sections of the society seem to have had of them. To others' derivation of the name Julaha from the Arabic *juhala* (meaning 'the ignorant class'), for instance, they responded with the suggestion that it was derived from *jils* (decorated), *jal* (net) or *ujla* (lighted up, or white) - from which last perhaps came one of the other names that the Julahas used for themselves in the nineteenth century, *nurbaf* or 'weavers of light'.[92] Already in the later nineteenth century (and more aggressively since then) Muslim weavers in many parts of northern India had come to reject the name Julaha altogether, and insisted that they be called Ansaris (after a claimed Arabic ancestor who practised the art of weaving) or Momins, that is, the faithful, or people of honour.[93]

Of the Ansaris, or Julahas, of U.P. it was said at the end of the last century not only that they were generally 'inclined to fanaticism', but that they displayed 'a strong clannish feeling, helping one another, and to a great extent settling disputes between members of their own caste among themselves'.[94] Those of Mau, Mubarakpur and Kopaganj in Azamgarh district would seem to have been among the leaders in this regard. J.R. Reid, writing in the 1870s, reported the existence of an interesting social custom that was peculiar to them. All marriages in the community took place together on one day fixed for the purpose every year.[95] The object was to reduce wasteful expenditure. The custom showed the solidarity and the single-mindedness of the Azamgarh Ansaris, factors whose influence persisted well into the twentieth century.

Over time the weavers of Mau appear to have attained a special status and a position of leadership relative to other, nearby weaving communities. In the 1880s, the Settlement Officer of Ghazipur (the district adjoining Azamgarh on the south-east) reported that the district had 'no counterparts to Mau and Mubarikpur', and that the district's major weaving centre - Banka, near Bahadurganj in pargana Zahurabad - was simply 'an offshoot from Mau'.[96] The Katuas of Mau were similarly said to be connected with those of Banaras, Bahadurganj (in Ghazipur) and Tanda (in Faizabad), apart from Kopaganj and Ghosi in Azamgarh district. They, too, claimed a distinguished ancestry. They were Bais Rajputs, according to their story, who had once been imprisoned for resistance to authority and released on the condition that they followed the woman's pursuit of spinning. They had then moved from Bheri Tal in Gorakhpur, first settling at Ghosi, then moving on to Mau and from there, at a later stage, spreading out to the various places mentioned above. In the latter half of the nineteenth century, they maintained their status as a distinct caste whose members wore the sacred thread - traditionally a privilege of the twice-born.[97]

The weavers and spinners of Mau, Mubarakpur and Kopaganj may have been a special case. But they were far from being unique in their self-image or their pride. The weavers of Tanda in Faizabad district, Jais in Rae Bareli district and other such centres traced back the origins of their privileged status to the days of the early Nawabs of Awadh and of their skilled production to a time much earlier. Thus the ancestors of Madar Baksh, whose figured muslin fabrics were said to be 'the finest specimens of this work', had been resident in Jais, Rae Bareli district, for eight centuries (as the family account had it).[98] Towards the end of the eighteenth century, a member of the family, Bhika, evolved a style of inter-weaving words, flowers and so on into patterns on fine muslins. He then devoted himself to the preparation of a kurta and pagri of the finest materials, elaborately interwoven with the names and praises of the Nawab of Awadh, Asaf-ud-daulah. The Nawab, greatly pleased with Bhika's effort, made to him a large grant of land in perpetuity. Later, Bhika made a similar kurta and pagri for Sikandar Jah, the Nizam of Hyderabad, and received for it a gift of Rs.5,000 - for which he was waylaid, plundered and killed by highway robbers while on his way home.

At the end of the nineteenth century, Bhika's direct descendants still held the land granted by Asaf-ud-daulah. They had abandoned their original craft, which passed to a younger branch of the family into which Madar Baksh was born. Madar Baksh specialized in the manufacture of caps and handkerchiefs (*rumals*) with words in Arabic or other languages interwoven into them. In the 1890s, some of his caps fetched as much as Rs.10, some of his rumals up to Rs.100. He took $3\frac{1}{2}$ to 4 months to weave a rumal that sold for Rs.50.

As the only working member of his family, Madar Baksh will certainly have been under pressure to weave more, and if necessary slightly less 'superior' goods. As far as is known, it was not a pressure to which he succumbed.

Whereas the line of Madar Baksh died out after him, the weaving industry of Mau and numerous other centres survived, as we know, in altered circumstances. How the developments of the nineteenth century, and the far more intrusive presence of usurious capital at every stage of the manufacturing process from the procurement of cotton to the sale of cloth, were viewed by the weaving communities of U.P. was noticed by some observers even at the time. We have earlier quoted from H.D. Robertson's comments on the loss of their independent position by the weavers of Saharanpur district at the time of the cotton famine in the early 1860s. Robertson concluded his remarks on the weavers' loss of independence with the following observation: 'I generally found that *they viewed this as more serious than the loss of income*, which has undoubtedly been considerable.'[99]

The vigorous and extended resistance offered to the factory system of production by weavers in many different parts of India (as elsewhere) is in line with this response. When weavers in Mau expressed their willingness to make the finest cloth 'cheaper than the coarser' during the American Civil War, they testified to the unprecedented reversal that had taken place: their labour and skills had become an entirely subsidiary consideration compared to the cost of the raw material. In some senses the plight of the men captured the tendency of the age as a whole - which was to reduce the man behind the loom to practical insignificance. What the Kayasth entrepreneur of Mau wanted at the turn of the century, and Rai Bahadur Goshain Bhawanipuri in Banaras a little earlier, was not craftsmen working on their own to produce articles of beauty, but more or less intelligent employees who could be told how to watch over a powerloom functioning at speed and producing cloth of a uniform quality on a larger and larger scale for distribution in farflung markets. The weavers' reaction, as we know, was a general refusal to take up employment in their factories.

There can be no explanation of this in simple economic terms. The Indian Industrial Commission's later strictures against the Indian artisan's 'conservatism, lack of ambition and present inability to appreciate a

Economic Dislocation

higher standard of living',[100] missed the point in this regard. The resistance of the artisans was a struggle for an autonomous culture as much as, if not more than, a protest against material deprivation. What the weavers of eastern U.P. appear to have feared above all was an alienation from their means of production,[101] and a fall from the position of proud independent producers to that of working dependants or mere wage earners. What they resented most was the indignity of being ordered about.[102]

9

It has been one aim of this paper to suggest that the decline of an artisanal industry in northern India in the nineteenth century cannot be measured merely in terms of the numbers employed in the craft: it must be viewed, too, in the light of their displacement from the position of manufacturing quality goods to one of producing inferior ones. It has been argued also that the process that has been designated the 'de-industrialization' of India, which we may never be able to quantify satisfactorily, was part of a broader economic dislocation that came about as a result of the progressive integration of the local economy with the economy of a commercially and, then, industrially powerful metropolis. Closely related to this is another point. While there were, without doubt, fluctuations in the standing of traditional crafts in one region and another long before the period here under study, the decline of the colonial era was of a rather different quality. For it occurred, as the U.P. example amply demonstrates, at a time when the buying up of property and other rights in land (both cultivated and waste), combined with a rigorous legal system and (though this is a relatively late problem) the growth of the population which altered the man:land ratio, had made a move to other areas or alternative employment far from easy.

The common objection that all this was inevitable, that older, less efficient modes of production must necessarily give way to more rational and modern ones, is deficient on two counts. The first, put simply, is that it overlooks the history of the generations who lived through the alleged 'period of transition': it is as though Raza and his untraced son might never have been. Secondly, it fails to take account of the particularities of the colonial experience. This is where

119

the very slow growth of modern industry created special problems, in India as in so many other Asian and African countries. There was a large-scale disruption of old forms, without a real transformation. The handicraftsmen of old, like vast numbers of the poorer peasants and agricultural labourers, found their means of livelihood in jeopardy: but their links with their rural homes were not completely severed. What was in western Europe a relatively short-lived if traumatic period of change became in the sub-continent and elsewhere a chronic condition.[103]

In eastern U.P. the reduced state of the artisanal classes, the survival of the weavers on sufferance, at the mercy of the moneylender and in pitiable conditions,[104] the effort to eke out a living from minute plots of land, and the necessity of 'semi-permanent' migration: all this continued. In 1941 emigrants from the tahsil of Phulpur in Azamgarh district alone remitted a sum of over Rs.60 lakhs to their relatives and dependants at home.[105] In 1942 the Magistrate of the district recorded that the Julahas of Mau could still think of nothing but 'their looms and their religion'.[106]

NOTES

Pandey, 'Economic dislocation in nineteenth-century eastern Uttar Pradesh: some implications of the decline of artisanal industry in colonial India'

In this paper 'U.P.' refers to present-day Uttar Pradesh, or, earlier, the United Provinces of Agra and Awadh. I owe thanks to the participants in the 'External Dimension' seminar held at SOAS, London, in December 1980; also to Shahid Amin, Amiya Bagchi, Barun De, Indrani Ray, Sumit Sarkar and, especially, Gautam Bhadra for their comments on an earlier draft.

Abbreviations

BTC Board of Trade (Commercial) Proceedings, West Bengal Archives, Calcutta

IESHR *Indian Economic and Social History Review*

SR Settlement Report

    1. Among the recent contributions are D. Thorner, 'De-industrialisation in India' in D. and A. Thorner, *Land and Labour in India* (Bombay 1962); J. Krishnamurthy, 'Changes in the Composition of the Working Force in Manufacturing, 1901-51', *IESHR* VI, 1 (1967); A.K. Bagchi, 'De-industrialisation in Gangetic Bihar, 1809-1901' in *Essays in Honour of Prof. S.C. Sarkar* (Delhi 1978), and 'De-industrialisation in India in the Nineteenth Century. Some Theoretical Implications', *Journal of Development Studies*, 12, 2 (1976) - see also M. Vicziany 'The De-industrialisation of India in the Nineteenth Century: A methodological critique of A.K. Bagchi', *IESHR* XVI, 2 (1979), and Bagchi's 'Reply', loc.cit. -; and R. Chattopadhyaya, 'De-industrialisation in India Reconsidered', *Economic and Political Weekly* X, 12 (22 March 1975).

    2. There is a considerable and growing body of literature on the textile industry in this period. See, e.g. Irfan Habib, 'Indian Textile Industry in the 17th Century' in *Essays in Honour of S.C. Sarkar*, and K.N. Chaudhuri, 'The Structure of Indian Textile Industry in the 17th and 18th Centuries', *IESHR* XI, 2-3 (1974). For the different levels of production and the role of intermediaries, see especially Hamida Hossein, 'The Structure of Cotton Textile Production for the East

India Company, 1750-1800', *IESHR* XVI, 3 (1979); S. Arasaratnam, 'Weavers, Merchants and Company: the handloom industry in south-eastern India 1750-1790', *IESHR* XVII, 3 (1980); G. Bhadra, 'The Role of Pykars in the Silk Industry of Bengal, c.1765-1830' (revised and expanded version of paper presented at the Indian History Congress, Aligarh 1975); and S. Bhattacharya, 'Industrial Production, Technology and Market Structure in Eastern India, 1757-1857' (*Cambridge Economic History of India*, vol.II, forthcoming).

3. Bhadra, Bhattacharya and Hossein,opp.cit.; also M.M. Martin, ed., *The History, Antiquities, Topography and Statistics of Eastern India, Vol.III* (1838, reprint New Delhi 1976), pp.971-8.

4. Bhattacharya, 'Industrial Production 1757-1857'; for the silk industry, also R.K. Gupta, 'Birbhum Silk Industry: A Study of its Growth and Decline', *IESHR* XVII (1980).

5. See Hossein, 'The Alienation of Weavers', p.324. As against this, it is necessary to note K.N. Chaudhuri's evidence regarding the strength of the specialised weavers' bargaining position; 'The Structure of Indian Textile Industry', p.155.

6. *Babarnamah*, tr. A.S. Beveridge (1970 reprint), p.487.

7. See A. Siddiqi, *Agrarian Change in a Northern Indian State 1819-33* (Oxford 1973); E. Whitcombe, *Agrarian Conditions in Northern India* vol. I (Berkeley and Los Angeles 1971); C.A. Bayly, 'The Age of Hiatus, the North Indian Economy and Society, 1830-1850' in C.H. Philips and M.D. Wainwright, eds., *Indian Society and the Beginnings of Modernisation* (London 1976); Bayly, 'Town Building in North India, 1790-1830', *Modern Asian Studies* 9, 4 (1975).

8. BTC vol.172, No.33, Letter from Resident, 'Gorruckpore', 26 March 1804, and 'Report on Commerce and Customs of Ceded Provinces' enclosed with Letter from Reporter-General of External Commerce, Patna, 20 October 1803.

9. Ibid., para 115.

10. J.R. Reid, *Report on the Settlement of the Temporarily Settled Parganas of Azamgarh District 1877* (Allahabad 1881), p.14; see also E.T. Stokes, *The Peasant and the Raj* (Cambridge 1978), p.67.

11. BTC, vol.172, No.33, Reporter-General's Letter, 20 October 1803, para.123.

12. Ibid., Report from Board of Trade-Governor General in Council, 17 December 1803, para.79.

Notes to pages 94-8

13. Ibid., para.51; also 'Account of Goods Received from the Ceded Provinces up to the present time' (from Export Warehouse Keeper, 29 March 1804).
14. BTC, vol.166, Pt.II, No.66, Resident, Mow and Azimgurh to President and Members of Board of Trade, 16 August 1803, paras.8 and 20.
15. BTC, vol.172, No.33, 'Report on Commerce and Customs of Ceded Provinces', para.77.
16. Ibid., Report from Board of Trade, 17 December 1803, paras.55 and 92.
17. By 1806, the 'investment' in Mau-Azamgarh piece-goods was already down to s.Rs.135,000; in 1818 it was a little over s.Rs.117,000 for the combined *aurungs* of Banaras, Mau and Azamgarh; BTC, vol.196, no.19 of 1 April 1806, and no.70 of 13 February 1818. For the experience of the sugar trade, which took a far larger share of the Company's investments for most of this period, see Shahid Amin, 'Sugarcane Cultivation in Gorakhpur, U.P., c.1890-1940' (Oxford University D.Phil. thesis, 1979), pp.13 ff.
18. Figures quoted in J. Thomason, *Report on the Settlement of Chuklah Azimgurh* dated Agra, 16 December 1837 (Art.XV of *Selections from the Records of Government, North-Western Provinces*, Pt.XII-XXI, Agra 1855) p.131.
19. Ibid., pp.131-2.
20. Ibid., p.128. Emphasis added.
21. Reid, Azamgarh SR, p.59.
22. Ibid., 159, 169 and also 144. See also Whitcombe, op.cit. pp.252-70; Vicziany, op.cit., and Bagchi 'Reply'.
23. Thomason, Azimgurh SR, pp.130-1; Reid, Azamgarh SR, p.170.
24. Ibid., p.147.
25. W. Hoey, *A Monograph on Trade and Manufactures in Northern India* (Lucknow 1880), p.28. See also Report of the Indian Industrial Commission, 1916-18 (Calcutta 1918), para.225.
26. C.A. Silberrad, *A Monograph on Cotton Fabrics produced in North-Western Provinces and Oudh* (Allahabad 1898), pp.45-6. See also A. Blennerhassett, *Monograph on the Cotton Fabrics of the Central Provinces* (Allahabad 1898), p.3.
27. Reid, Azamgarh SR, p.169.
28. Ibid., p.170.
29. Papers Connected with the Industrial Conference held at Naini Tal, 1907. 'Note by the Honourable Rai Sri Ram Bahadur, C.I.E. on the Handloom Industry', p.44;

A.C. Chatterji, Notes on the Industries of the United Provinces (1908), pp.10-11. For India as a whole, during the five years 1924-25 to 1928-29, handlooms still provided some 25 per cent of the total consumption of about 5000 million yards of cloth, while 40 per cent was supplied by Indian mills and about 35 per cent was imported. Report of the U.P. Provincial Banking Enquiry Committee 1929-30, vol.III (Allahabad 1930), pp.386-7.

30. This argument was put forward by M.D. Morris, 'Towards a Reinterpretation of Nineteenth Century Indian Economic History', *IESHR* V, 1 (1968). It has been reasserted by Vicziany, op.cit., p.158.

31. Hoey, *Monograph*, p.28. A.F. Millett, *Report on the Settlement of the Land Revenue of the Fyzabad District* (Allahabad 1880); Silberrad, *Monograph*, pp.32,46. For the same in central India, see Blennerhassett, *Monograph*, p.2.

32. A.C. Turner, *Census of India, 1931. United Provinces of Agra and Oudh. Vol.XVIII, Pt.1 - Report* (Allahabad 1933), p.426.

33. See Blennerhassett, *Monograph*, p.2.

34. BTC, vol.166, Pt.II, No.66, Resident Mow and Azimgurh to Board of Trade, 16 August 1803, para.14.

35. Ibid., para.16.

36. Thomason, Azimgurh SR, pp.136-7.

37. J. Deloch, ed., *Voyage en Inde du Comte de Modave, 1773-76* (Paris 1971), pp.140-1 (I am indebted to Aniruddha Ray for this reference); Reid, Azamgarh SR, p.150.

38. Ibid., 15.

39. BTC, vol.166, Pt.II, No.66, Letter of Resident Mow and Azimgurh, 16 August 1803, paras.13-20. For Mubarakpur, see Reid, Azamgarh SR, p.148.

40. The quotations are from Thomason, Azimgurh SR, p.130; Reid, Azamgarh SR, pp.147 and 170.

41. *Selections from the Records of Government, North-Western Provinces, Part XL* (Allahabad 1864), Art. IV - 'Information Regarding the Slackness of Demand for European Cotton Goods', p.149. For the adjoining district of Ghazipur, e.g., where the number of looms at work fell by half from 7,000, see ibid., p.152.

42. Reid, Azamgarh SR, pp.168-9.

43. Silberrad, *Monograph*, p.46. The exports went chiefly to neighbouring areas in U.P., Bihar and Central India, and a little also northwards to Nepal.

44. C.E. Crawford, *Final Report on the 7th Settlement of the Azamgarh District of the United Provinces* (Allahabad 1908), p.8; D.L.Drake-Brockman, *Azamgarh: A Gazetteer*, vol. XXXIII of U.P. Gazetteers (Allahabad 1911), p.62. H.R.Nevill,

Allahabad Gazetteer, vol.XXIII of ibid, p.273; H.R. Nevill, *Benares Gazetteer*, vol.XXVI of ibid. (1909), p.27.

45. Drake-Brockman, Azamgarh District Gazetteer, p.255. Sharp fluctuations have occurred since then as well. The national movement gave a considerable fillip to the indigenous handloom industry, especially in the 1920s and 1930s. Then the introduction of the power-loom in the 1960s restored the fortunes of the local cloth industry. Mau and Mubarakpur are probably bigger centres of weaving today than they were before; but the conditions of the trade now are very different.

46. Drake-Brockman, Azamgarh District Gazetteer, p.255.

47. Crommelin, the Commercial Resident for Mau and Azamgarh, was given a figure of about 10,000 as the population of Mau in 1803, which he considered exaggerated, however. But Reid in his report on the district in 1877 clearly declared his opinion that, in the 1780s, the town of Mau was 'larger than now', Azamgarh SR, p.15.

48. Such an equation is often made: see C.E. Crawford, Azamgarh SR (1908) p.9.

49. Judgement in Trial no.13 of 1863, Court of A. Ross, Sub-Judge: Government v Sheonarian Rai and others, Appendix D to 'Petition of Hindu Inhabitants of Mhow, to Secretary of State for India in Council' (1893?). (I am grateful to Shri D.N. Pandey of Mau, Azamgarh, for allowing me to consult this document which is preserved in the library of his late father, a prominent Hindu of the town.) Drake-Brockman, Azamgarh District Gazetteer, p.62. It speaks of the transitory nature of the local weavers' trade in the nineteenth century that no-one in Mau appears to be able to recall what exactly the *dakhini pagri* was and for what market it was produced.

50. *Census of India, 1961, Vol.XV, U.P. Pt.VII. Handicrafts Survey Monograph No.6*, R.I. Verma, 'Cotton Textiles Industry in U.P. with special reference to Maunath Bhanjan, Azamgarh'. Mubarakpur suffered a similar dislocation. Famous for a silk-and-cotton mixture like satin, woven into fabrics known as *sangi* and *ghalta*, the weavers of Mubarakpur, it was said, at the turn of the century, had 'owing to the trade depression ... been compelled to resort to the weaving of cotton handkerchiefs and *pagris*, which are now more in demand than satins'; Drake-Brockman, Azamgarh District Gazetteer, p.62. Such dislocation was in fact a

Notes to pages 104-6

very widespread phenomenon. Hites Sanyal gives me the following example regarding Ramjiwanpur (Midnapur district) from his researches on West Bengal. Ramjiwanpur, situated near the junction of the old Burdwan-Puri main road and the chief trading road from Midnapur towards the north-west, and surrounded by a number of smaller cloth-manufacturing villages, was the nodal point of a thriving inter-district and also longer-distance trade in textiles at the beginning of the nineteenth century. At this time, the cloths produced in the region were chiefly *garah*, fine cotton cloth, silks and some *tassar*. For several decades from the early nineteenth century, local manufacturers were able to concentrate their attention on silks and fine cotton cloths, for which there was considerable demand. Sometime around the middle of the century, silks began to lose their importance, and coarser cotton dhotis and saris joined the finer cotton cloths as the chief products of the region. By the end of the century, the market for the fine cottons had also collapsed, and the weavers were occupied in the production only of coarse cotton cloths for a local market.

51. Blennerhassett, *Monograph*, p.5.

52. A. Yusuf Ali (comp.), *A Monograph on Silk Fabrics Produced in the North-Western Provinces and Oudh* (Allahabad 1900), p.103, writes of Azamgarh: 'In silk fabrics, especially of the mixed kind manufactured in this district, there is a peculiar adaptation to local conditions and prejudices, which enables the industry to hold its own, or at least to decline less slowly than it would otherwise have done'. For a different view of the significance of old tastes, see Silberrad, *Monograph*, p.46.

53. 'Slackness of Demand for European Cotton Goods', p.116.

54. Ibid., p.119.

55. Silberrad, writing in 1898, accounted it as a specially powerful argument in favour of handmade cloth in the cotton-growing districts: the women of the cultivator's household spin some of their home-grown cotton into yarn, which the Kori then weaves for them; *Monograph*, p.46.

56. See, for the example of sugar-cane cultivators in an era of considerable expansion of the area under the crop and, indeed, of the establishment of modern factories for the refining of sugar, Shahid Amin,, 'Sugar-cane Cultivation in Gorakhpur, c.1890-1940', passim.

57. 'Slackness of Demand', p.119.

58. Ibid., p.118.
59. Ibid., p.148.
60. Ibid., p.121.
61. Siddiqi, *Agrarian Change*, p.155.
62. *The Imperial Gazetteer of India. The Indian Empire*. III (Oxford 1908), p.465. See D.R. Gadgil, *The Industrial Evolution of India in Recent Times, 1860-1939* (Delhi 1972), pp.21-2, 65; and Whitcombe, op.cit., pp.102-3, 178-9 and Fig.3 at end of book. These present some of the evidence regarding general price movements during the period.
63. See M. Vicziany, 'Bombay Merchants and Structural Changes in the Export Community, 1850-80', in K.N. Chaudhuri and C.J. Dewey, eds., *Economy and Society. Essays in Indian Economic and Social History* (Delhi 1979).
64. Naini Tal Industrial Conference Papers 1907, p.44. See also Indian Industrial Commission Report, p.7.
65. Drake-Brockman, Azamgarh District Gazetteer, p.118.
66. Naini Tal Industrial Conference Papers 1907, p.44; R. Baird-Smith, *Report on the Famine of 1860-61* (Roorkee, May 1861), p.31; F. Henvey (comp.), *A Narrative of the Drought and Famine which prevailed in the North-Western Provinces during 1868, 1869 and 1870* (Allahabad 1871), p.2; Gorakhpur Commissioner's Record Room, Dept.XIII, File 40/1905-9, 'Rules for the Relief of Distressed Weavers'.
67. 'Slackness of Demand for European Cotton Goods', p.146.
68. Government of India, Revenue and Agriculture Dept., Famine. Progs.1-24, December 1888, 'Reports on the Condition of the Lower Classes of the Population of India', Report from Banaras Division, para.17. Blennerhassett, *Monograph*, p.3, writes of how thirty years ago, the weavers were 'a prosperous community', common weavers, let alone those of special skill, earning Rs.50 per month, whereas now the average income was probably as low as Rs.3 to Rs.5 a month.
69. Silberrad, *Monograph*, p.49.
70. 'Condition of the Lower Classes', Banaras Division Report, para.17.
71. Silberrad, *Monograph*, p.46.
72. Reid, Azamgarh SR, p.129; A.K. Bagchi, *Private Investment in India 1900-39* (Cambridge 1972), p.221, n.8.
73. 'Slackness of Demand for European Cotton Goods', p.91.

74. G.A. Grierson, *Notes on the District of Gaya* (Calcutta 1893), p.91.
75. Ibid., p.95. Emphasis in the original.
76. Ibid., p.107.
77. Drake-Brockman, Azamgarh District Gazetteer, p.118. J.R. Reid noted in 1877 that employment on public works in the Azamgarh district did not compensate for the loss of service 'in the Native Army and with Native Princes' from which 'extraneous source a good deal of money used to come into this part of the country', cited in Whitcombe, op.cit., p.140.
78. R. Das Gupta, 'Factory Labour in Eastern India: Sources of Supply, 1855-1946', *IESHR*, XIII, 3 (1976), pp.289-91, 310, 312.
79. L. Chakravarty, 'Emergence of an Industrial Labour Force in a Dual Economy - British India, 1880-1920', *IESHR*, XV, 3 (1978).
80. E.P. Thompson, *The Making of the English Working Class* (Harmondsworth 1968), p.297.
81. See Blennerhassett, *Monograph*, p.1.
82. R. Guha, *Report on an Investigation of the Gauripur Raj Estate Archives* (Annual Report, Regional Record Survey Committee, West Bengal, 1955-56), p.29. I am grateful to Gautam Bhadra for drawing my attention to this report.
83. There were a few exceptions in special circumstances, such as migration in times of famine, or the hijrat of Patidar peasants from Kheda and Surat districts during the Civil Disobedience Movement of 1930-31 which was made possible by 'the jigsaw-like juxtaposition of British and Baroda territory in the area'; D. Hardiman, 'The Crisis of the Lesser Patidars: Peasant Agitations in Kheda, Gujarat, 1917-34', in D.A. Low, ed., *Congress and the Raj* (London and Delhi 1977), p.63.
84. Quoted in D.P. Saxena, *Rururban Migration in India. Causes and Consequences* (Bombay 1977), pp.175, 178.
85. Blennerhassett, *Monograph*, p.4.
86. I owe this point to Gautam Bhadra. For an elaboration, see his *'Mughal Juge Bhartiya Krishi Arthaniti te Sreni Vinyas O Sreni Dwanda'*, *Anya Artha*, 7 (January-February 1975).
87. Both these examples are from W. Crooke, *A Rural and Agricultural Glossary for the North-Western Provinces and Oudh* (Calcutta 1888), p.181.
88. U.P. Regional Archives, Allahabad, COG (Gorakhpur), Judicial (Azamgarh), vol.68, File 47, 'Outbreak

Notes to pages 115-20

in the Town of Mubarikpur, Azamgarh 1845'. Drake-Brockman, *Azamgarh District Gazetteer*, pp.261-1. For a fuller discussion of this subject, see my 'Sectarian Strife in the Bhojpuri Region, c.1806-1917' (forthcoming).
    89. Naini Tal Industrial Conference Papers (1907), p.40.
    90. Ibid.
    91. U.P. Regional Archives, Allahabad, COG (Gorakhpur), Revenue (Azamgarh), vol.27f, File 331, J. Thomason, Collector Azimgurh to F. Currie, Commissioner Revenue 5th Division, 22 June 1836, para.22; Reid; Azamgarh SR, pp.146-7.
    92. Silberrad, *Monograph*, p.1; W. Crooke, *The Tribes and Castes of the North-Western Provinces and Oudh* III (Calcutta 1896), pp.69-70.
    93. Ibid.; also interviews with Maulvi Kamruzzaman, Mubarakpur, Azamgarh.
    94. Silberrad, *Monograph*, p.1.
    95. Reid, Azamgarh SR, p.147n.
    96. W. Irvine, *Report on Revision of Records and Settlement Operations in the Ghazipur District, 1880-85* (Allahabad 1886), p.127. See also Collector of Mirzapur's report, in 'Slackness of Demand for European Cotton Goods', p.149.
    97. Reid, Azamgarh SR, p.147.
    98. The following account is based on Silberrad, *Monograph*, pp.32-3.
    99. 'Slackness of Demand', p.148.
    100. Indian Industrial Commission Report, p.195.
    101. The point is made by S. Bhattacharya, 'Cultural and Social Constraints in Technological Innovation', *IESHR* III, 3 (1966).
    102. See Thompson, op.cit., p.338.
    103. See Bagchi, 'De-industrialisation in Gangetic Bihar', pp.500-1, and 'De-industrialisation in India', pp.136-7.
    104. See, for example, K. Nair, *Blossoms in the Dust* (London 1961), pp.35-6.
    105. Ram Rup Singh, *Assessment Report of Tahsil Phulpur, District Azamgarh* (Allahabad 1944),p.4.
    106. U.P. Regional Archives, Allahabad: List 35, R.H. Niblett, District Officer (1 December 1939 to 22 August 1942), 'Who's Who in Azamgarh District', entry no.86.

RURAL LABOUR IN THE BOMBAY TEXTILE INDUSTRY
AND THE ARTICULATION OF MODES OF ORGANIZATION

Dick Kooiman

Introduction

One of the most fundamental problems of historical
analysis is the specification of particular modes of
production within a given social formation and the way
in which one mode requires for its own reproduction
dominance over the other. Recently, this claim has
been put forward most emphatically and persistently by
adherents of the so-called mode of production school of
thought. And it must be conceded that this approach
has proved its worth and has yielded interesting
results as far as African and Latin American studies are
concerned. Asian studies, however, seem to be lagging
behind in this field of research. It may be that the
lack of written sources, especially for Africa, has
prompted historians to investigate the past by extra-
polating from the present with the help of comprehensive
theories, whereas in the field of South Asian studies
historians, worming their way through huge piles of
documentary evidence, are more inclined to cling to
the established practices of their profession. Nevertheless, mode of production studies on South Asia do
appear occasionally and in all probability have come
to stay.[1]

Most studies made from this perspective agree that
imperialism, by imposing private property and establishing large scale commodity production, subordinated
indigenous agriculture to the exigencies of the world
market. But although imperial power drastically
changed the existing relations of production in agriculture, it prevented native societies from fully
industrializing. Consequently, the majority of the uprooted peasants could not be absorbed by industrial
growth but had to fall back upon village society and
thus the essential backwardness of agriculture was maintained.

As a matter of course, this quite general picture
needs further elaboration to fit specific situations.
But the filling in of more details generates a lot of
discussion about the extent to which capitalism succeeded in transforming indigenous society, the exact
definition of the agrarian, non-capitalist sector

and the existence or non-existence of free wage-labour in agriculture.[2]

It is not the purpose of this paper to bother about the many niceties of this ongoing debate. Rather, it focuses on one central notion, the articulation of two different modes of production. This articulation can be conceptualized as the co-existence of a non-capitalist (agrarian) mode of production and a capitalist (industrial) one within a given social formation. But this dualism does not imply a complete separation or lack of communication between the two modes of production. Peasant social formations in the Third World have been penetrated by foreign as well as indigenous industrial capital, which drew its labour from the agrarian sector. But as Meillassoux has pointed out for Africa, industrial capitalism became interested in the maintenance of that agrarian society (the 'communauté-domestique'), as it represented a source for the reproduction of labour, that is the provision of social services, care of the sick and aged, child-rearing and so on. For the wage-earners also, the preservation of village and family ties was of utmost importance, as the agricultural self-sustaining community fulfilled the vital functions of social security that industrial capitalism refused to assume. Whereas in Europe capitalism arose by destroying feudalism, in the Third World it developed by maintaining previous modes of production and Meillassoux concludes that 'the agricultural communities ... are being both undermined and perpetuated at the same time, undergoing a prolongated crisis and not a smooth transition to capitalism'.[3]

An attempt to apply this frame of analysis to colonial India has recently been made by Gail Omvedt. She emphasizes the lack of a family wage as the main mechanism through which cheap labour could be employed and manufacturing costs reduced. By leaving the costs of reproduction of labour power to the non-capitalist agrarian sector, capitalism also forced a sexual division between the villages, where most women and family members remained, and the new centres of employment to which the male workers migrated in large numbers. Although Omvedt is laying more stress on the crucial role of the colonial state, she reaches the same conclusion as Meillassoux in the sense that the development of the capitalist mode of production is furthered simultaneously with the maintenance of feudal relations in agriculture.[4]

In this paper, I want to carry the argument of

Dick Kooiman

Gail Omvedt a bit further. First of all the concept of a dominant capitalist and subordinated feudal mode of production will be narrowed down and its applicability tested by focusing on the city of Bombay and its surrounding hinterland before World War II. The textile industry of this city represented one of the most developed sectors of the British-Indian economy, while the surrounding village societies may be called non-capitalist or even feudal in the sense that their economy was characterized by personal relationships of dependence based on the differential access to land and (mainly agrarian) employment opportunities. Next, attention will be paid to the so-called jobber, who as a recruiter of labour served as a linkage between these rural localities and the wider world of urban industry. Finally, the most important question will be, to what extent the articulation of two different modes of production determined the character of the emerging trade unions in the Bombay textile industry and how far our analysis may benefit from the introduction of the concept of articulation of modes of labour organization.

Bombay and the Textile Industry: Migration of Labour

The Bombay textile industry was started in the mid-nineteenth century by native enterprise. It combined indigenous capital with European management and technical equipment. After a period of extensive growth it very soon came to dominate the city's economic life. By World War I the industry numbered more than eighty mills and employed one quarter of the total working population. Except for its textile mills Bombay had little claim to be called an industrial city and economically it may be characterized as a city which combined the textile specialization of Manchester with the trade and shipping of London.

The labour needed by the growing number of mills was mainly drawn from the surrounding districts, and, of course, this labour drain had far-reaching consequences both for city and countryside. The peculiar composition of Bombay's urban population in terms of sex and age bore testimony to this and may be seen as a clear example of the way in which industrial capitalism made use of labour from the non-capitalist sector.

First of all, Bombay was primarily a city of immigrants. According to the census, the percentage of

Rural Labour in the Bombay Textile Industry

the urban population born outside Bombay was 69 per cent in 1872 and never fell below the 70 per cent level in any subsequent census. There is, however, some inflation in this figure, owing to a widespread female custom of returning for confinement to the village of origin.[5]

Most migrants went to Bombay alone in search of employment. A married man would leave his family behind until such time as he might decide to make a home for them in the city. In most cases, however, that time never came and thus the worker had to pay periodical visits to his village to fulfil the necessary family obligations. Therefore, the proportion of females was very low among the immigrant groups and in 1931, for example, amounted to only 541 females for every thousand males coming from Ratnagiri, the main labour-supplying area. This figure does not distinguish between textile workers and other types of migrants. On the basis of census data, however, the sex-ratio of immigrant textile workers from the main labour catchment areas can be calculated at least approximately (as in table 1).[6]

Table 1: *Sex-Ratio among Immigrants in Bombay (1931) - Females per 1,000 Males*

Place of Origin:	Sex-Ratio (General)	Sex-Ratio (Textile Labour Only)
Poona	661	599
Kolaba	619	375
Satara	545	274
Ratnagiri	541	459
United Provinces	211	38
Total	489	323

As might be expected, the sex-ratio of textile workers turns out to be considerably lower than that of the whole migrant group from the corresponding region, and the far-away districts of U.P. were represented by a low of 38. The number of females per 1,000 males for Bombay as a whole was 554 and the general census report mentioned that the sex-ratios of Bombay City and Ratnagiri district offered interesting complements to each other.

Not only was the sex-ratio in Bombay exeptional, but the age composition of the urban population also differed markedly from the rural hinterland. The censuses show a great preponderance of adults in the active wage-earning periods of life. Whereas in the Presidency as a whole the 15-40 age-group year numbered 41.8 per cent of the total population, in Bombay City its proportional representation was no less than 61.3 per cent. Especially in this age-group there was a marked deficiency of females (248 per 1,000 males) and only in the lower and higher age-groups did the female ratio approach a more even distribution. This very particular demographic structure clearly reflects the special economic needs and labour recruitment in Bombay's capitalist mode of production. It proves that the greater number of workers born outside Bombay did not reside in the city permanently. They spent the most productive period of their lives there, then left the city when they ceased working.

In 1931 the census concluded that Bombay 'has become less and less a place for children and old people'. It even discerned a tendency for workers to retire from factory work at an earlier age than formerly, suggesting that Bombay was also becoming 'progressively a place for younger and younger workers'.[7] The average age of the male operatives was computed at 26 years.[8]

The 1908 Labour Commission reported that the migrant worker could return to his village the moment he came to dislike factory labour. Back home he could always find some work to do, while the joint family system secured him against want.[9] But that is a much too rosy picture of the situation. From an interview with returned workers, a *mamlatdar* in one of the main labour supplying areas concluded 'that the lot of these persons is a hard one and that if they take to mill life it is not so much out of love as out of necessity'.[10] As their villages did not offer sufficient work they had to seek employment elsewhere. Or, as the Whitley Commission had it, in its classical phrase, the migrant workers 'are pushed not pulled'.[11] The areas they came from suffered from a poor agriculture hampered by too heavy or scanty rains, an increasing population pressure and the dwindling importance of local handicrafts.[12]

A frequently observed and much discussed aspect of this labour migration was the workers' habit of returning to their villages quite regularly. Apart from family obligations, considerations of health and climate also afforded strong motives for temporary retirement. The modern factory with its deafening noise, lack of ventilation and artificial humidity tested the villagers' staying capacities to the utmost, let alone their working capacities. Especially during the summer with its suffocating heat were they exhausted. A periodical return home, it may be presumed, was absolutely necessary to recover from the fatigue caused by continually working under these circumstances ten hours a day, twenty-six days a month.

There are also some indirect indications of a continuing influence of the agrarian cycle on the movements of labour. Although in the twentieth century the Bombay mills had generally passed the stage of being compelled to adjust their production to the agrarian season, government officals kept reporting on a largely seasonal migration of labour from their districts. In May, as the flow-back to the countryside began, some mills increased their piece-rates and those in charge of recruitment had to make more efforts to enlist the normal complements. And big textile strikes, like those in 1928, 1929 and 1934, invariably began in the month of April. On the eve of the summer rains, the call to stop work with the implicit consequence of returning to the village was sure to fall on fertile soil.[13]

According to all descriptions, the workers' dwellings were distinctly dark, damp and ill-ventilated. They were surrounded by narrow gullies for carrying off waste and sewage, which permeated the whole of the surrounding atmosphere with an offensive odour. Moreover, they were terribly overcrowded. The very great majority of the working-class population lived in single room tenements and a single room was very often shared by several groups or families. The miserable housing conditions and bad sanitary arrangements had a most disastrous effect upon the health of the workers, and a contemporary observer called these *chawls* 'pestilential plague spots'.[14] Death-rates were very high and during the 1918-1922 period the average infant mortality in these chawls amounted to 572 deaths per 1,000 births.[15]

The working-class population was also frequently harassed by epidemics and plague. But respiratory diseases, caused by the breathing of foul or dust and fibre-laden air constituted the determining factor in the high death rate in the workers' chawls. Malaria was also a standing menace and health officers pointed to the striking correlation between the intensity of malaria and the proximity of the mills.[16] These highly unsatisfactory conditions of health are also clear from another expert's statement that the average of 99 pounds in weight for all mill operatives was below the minimum weight for police recruits of the same average height.[17]

There was no sustained and convincing effort on the part of the employers to create a more settled labour force and to incorporate the workers more permanently into the capitalist sector. Some mills boasted of their dispensaries for medicines and of their attendance by qualified medical practitioners. But in fact these were mere first-aid centres. So, if in case of illness the house remedies failed, the worker went to see a country *vaidya* (practitioner) and returned home to be nursed by his family. The mills profited from his improvement in health, although they frequently complained of absenteeism.

Apart from the lack of medical attendance there was also a marked neglect of the workers' housing. Employers and government had both started housing schemes to provide accommodation to at least a small section of the labouring poor. But a considerable number of these one-room tenements remained unoccupied or were sublet to outsiders. In 1925 76 per cent of the chawls built by the government Development Department stood empty and a representative of the Bombay Millowners' Association (B.M.O.A.) wondered with slightly concealed annoyance, why the Bombay millhand 'should prefer to live in horrible slums to the sanitary and up-to-date chawls which had been built for him'.[18] But he glossed over several important objections. The workers were reluctant to take advantage of the employers' chawls, as experience had shown that their independence was severely curtailed by living there and they might instantly be evicted in case of strike. As for the Development Department chawls, the rent was prohibitive and their concrete construction made them too hot in summer and too cold in winter. These and other disadvantages made the workers prefer to stay in their comparatively cheap but unhealthy environments, where the traditional relationships with their co-villagers could be maintained.[19]

To the children and the aged the mill industry had nothing to offer to make life in the city an attractive proposition. Since successive Factory Acts had rigorously reduced the maximum working-day for children, primary schools had been established in some mill compounds. But in the majority of cases mill managements used these schools for the sole purpose of having a hidden reserve pool of labour at hand. And workers who had spent their productive years in the mills had no source whatsoever to depend upon after retirement, as pensions and provident funds were lacking. They had to return to their village to eke out a meagre existence among their family members.

Now it is remarkable that the very mill-owners, who were primarily responsible for this state of affairs, consistently complained of the migratory habits and unsettled character of their work force. Their reading of the facts was bitterly disputed by welfare workers and trade unions, who claimed that workers generally stuck to their mills, often serving ten or twenty years or even more. In the absence of reliable and accurate data, however, the least that can be said is that the employers are under the strong suspicion of exaggerating the migratory charactor of their labour in order to shirk their duties in the field of personnel management. And the Bombay Textile Labour Union was very much to the point in remarking that the mill-owners' inability to build up a permanent industrial workforce reflected little credit on their reputation as efficient managers (as they claimed to be).[20]

As has been postulated by the mode-of-production theorists, the crucial characteristic of colonial labour was that it was paid no family wage. The capitalist sector paid the worker just enough to maintain himself but relegated him to village society for the maintenance of his family. Remittances sent home or savings brought back are not supposed to have been substantial.[21]

As was the case with migration, a discussion of wages and costs of living has to cope with the problem of lacking or unsatisfactorily based statistics. Therefore, one has to find one's way through a jungle of contradictory statements and impressionistic views.

Before World War I, the employers, in defence of their wage policy, emphasized the workers' 'extravagent habits' like drinking, gambling and other vices, whereas government reports tended to express the opinion that the mill-workers as a thriving community yearly sent large sums home, which were partly invested in buying land.[22] A third viewpoint was put forward by N.M. Lokhande, renowned as Bombay's first labour organizer and himself employed in several mills as storekeeper. In 1884 he petitioned government on behalf of the operatives 'who as a rule save nothing and are mostly involved in debt'.[23]

After the war the Bombay Labour Office was

inaugurated by the government to examine in a scientific and exact manner the real conditions of work and wages. In 1922-23 it conducted one of its first and most frequently quoted reports on working-class budgets in Bombay.[24] This inquiry, based on about 3,000 budgets of families and single men, nearly 50 per cent of which were mill-workers' budgets, disclosed the monthly remittance of considerable sums of money, from Rs.1/11/1 in the case of families to Rs.11/7/1 in the case of single men. But at the same time it concluded that half the mill population was in debt and that every worker earning less than Rs.30 per month added one rupee to his burden every month. As might have been expected, this report in no way solved the dispute. The mill-owners missed no opportunity to quote the remittances, whereas labour sympathizers kept referring to the existence of mass indebtedness.

There were, however, some fundamental weaknesses in the report as has been shown very competently by the Bombay Textile Labour Union.[25] First of all, the finding that the textile worker's average earnings were Rs.30/10/1 per month was greatly misleading, as the salaries of highly paid mill officials (masters, storekeepers, jobbers) were included in the calculations made. Equally erroneous was the report's failure to take account of the many deductions from the wages in the form of fines, interest or partial withholdings. Also, it was unmistakably clear from the report's own pages that remittances were sent in spite of the excess of expenditure over income, resulting in increasing indebtedness. Therefore, it is very difficult to accept remittances as an accurate index of the economic position of the worker.[26]

For our purpose the main point to note is that, if remittances were sent home, in most cases it was to the detriment of the workers' health, the recovery of which had to be paid by the same village society. And the most significant finding by the report might well be that industrial workers consumed less cereals than the diet prescribed by the Bombay Jail Manual, although 57 per cent of their income was spent on food.

In the introduction of this article we have outlined the model of a dominant capitalist mode of production that maintained and exploited the old village economy for the (re-) production of its labour. The discussion that followed tends to qualify but in the main to confirm that model as applicable to the situation in Bombay. But a comparison of Bombay with

Ahmedabad, the Gujarat centre of the textile industry, creates new problems that possibly contradict our analysis.

In 1929 the Ahmedabad mill-owners told the Whitley Commission that 80 per cent of their work-force was permanent, that only 10 or 20 per cent of workers went to the villages for about a week during festive seasons and that most of the workers brought their families with them to the city.[27] This more settled character of Ahmedabad labour can clearly be seen from the sex-ratio, that stood at 765 to 1,000 in 1921 (Bombay 525). But although most workers lived by wage labour alone and presumably did not fall back on village society, mills in Ahmedabad paid wages that were not higher, but even a bit lower than those in Bombay: the average monthly earnings of all workers in Bombay were Rs.16/6/3 in 1914 and Rs.30/10/1 in 1923 as against Ahmedabad Rs.13/9/9 and Rs.29/7/0 respectively.[28]

Some authors have attributed this wage difference to the many alternative jobs that were available in Bombay as a seaport. Migrant workers going to East Africa, for instance, were said to receive wages considerably higher than those paid by the Bombay mills.[29] This line of reasoning seems to imply that on the Bombay labour market the competition was for workers rather than for jobs, which contradicts the widely accepted view that generally Bombay enjoyed a more than adequate labour supply.[30] But for our argument the main point to note is that if Bombay's alternative employment opportunities did exert an upward pressure on wages, the mills must have paid their workers rates that were higher than the mere subsistence level.

Several contemporary witnesses advanced the view that the Bombay wage level was nothing but a reflection of the higher costs of living in this city. These costs were alleged to be very high and it was argued that after World War I it was absolutely impossible to live on wages less than Rs.30 p.m.[31] Now, unfortunately, there is no comparative cost-of-living index available for Bombay and Ahmedabad covering all the items of food, fuel, cloth and house-rent. But at least a comparative index for food prices has been computed every month since July 1921. Figures from this index show marked differences and fluctuations in food prices, but do not unequivocally suggest that in Bombay they were so much higher than in Ahmedabad.[32] And even if it could be shown that Bombay's slightly higher wages did indeed keep pace with its slightly higher costs of living, the point still remains that in Ahmedabad more people had to live on more or less the same real wages. However, as the extant figures and statistics are far from reliable, they have to be treated with considerable reservation. And further research will be needed into the position of the millworkers' women, who in Ahmedabad may have contributed to the family's income with earnings from the informal sector. So, we come back again to the problem of sources, because what we urgently need, like Thomas Gradgrind, is 'facts, nothing but facts'.[33]

The Textile Industry and the Jobber System: Recruitment of Labour

It was the recruiters of labour who performed the vital function of linking village society with the urban capitalist mode of production. From the inception of the Bombay textile industry this task of recruitment was entrusted to so-called jobbers. Coming from the rank and file, these jobbers were empowered to engage, to discipline and to dismiss workers and to give what elementary training was required. Unfortunately, as most jobber dealings were off the historical record, information is scarce and little research has been done in this field.[34]

In the early days of the industry the rural population had not yet found its way to the factory gate. Therefore, the mill management itself had to go on the road to supplement the shortage of labour in the city. For that purpose, the first jobbers went up country and lured the economically affected villagers by picturing urban factory life in bright colours and offering them travel expenses as an additional inducement. By this personal approach special ties which lasted for years were established between certain mills and villages.

In the course of time, it was no longer necessary - apart from exceptional circumstances - to recruit labour in the countryside. Population pressure had increased, the employment opportunities in the textile mills had become sufficiently well known and migration had considerably swelled the number of willing recruits in the city. The itinerant jobber became a thing of the past, as well as the migrant labourers came more and more to the factory gates on their own. In spite of these changes on the labour market, the jobber remained in charge of the recruitment of labour for his department. His recruiting activities, however, became progressively more than an aspect of his role as foreman and supervisor.

The main qualification of a jobber was his ability to control a number of men. Most probably, in the initial period, when industrial experience was still largely lacking, the wielding of some influence over labour was the sole criterion for appointment as a jobber. More often than not physical force constituted an important element of that influence and probably in the beginning the most aggressive mill-workers were designated as jobbers.[35] In any case, it remained usual to speak of the jobber as the *dada* or 'the strong tough guy, who can terrorize the people'.[36] The frequent association of jobbers with *akhadas* or wrestling-schools also points to the use of violent mechanisms of control.

The oldest historical documentation on jobbers can be found in the Factory Commission Report of 1875. Of the two jobbers heard by the Commission - a Muslim weaver and a Koli spinner - the former had been a resident of Bombay for more than twenty years and the latter had been born there.[37] This leads to another, more or less obvious conclusion, namely that the first jobbers were drawn from the more urbanized groups. The textile mill was only one, although the most obvious sector of the jobber's activities. Apart from that, he might run a shop, let rooms, head an akhada or pursue other interests that tied him to the city.

A second generation of jobbers could be expected to have at least some technical knowledge and experience. According to some observers that was indeed the case,[38] but even in the 1920s complaints persisted of jobbers who could never tackle a loom or make a repair.[39] In the latter case, a jobber's lack of technical skill was tolerated, simply because some managers or department heads were not completely indifferent to the possibility of material gain. They expected financial compensation for the grant of appointment and first of all weighed a prospective jobber's ability to pay, a burden that the jobber passed on to his gang of labourers (as discussed below). In many mills a community of interest developed between management and jobbers, based on a joint exploitation of labour.[40]

In reeling and winding departments, where mainly women were employed, labour was recruited and supervised by *naikins*, the jobbers' female counterparts. What has been said of the jobber also applied to her. But according to some, an additional requirement pertaining to the naikens was the possession of an attractive appearance and a willingness to please the manager or department head in all respects. Therefore, mills sometimes found difficulty in getting naikins, as this position was not considered to be respectable and many women refused the job in spite of its remunerative prospects.[41]

Since management had delegated the distribution of eagerly-sought employment opportunities to him, the jobber could build up a position of considerable strength. As a result, the jobber and his men maintained a relationship of mutual but unequal interdependence, that can most aptly be described as a form of patronage.

Although formally the authority to hire and to fire rested with the management, in actual practice it was the jobber who assigned vacant places. Therefore, the employment relationship may be said to have been set up primarily between the jobber and his labourers, even though the jobber was not in charge of wage payment as was the *maistry* on South Indian plantations.[42] Kinship or common origin usually served as the main basis for this employment relationship. But if the immigrant labourer did not belong to the jobber's personal acquaintances, he could be introduced to him by co-villagers or family members, who had already found their way in the urban industry.

Protection of his labourers' interests - which were partly his own - was another aspect of the jobber's patronage. Labourers used to address their complaints not to the mill officers but to the jobber, who was expected to act as their spokesman. To keep their confidence the jobber had to use his contacts with management to get the grievances of his men redressed or their conditions of work improved. In that way, the jobber represented an important, if not the sole channel of communication through which managers or department heads could remain informed as to their employees' opinions and well-being. In the majority of cases, however, this channel was used for information in the oppositie direction and instructions to the men were issued not directly to them, but via their jobbers. As a matter of course, there was a strong tendency for these intermediaries to colour this information in the process of transmission in accordance with their own particular interests.

Immigrant labourers arriving in Bombay generally possessed little hard cash. In addition, they generally did not find work overnight and mills used to keep wages in arrears. Therefore, most newcomers soon ran into debt. Fines, illness or marriage sometimes increased their indebtedness beyond redemption. In contracting loans the jobber played an important part. Sometimes, he acted as a moneylender himself. But as his means were limited, the jobber usually introduced his men to other moneylenders, like mill officers, grain-dealers or Marwari merchants, and stood security for them. By providing or mediating the necessary loans the jobber not only profited financially, but also considerably strengthened his control over the men. But the dependence was mutual and so was the risk. If a labourer left before the debt was cleared, the jobber had to bear the loss. His risk, however, was small, as he maintained a wide set of personal relations with the labourers of his gang. He guided fresh recruits in the difficult process of urban adjustment, advised them in accommodation and family affairs and provided many services, which the industry and the government were unable or unwilling to provide. His strategic position in a network of social relations enabled him to act as a professional mediator in communication and distribution, strongly resembling the culture broker as described by Neale.[43] The preservation of customary social relationships in a new urban context made him also very much look like 'a city equivalent of the village headman' and the jobber was very commonly referred to as *mukadam* or traditional leader.[44]

The emergence of the jobber system may be attributed to the social and linguistic differences between the mill-owners and their management cadre on the one hand and the labourers on the other. The mill-owners came from prominent merchant communities like Parsis, Gujaratis and Iraqi Jews, and the management functions in their mills were filled by Europeans or Indians with an educated middle-class background, whereas the immigrant rural labour force was of Marathi-speaking peasant origin. Therefore, a system of intermediaries, like jobbers, would seem to be an obvious solution. To take personnel management in their own hands, the mill officers had to devise recruitment strategies for a culture they found difficult to understand and to communicate through interpreters with all the concomitant frustrations and waste of time. And as available labour was largely unskilled, no further selection was required than a cursory examination of the candidate's physical fitness. When later on management became more Indianized, the established practice was left untouched.[45]

Another, partly complementary explanation suggests that from the beginning the jobbers were intended to play the role of a middle management cadre. Primarily interested in the making of quick profits, the millowners were reluctant to invest in an expensive and perhaps no more efficient personnel office to recruit and discipline the work-force. Apart from that, the Indian entrepreneurs had little personal experience in labour administration, as their previous activities were mainly in trading, banking and brokerage. Therefore, as long as the level of technology was very low and the necessary skills could easily be acquired, no one more sophisticated than a jobber was needed. Exactly this lack of a well-organized personnel office enabled the jobber to emerge as the key-figure in labour relations and to assume the wide responsibilities of hiring and disciplining the workforce.[46]

Whatever explanation we prefer, for the purpose of our paper they amount to the same, namely the basic non-interference by the industry in the nature of village society with which it was linked and in the social relationships that were prevalent there. As long as the machines were properly manned and industrial peace was maintained, managements would not bother their jobbers with irksome questions about how exactly they dealt with their men. Therefore, one may say, the capitalist mode of production not only preserved village society for the reproduction of its labour, but also by its adoption of the jobber system perpetuated social relations of a feudal kind within the industrial framework itself.

The mill-owners readily used every opportunity to stress the essentially alien character of their workers' social background. When after the first world war enquiries by government and labour sympathizers brought to light the manifold malpractices connected with the jobber system, the employers in defence referred to the existence of vital differences in social position, caste and language. For recruiting to be successful, the Bombay Millowners' Association (B.M.O.A.) declared in 1926, the recruiting officer needs some point of contact with the men. The jobber, coming from practically the same class as the worker, is 'naturally in touch', but the mill officers above him belong to very different strata of life. Therefore, a jobber was indispensable in the recruitment of labour, as 'you cannot easily get at them unless you have some point of contact with them, ...'[47] One may add that stressing the social distance had the additional advantage of exempting the mill-owners from all further obligations they might have in regard to their labour. In the Sinhalese plantations described by Meyer the planters even deliberately fostered the alien character of their Tamil workers to create a submissive labour force and to prevent its integration into Sinhalese society.[48]

The malpractices, mentioned in the preceding paragraph, were mostly of a financial nature. The jobber used to demand *dasturi* (fee or commission) as the price of engagement or of re-employment after a period of absence. Tha amount of dasturi could range from some annas to a full month's wages and varied according to time, place and the closeness of the jobber's relations with his men. The Factory Commission of 1875 already felt obliged to make investigations into this matter and the B.M.O.A. included a prohibition of taking or paying bribes (meaning dasturi) in its 1891 draft work regulations. Nevertheless, in the first quarter of this century the payment of dasturi to the jobber was a fairly general condition for getting a job.

Summarizing, this meant that as long as the jobber was considered to be an indispensable benefit or at least an equally indispensable evil, he could reap financial benefits from two different structural contexts. First of all, he received from the mill management his normal monthly wages that were paid on time-rates or on piece-rates and exceeded the average worker's earning twice or thrice. But apart from that, he enjoyed an additional income, derived from sources outside the capitalist industrial framework and based on his informal position of labour recruiter.

The connection between the jobber's regular wages and the capitalist mode of production is obvious. It is less clear how far dasturi has to be seen as a form of payment originating from Indian village society. One may argue that it was a well-established custom to offer gifts or render services to landlords in return for their grant of protection or lease of land. Familiar with this custom in the countryside, the migrant worker could not regard the gift of dasturi, after its transplantation to an urban industrial soil, as unusual or unreasonable. The workers' lack of opposition to the payment of dasturi as such may also be put forward to strengthen this interpretation. However, no dasturi was paid in critical periods of labour scarcity, as during the plague of 1897. This suggests that dasturi was also closely linked with the economic law of supply and demand and that capitalist mechanisms were operating within forms which appear on the surface to be traditional institutions of peasant society.[49]

It was well-meaning outsiders, government officials and trade-union leaders, who in the 1920s began to challenge this custom, which they branded as 'sheer corruption' and 'actual extortion'.[50] But also, no sharp distinction can be drawn between dasturi as attribute of patronage and as form of corruption. The only thing that can be said is that patronage always bears an element of exploitation, as it is based on a difference in power that can be used by the patron - as the stronger partner in the relationship - in his own favour. It might very well be that interpretations of dasturi, stressing the corruptive and exploitative element in it, are strongly coloured by value-judgements derived from a capitalistic rationalism. This suggestion does not imply that ethical judgements are completely ruled out. It does mean, however, that dasturi has to be understood first and foremost as part and parcel of its specific socio-economic context.

Finally, the payment of dasturi also throws new light on the absence of a well-organized personnel office. For, entrusting the jobber with the recruitment, instruction and supervision of labour not only meant that the employers shirked all their duties in this field; it also implied that the costs that went with these duties fell back upon labour itself in the form of dasturi.

Jobbers and Labour Unions: Organization of Labour

Textile labour, far from being unorganized, was composed of a multitude of particularistic jobber units. This may explain much of Bombay's labour mobility. The workers cnsidered their fortunes to be bound up with their jobber, more than with the mill. Therefore, when a jobber conflicted with his management or received a more attractive offer elsewhere, he could change mill and 'his' workers would follow him. Before World War I protracted strikes were very rare and most conflicts remained confined to one mill, or more often, to one department. Jobber moves were at the centre of most of these early labour disputes and the isolated and shortlived strikes before the 1920s coincided in their scope with the jobber's personal network. Sometimes it happened the other way round: workers dissatisfied with their working conditions left their mill, and the jobber, unable to control labour unrest, preferred to become the leader of a strike rather than lose his influence with the men. But in all these cases vertical loyalties dominated any sense of horizontal or collective solidarity. Different jobber gangs competed for the same employment opportunities, whereas conflicts with managements about wages or work-rules were fought independently.[51]

The multicellular composition of the labour force greatly influenced all attempts to organize the textile workers into a larger whole. As long as the limitations of the small, particularistic groups could not be overcome, gaining the jobber's support was the sole way to mobilize labour on a wider scale. So, for organizing purposes the combination of a number of jobber units was an obvious starting-point.

According to Gail Omvedt in her recent contribution, labour recruitment through intermediaries began to end when union organizing among the workers started to develop. Workers organizing themselves into unions fought the jobbers and she mentions the Bombay textile mills as the first place where by 1930 their influence was on the decline as a result of militant labour strikes.[52]

Personally, I do not find this view, quite current among most labour historians, to be completely acceptable. Capitalism in the Third World did not completely destroy previous modes of production. By the same token, unionization did not rise from the ashes of earlier organizations like the jobber unit. Therefore, if modes of labour organization are also analysed in terms of mutual penetration and articulation, a deeper insight can be gained into the processes at work in the emerging trade-union movement. I will briefly present some empirical data to substantiate my point.

The first attempts to organize Bombay textile labour were made as part of a wider non-Brahman movement, which worked for the general uplift of the lower castes. In 1884 Lokhande, its most prominent leader in Bombay, organized two mass meetings to petition government on behalf of labour. For this purpose Lokhande made use of an existing jobber association that had been set up with the quite different intent of collecting funds for the building of a *dharamshalla*. Through this association other jobbers were summoned to the meetings and five thousand workers attended as a result. The Millhands' Association formed in its wake also found its organizing basis in the jobbers, but very soon disintegrated into its constituent parts. [53]

From the same socio-political background, but more important, was the Kamgar Hitwardhak Sabha (K.H. S.), established in 1909. Founded by educated middle-class non-Brahman leaders, the K.H.S. was essentially a labour welfare association. Although it was not exclusively meant to look after the interests of textile labour, its following was chiefly drawn from that source. The membership was small, about two or three hundred, but consisted of a great many jobbers and other influential elements, so that its total support may be reckoned at ten thousand workers. In spite of their crucial position in the K.H.S.'s organization, few jobbers served on its managing committee. This was mainly because of the strong opposition exerted by the employers against their workforce combining into larger associations. [54]

The important point to make here is that the cases of the Millhands' Association and the K.H.S. prove that jobbers were not completely averse to concerted action. They also prove that outsiders, to a certain extent, could enrol the jobbers for joint action in accordance with their own, that is non-Brahman, interests. Later political movements did not fail to take this lesson to heart.

After the first world war the nationalist movement in India gathered momentum. The exigencies of the war, the policy declarations by the British government and the echo of the 1917 Revolution in Russia created a suitable climate for political leaders to press their demands. The Montford reform proposals fell far short of the expectations raised. Therefore, the nationalist leaders sought to strengthen their agitation for Home Rule by broadening their political base and came to appreciate support from an urban, concentrated labour force as an invaluable asset to their political struggle. In Bombay, Home Rulers of different shades of opinion launched their own labour associations but they did not strike root. Not until the Bombay Textile Labour Union (B.T.L.U.) was formed (in 1925) did trade-unionization really begin. This B.T.L.U. had grown out of a Committee of Assistance which during the 1925 textile strike organized relief for those workers who had remained in the city. After the strike this Committee was transformed into a permanent union, led by labour politicians and social workers and presided over by the well-known N.M. Joshi. In fact, the B.T.L.U. represented a master union comprising several smaller labour associations in a more centralized bureaucratic framework.

After one year the B.T.L.U. numbered approximately 10,000 members. Most of these were employed in mills on the southern fringe of the Bombay mill area and in two northern mills in Kurla. This very uneven spread of membership was partly a legacy of the smaller associations incorporated by the B.T.L.U. and partly a result of the B.T.L.U.'s communal composition, its main areas of strength being in Muslim-dominated wards. But first and foremost this strongly localized membership has to be seen as evidence that in fact the B.T.L.U., its formal bureaucratic structure notwithstanding, had to rely on jobbers and other locally-influential leaders among labour. This may be called the fundamental dilemma of the B.T.L.U. as it was of all labour unions during the inter-war period.

For the enlistment of a membership or the setting-up of mill committees, it was absolutely necessary for the B.T.L.U. to gain the support of the jobbers or at least to convince them that the union's intentions were not detrimental to their position. In some mills the B.T.L.U. proved successful in this endeavour and in consequence it sometimes even came to champion specific jobber interests. In many cases, however, this method yielded no result. When the union arranged a meeting with the jobbers and head jobbers of a mill in order to persuade them to join the union along with their men, it very often happened that the jobbers concluded that a union did not suit their interests. They would refuse to have any dealings with the union and their labourers, if members, would withdraw. And if in case of labour disputes the union could not reach a settlement that was favourable to its members, many jobbers would back out again, as their B.T.L.U. connection had not turned out to be a strengthening of their existing powers.[55]

A completely different type of labour union had

been founded the year before, the Girni Kamgar Mahamandal (G.K.M.). Whereas the B.T.L.U. was primarily an outside initiative, the G.K.M. was formed by labourers themselves, at least by a more skilled and better paid section of them. Its leaders were mainly jobbers, who were joined by some clerks, shopkeepers and akhada-owners, D.R. Mayekar, A.A. Alve and G.R. Kasle being the most prominent among them. As their union was built on their respective client networks, it suffered basically from the same weaknesses as the B.T.L.U.: lack of centralization and a membership concentrated in some local bulwarks.

A special characteristic of the G.K.M. was its rejection of all outside interference. On several occasions the G.K.M. leaders declared the labour politicians from the middle class to be of no use, as they were completely unacquainted with the millworkers' conditions. They even openly distrusted the outsiders' motives in trying to lead labour.[56]

Nevertheless, this attitude did not prevent outsiders, mainly of a communist persuasion, from taking increasingly more interest in the affairs of the G.K.M. Initially, the activities of the Bombay communists remained confined to the study of Marxism-Leninism and the dissemination of their newly-acquired views in English-language publications. However, they were unable to radicalize the Bombay Congress in labour matters or to make any inroads into the established nationalist trade-union movement controlled by N.M. Joshi. So, in 1927 they set up a Bombay Workers' and Peasants' Party (B.W.P.P.), which operating independently within the Congress aimed at the organization of workers and peasants and at the transformation of the parent body into a real mass party.[57] This was an enormous, if not impossible, undertaking, in view of the fact that the B.W.P.P. numbered about twenty members, mostly Brahman students, and had no connection with labour at all.[58]

In this situation, the jobber-led G.K.M. offered the communists an opportunity to establish the much-desired connection with the workers. But because of its special character, the G.K.M. had to be dealt with very carefully. Through a local Congress Committee K.N. Joglekar (B.W.P.P.) managed to develop a fragile relationship with Mayekar, the G.K.M.'s secretary. This was going to be the vital link. Joglekar spared no effort to introduce his friends into the G.K.M. as political advisers and - to use his own words - 'was doing consistently the boring work on behalf of the Party'.[59] This enabled the communists to pass themselves off as leaders of this textile union, a status that gained them important positions in the national trade-union federation. But in actual fact they were only marginally involved and were merely tolerated in their capacity as self-appointed advisers.

Economic developments, however, were to promote closer co-operation at least for the time being, between labour politicians and jobbers in general. After about 1924 Bombay suffered from an economic depression and to check this trend the mill-owners considered the introduction of rationalization schemes. Although these schemes generally implied increased efficiency, to the workers their implementation meant retrenchment, heavier workloads and, to some categories of labour, reduced earnings. In addition, the jobbers would have to face a drastic curtailment of their freedom of recruitment by increased demands for skill and efficiency. Introduction of these measures, therefore, provoked a wave of labour unrest, which provides the background to the 1928 and 1929 general strikes.

On the eve of this strike movement serious tensions arose in the G.K.M. Whereas Mayekar came to resist all further encroachments by the educated outsiders, Alve thought he could use them in the workers' fight against the new work schemes. Connected with this conflict was a dispute over the feasibility of organized opposition, Alve being more inclined to radical solutions. These tensions which divided the G.K.M. enabled the B.W.P.P. members to strengthen their influence, and in March 1928 the B.W.P.P. could report truthfully that 'at present Party members are more or less connected with the Textile Workers' Union'.[60] After a general strike had been called the B.W.P.P. influence grew further. When in May the Alve-led G.K.M. wing had itself formally registered as the Girni Kamgar Union (G.K.U.), jobbers and other labour leaders like Alve and Kasle sat on its managing committee alongside communist students like Joglekar and S.A. Dange. Again the co-operation of jobbers with politically-motivated outsiders proved to be the formula for trade-union formation.

The G.K.U. had its heyday during and immediately after the 1928 strike. The imminent rationalization of the industry had given rise to a broad resistance movement, which overstepped the limits of the small, particularistic group. This situation required a more general leadership, able to negotiate with the employers concerning the little-articulated grievances of labour and the economic problems of the industry in a long-term perspective. As the jobbers could not meet these requirements, the labour politicians of the G.K.U. together with representatives of the more moderate unions filled in the gap and emerged as leaders by acting as spokesmen. This was especially true of the G.K.U. leaders, who formed the most energetic part of the Joint Strike Committee and whose militant speeches attracted large audiences.

During and after this strike jobbers co-operated at two distinct levels. A small number of them co-operated at the highest administrative level and made the union more identifiable to labour by acting as its president or sitting on its executive. A majority, however, co-operated by supporting the strike on the spot. They might have had private leanings toward the union but primarily they fought the new work schemes and did not mind that interested outsiders gave new names to their traditional practices.[61] Alve and Dange held special meetings with these jobbers to exchange information, and thanks to their support the fight was kept up for six months. After the strike the G.K.U. sometimes effected the dismissal of hostile labourers, revealing the active influence of jobbers who made use of victimization to serve union purposes. Also, in as far as the G.K.U. succeeded in enforcing some discipline, it was through the jobbers who by their personal influence prevented the workers from using violence.[62]

The G.K.U. numbering about 60,000 members and 40 mill committees in the beginning of 1929, showed marked progress over its various predecessors. But in the last analysis it also had to keep a precarious balance between using and losing the jobbers. At the end of the same year, the G.K.U. membership had dwindled to fewer than a thousand and it faded into insignificance. To explain this spectacular decline much has been made of the mill-owners' opposition and government intervention (the Meerut trial). But at the root of the problem, again, we find the jobber.

The G.K.U. constitution permitted the mill committees to deal with grievances and to collect union fees, but it did not authorize them to call a strike. Mill committees, according to Dange, were meant 'to control the workers' and the G.K.U. and its main enemy the B.M.O.A. fully agreed on the need for control.[63] Lightning strikes and irregular operation of the mill

Rural Labour in the Bombay Textile Industry

committees, however, demonstrated that the workers could not be confined within the officially-prescribed rules as laid down by the communists in conjunction with the employers. In some places committee members claimed special privileges on the shop floor; elsewhere they agitated for the dismissal of jobbers who were disliked by their men.[64] In numerous ways the hierarchy of productive relations was disturbed and the resulting disorder made working impossible for mill and union alike.

Not only the mill managements, but also the jobbers began to resist the mill committees. That was a very critical development, as to a great extent the G.K.U.'s achievements had to be credited to the jobbers. From the fact that the mill committees were distributing jobs and material we may infer the jobbers' active participation. But slowly the jobbers began to change sides. After they had realized that some kind of rationalization had become inevitable, they came to discover the G.K.U. mill committees as a new and greater menace. These mill committees further reduced their freedom of action, and by dealing with grievances threatened to undermine their traditional mediation. These considerations made many jobbers decide to dissociate themselves from the union. During the 1929 strike they were conspicuous by their activities as strikebreakers and the G.K.U. lost the strike and its organizing base.

Following Joglekar's example, many labour politicians in Bombay associated themselves with rank-and-file labour leaders for the purpose of building new organizations by using traditional social networks. After 1929 leftists like B.T. Ranadive and S.V. Deshpande applied this formula by co-operating with the jobber G.L. Kandalkar and his group in the G.K.U. (Red Flag) and after 1934 the Royists conducted their Bombay G.K.U. in co-operation with the Muslim jobber Abdul Majid.[65] During the 1930s the jobber system came under heavy pressure from industrial reform and government legislation. But the jobbers remained active and proved influential enough to become towers of strength to the Rashtriya Mill Mazdoor Sangh, the nationalist textile union established in 1945.[66]

Conclusion

As has been said, the articulation of different modes

of production seems to be a useful concept to organize and clarify most of the historical data concerning the Bombay textile industry. The migration of mainly male labour, their preservation of village ties for reasons of social security and the apparent lack of substantial remittances back home all clearly testify to the subordination of a weakened village economy to the needs of the capitalist mode of production. This penetration of peasant society by the capitalist mode created also new phenomena, the most conspicuous being the jobber, who transferred labour from the village to the urban industry or recruited co-villagers at the factory-gate. In fact, the jobber was the focal point in the whole process of articulation, and around him the jobber-unit was formed as an organization of labour that adapted existing social relationships to new industrial needs.

We may discern the trade union and the jobber-unit as two clearly distinct modes of labour organization. The trade union tended to treat the workers as if they were a category and therefore to negotiate for wages and employment in the industry as a whole. The individual worker, however, remained personally dependent on his jobber for a job or a loan and thus a jobber-unit comprised a wide set of relations, maintained even in situations of industrial peace or temporary unemployment. Whereas the trade union's approach was specific and bureaucratic, the jobber's relations with his men were multi-purpose and face-to-face. Therefore, the Bombay textile unions, their ideological differences notwithstanding, had to build on the jobbers as their main organizing base. Fundamentally, the modes of organization of trade union and jobber may be opposed, but in actual fact they proved to a large extent to be complementary. The jobber's personal hold on the men was supplemented by the outsiders' administrative skills and their ability to translate the workers' grievances into a political idiom.

We may conclude from this case-study that the articulation concept is fruitfully applicable to the field of labour organization. Therefore, elaborating the opening sentence of this article, one of the fundamental problems of historical analysis may be seen as the specification and articulation of particular modes of organization within a given association of labour.

As for Bombay, one may say that just as the

Rural Labour in the Bombay Textile Industry

capitalist mode of production developed by the exploitation of village society for the cheap production of labour, in the same way trade unionism as a concomitant phenomenon could emerge by using the jobber-unit for the easy recruitment of a following. The high points of trade-union development in Bombay were reached when the union became the dominant mode of organization and succeeded in effectively subordinating these jobber-units. Thus, the decisive point in the development of the Bombay textile unions was not so much the mounting resistance of a class-conscious workforce against the jobber influence. Rather it was the relative success of the attempts to institutionalize informal, short-term interest organizations in bureaucratic frameworks.

There is yet another striking parallel. The mill-owners frequently complained of the migratory habits of their workers, but kept silent about the ways in which the maintenance of village ties contributed to the economic well-being of their industry. Likewise, trade-union leaders openly condemned the evils of the jobber-system, but were absolutely unwilling to acknowlege that the jobber represented an indispensable link in their organizational set-up. During my own interviews with pre-war union-leaders I found them rather tight-lipped as far as the jobbers were concerned and most of them contented themselves with classifying them as part of labour, if not as hand-in-glove with the employers.

Finally, village society also served union purposes by supporting workers in times of strike. So, in the 1920s strike committees actively furthered the workers' return to the countryside, even to the extent of dealing out steamer tickets, as strike funds in the city fell far short of wants.

However, there are also some differences which may prevent us from stretching the conceptual analogy too far. First of all, the political leaders of the trade union looked upon the jobber as a practical device which had to be used for a short time only but in the long run must be got rid of. Therefore, they were much more intent upon the final destruction of the jobber system than the capitalists were with regard to village society. Further, subordination to the trade union organization was not always as detrimental to the jobber as subordination to the urban industry was to village society. Many jobbers used the union in the struggle for their own immediate interests or as a protective cover against threats like rationalization. Some of them even rose to prominence as the union offered an opportunity of upward mobility which they lacked in the mill. But sooner or later most jobbers became convinced that the outside union leaders only seized upon the problems of labour to further vague and distant political ends and they turned away in bitterness. On trial in Meerut, Kasle lamented that if the outsiders 'have made some secret plot behind the backs of us workers ..., taking advantage of our ignorance, ... only God knows it.'[67]

Finally, an increasing rationalization of production and personnel management (such as the introduction of labour officers in the 1930s) was accompanied by a further bureaucratizing of labour organization. There was an ambivalent but undeniable trend discernible towards a growing dominance of the union mode of organization, especially after World War II. But for the greater part of this period the most essential characteristic of the Bombay textile unions was - to use Meillassoux's phrase in a slightly different sense - that traditional jobber-units 'were being both undermined and perpetuated at the same time, undergoing a prolonged crisis and not a smooth transition to' trade-unionism.[68]

NOTES

Kooiman, 'Rural labour in the Bombay textile industry and the articulation of modes of organization'

My thanks are due to Diane Papstein for help with the English text.

1. Apart from contributions to the *Economic and Political Weekly* (Bombay) by Ashok Rudra, Utsa Patnaik, Paresh Chattopadhyay and Hamza Alavi, mention may be made of Irfan Habib, 'Potentialities of Capitalistic Development in the Economy of Mughal India', *Journal of Economic History* XXIX (1969), pp.32 ff.; Brian Davey, *The Economic Development of India - A Marxist Analysis* (Bristol 1975); Kathleen Gough, 'Modes of Production in Southern India', *Economic and Political Weekly* Annual Number (February 1980), pp.337 ff.
2. D. McEachern, 'The Mode of Production in India', *Journal of Contemporary Asia* VI, 4 (1976), pp.444 ff.
3. C. Meillassoux, 'From Reproduction to Production - A Marxist Approach to Economic Anthropology', *Economy and Society* I, 1 (1972), p.103.
4. Gail Omvedt, 'Migration in Colonial India - The Articulation of Feudalism and Capitalism by the Colonial State', *Journal of Peasant Studies* VII, 2 (1980), pp.185 ff.
5. See Report of the Lady Doctor, Bombay, *Labour Gazette* II, 1 (1922), pp.31 ff.
6. This table has to remain an approximation, as the census succeeded in an occupational breakdown for only some of the immigrants classified as actual workers.
7. Census of India 1931, IX, I, pp.27-9.
8. Official Report on Mill Humidification (1923), quoted in Royal Commission on Labour in India (Whitley Commission), Calcutta 1931, Evidence I, 1, p.29.
9. Indian Factory Labour Commission, Simla 1908, Report I, p.19.
10. Textile Factories Labour Committee, Bombay 1907, Evidence (in Proceedings of the Department of Commerce and Industry), p.75.
11. Royal Commission on Labour 1931, Report, p.16.
12. Lalita Chakravarty has recently mapped out these and other prominent labour catchment areas of colonial India, laying great stress on the economic factor in labour migration, L. Chakravarty, 'Emergence

of an Industrial Labour Force in a Dual Economy - British India 1880-1920', *Indian Economic and Social History Review* XV, 3 (1978), pp.249 ff.

13. A.R. Burnett-Hurst, *Labour and Housing in Bombay - A Study in the Economic Conditions of the Wage-earning Classes in Bombay* (London 1925), p.51; Report of the Indian Tariff Board (Calcutta 1927) III, pp.553 ff.; Indian Factory Labour Commission 1908, Evidence II, p.84; R.G. Gokhale, *The Bombay Cotton Mill Worker* (Bombay 1957), p.70.

14. Textile Factories Labour Committee 1907, Report, pp.3 ff; Report of the Lady Doctor, Bombay, op.cit.; A.R. Burnett-Hurst, op.cit., pp.30 ff.

15. Annual Reports of the Executive Health Officer for the City of Bombay, quoted in A.R. Burnett-Hurst, op.cit., p.35. One has to bear in mind, however, first that these were the years of the influenza epidemic and second that deaths were more accurately registered than births (partly outside Bombay).

16. J. Sandilands, M.D., 'The Health of the Bombay Worker', *Labour Gazette* I, 2 (1921), pp.14-16; Royal Commission on Labour 1931, Report, p.24.

17. Quoted in the Royal Commission on Labour 1931, Evidence I, 1, p.317.

18. *Times of India* 25 December 1925.

19. Indian Factory Labour Commission 1908, Evidence II, pp.72, 86; Report of the Indian Tariff Board, Calcutta 1927, I, p.140; III, pp.449, 563; Royal Commission on Labour 1931, Evidence I, 1, p.24; I, 2, p.256; S.D. Mehta, *The Cotton Mills of India 1854-1954* (Bombay 1954), p.154; A.R. Burnett-Hurst, op.cit., p.62.

20. Indian Tariff Board 1927, III, p.452; Royal Commission on Labour 1931, Evidence I, 1, pp.296, 394.

21. For instance Gail Omvedt, op.cit., p.195.

22. Indian Factory Labour Commission 1908, Evidence II, pp.66, 85, 116; Royal Commission on Labour, II, *The Colonies and the Indian Empire* 1892 (Parliamentary Papers XXXVI: 5 1892), p.174; Gazetteer of the Bombay Presidency, X (Ratnagiri and Savantvadi) (Bombay 1880), p.143.

23. Petition in Factory Commission Report, Bombay 1885, pp.230-1.

24. Labour Office, Government of Bombay, Report of an Enquiry into Working Class Budgets in Bombay (Bombay 1923).

25. B.T.L.U. in Indian Tariff Board 1927, III, pp.443-7 and in Royal Commission on Labour 1931,

Notes to pages 138-41

Evidence I, 1, pp.344-5.

26. Harold Mann, who did research in what allegedly was the receiving end of the remittances, a Deccani village, estimated the amount of money brought or sent back to be much smaller than was often supposed; H.H. Mann and N.V. Kanitkar, *Land and Labour in a Deccan Village* (Bombay 1921), pp.111 ff.

27. Royal Commission on Labour 1931, Evidence I, 1, pp.258-9.

28. Indian Tariff Board 1927, I, pp.111-13; Royal Commission on Labour 1931, Evidence I, 1, pp.166-7.

29. K.L. Gillion, *Ahmedabad, A Study in Indian Urban History* (Berkeley 1968), p.102; L. Chakravarty, op.cit., pp.267, 284.

30. Morris D. Morris, *The Emergence of an Industrial Labor Force in India - A Study of the Bombay Cotton Mills 1854-1947* (Berkeley 1965).

31. Indian Tariff Board 1927, III, p.472; Royal Commission on Labour 1931, Evidence I, 1, p.300.

32. Comparative Retail Prices of Food for Bombay and Ahmedabad, based on the prices for seventeen commodities commonly consumed by the working classes (cereals, pulses, sugar etc.), are given in every issue of the Bombay *Labour Gazette* since 1921. The index for Ahmedabad (Bombay prices = 100) was in July 1921: 101; 1922: 98; 1923 : 92; 1924 : 96.

33. Charles Dickens, *Hard Times* (London 1854), p.1.

34. Mention may be made of M.D. Morris, op.cit.; R.K. Newman, 'Labour Organisation in the Bombay Cotton Mills 1918-1929', Unpubl. Ph.D. Thesis, University of Sussex 1970; D. Kooiman, *Koppelbazen, Kommunisten en Ekonomische Krisis - Arbeidersorganisatie in de Textielindustrie van Bombay 1917-1937* (Jobbers, Communists and Economic Crisis - Labour Organization in the Bombay Textile Industry 1917-1937) (Amsterdam 1978) (Dutch with English summary).

35. S.M. Rutnagur, *Bombay Industries, the Cotton Mills* (Bombay 1927), p.326; M.D. Morris, op.cit., p.130.

36. H.S. Poredi, Labour Office Bombay Millowners' Association, Bombay, 12 November 1974.

37. Report of the Factory Commission (Bombay 1875), pp.88-90.

38. S.M. Rutnagur, op.cit., p.326; Royal Commission on Labour 1931, Report, p.23; *Labour Gazette* XIII, 2 (1933), pp.111 ff.

39. Indian Tariff Board 1927, IV, pp.178, 193; Royal Commission on Labour 1931, Evidence I, 1, p.296.

40. In 1929 the Millowners' Association drafted

new work-rules including 'that any heads of departments, assistants or jobbers accepting bribes from the work-people would be instantly dismissed', *Report of the Bombay Millowners' Association* (Bombay 1929), p.60.

41. J.H. Kelman, *Labour in India, A Study of the Conditions of Indian Women in Modern Industry* (London 1923), pp.110-11; Maniben Kara and Ushabai Dange, former trade-union leaders, Bombay, 9 and 23 November 1974.

42. See Nurit Bird in this volume, above.

43. Walter C. Neale in this volume, below.

44. Royal Commission on Labour 1931, Evidence I, 1, p.10; W.L. Rowe, 'Caste, Kinship and Association in Urban India' in A. Southall, ed., *Urban Anthropology* (New York 1973), p.231; the quotation is from Gail Omvedt, *Cultural Revolt in a Colonial Society, the Non-Brahman Movement in Western India 1873-1930* (Bombay 1976), p.252.

45. R.C. James, 'Labor Mobility, Unemployment and Economic Change, an Indian Case', *The Journal of Political Economy* LXVII, 6 (1959), p.546; S.C. Jain, *Personnel Management in India, its Evolution and Present Status* (University of North Carolina, Chapel Hill 1968); H. Crouch, *Trade Unions and Politics in India* (Bombay 1966), pp.17-18; see also the Open Letter from a mill-agent in *Indian Textile Journal* XX, 229 (1909).

46. M.D. Morris, op.cit., pp.131-2; R.K. Newman, op.cit., p.22. A slightly different analysis of the jobber system, stressing the concepts of risk and uncertainty, has been offered by M.D. Morris, 'Modern Business Organisation and Labour Administration', *Economic and Political Weekly* XIV, 40 (1979), pp.1680 ff.

47. Indian Tariff Board 1927 II, pp.348, 350.

48. Eric Meyer in this volume, above.

49. D.B. Miller, ed., *Peasants and Politics, Grass Roots Reaction to Change in Asia* (London 1979), pp.13, 106; for the 1897 plague and the labour market see *Annual Factory Report of the Presidency of Bombay* (Bombay 1897, p.8.

50. See for instance Royal Commission on Labour 1931, Report, p.24.

51. Royal Commission on Labour 1892, pp.123-4, 174; Indian Industrial Commission 1916-1918, Evidence IV, London 1919, p.341; Indian Tariff Board 1927, II, p.224; III, p.542; IV, p.204; D.H. Buchanan, *The Development of Capitalistic Enterprise in India*

(London 1966), p.124; R.C. James, op.cit., p.547.
  52. Gail Omvedt, 'Migration', p.195.
  53. Factory Commission 1885, pp.98-105, 230-321; *Times of India* 25 September 1884, 6/7 and 13 October 1884 and 26 November 1884.
  54. B.G. Meher, 'Early Labour Movement in Bombay City 1875-1918', Unpubl. Master Thesis, Tata Institute of Social Sciences, Bombay 1965, Chapter VI.
  55. Indian Tariff Board 1927, III, pp.455 ff., 460, 541, 552-3; P.S. Lokanathan, *Industrial Welfare in India* (Madras 1929), pp.172-3; R.K. Newman, op.cit., pp.201 ff.
  56. *Times of India*, 23 February 1924, Indian Tariff Board 1927, III, p.567.
  57. G. Adhikari, ed., *Documents of the History of the Communist Party of India* (New Delhi 1979), III B, Chapter IV; S. Choudhary, *Peasants' and Workers' Movement in India 1905-1929* (New Delhi 1971), p.238.
  58. Later, the Bombay communist Dange admitted that the B.W.P.P. 'had never its roots in the masses'; S.A. Dange, 'The Situation in India', no date (1930) Meerut Exhibit p.2512, in S.A. Dange, *Selected Writings* (Bombay 1977) II, p.508.
  59. *Meerut Judgment - Judgment delivered by R.L. Yorke, Esqr, I.C.S. Additional Sessions Judge, Meerut on 16 Jan. 1933 in the Meerut Communist Conspiracy Case ...* Simla 1932, I, p.251; II, pp.370, 415.
  60. Ibid. I, pp.250-1; II, pp.414-16; the quotation is from p.415.
  61. D. Kooiman, 'Jobbers and the Emergence of Trade Unions in Bombay City', *International Review of Social History* XXII, 3 (1977), pp.321 ff.
  62. In S.C. Ghate, *Our First General-Secretary - A Memorial Volume* (New Delhi 1971), p.105, the communist M.B. Rao vividly describes how the *Lal Bavta* (G.K.U. Red Flag) prevented an angry crowd of Hindu and Muslim labourers from coming to blows at Byculla bridge during the communal riots of February 1929. But he does not mention that the leader whose words had so much influence on the men was Alve.
  63. Dange in Report of the Court of Inquiry, Bombay 1929, summarized in *Indian Textile Journal* XXXIX; 468 (1929), p.432.
  64. Ibid, in *Indian Textile Journal* XXXIX, 468 (1929), pp.433-4, and Evidence from the Court of Inquiry, quoted in R.K. Newman, op.cit., p.308.
  65. D. Kooiman, *Koppelbazen*, Chapters VII and VIII.

Notes to pages 153-6

66. P.N. Inamdar, Rashtriya Mill Mazdoor Sangh official, Bombay 22 November 1974.
67. Meerut Judgment II, p.428.
68. See above, note 3.

THE ROLE OF THE BROKER IN RURAL INDIA

Walter C. Neale

Money-lenders and money-lending merchants have long been villains in Indian oral tradition and in the literature about the economic problems of India's villages. One need only read Malcolm Darling's *The Punjab Peasant in Prosperity and Debt*[1] to get the flavour of the tradition, or consult the Reserve Bank of India's *All-India Rural Credit Survey*[2] to learn how money-lenders exacerbated the problems of rural credit. They were said to charge outrageous rates of interest; to charge unconscionably high prices; to falsify the books; to cheat on weights and measures; to absorb an undue portion of the peasantry's saleable crop and thereby reduce the peasants' investment in agricultural improvement and lower the peasants' standard of living; to thrive on the peasants' ignorance and to abuse a monopoly position.[3] They were exploiters without socially redeeming traits.

Such was and is a common view, and from this common view followed programmes varying from legislative requirements that written receipts be given; through the establishment of the Indian Co-operative Movement and the proposal that the peasantry should be taught to read, write, and figure in order to prevent money-lenders from cheating; to the employment of a variety of extension officers to deal directly with the villagers.

If one pauses, however, to consider the money-lender's history, one is struck by certain peculiarities. First, the money-lender not only exploited the lower orders of Indian rural society but also exploited the higher orders, members of dominant castes in the villages.[4] Second, the money-lender and money-lending merchant antedate the 'capitalist' or market system in India by many years.[5] Third, the money-lender and money-lending merchant survived the introduction of the co-operative movement and later survived the India-wide spread of community development. In fact, they more than survived, for they have been blamed for the failure of the co-operative movement and observers have noted that villagers often turned to the money-lender in preference to other sources of finance and goods.

The money-lender's first peculiarity, the length

of his history, indicates that he was not only a capitalistic or commercial exploiter - or at least that, in his origin, he did have other functions. The second peculiarity, that he exploited the powerful as well as the weak, raises the question of why the powerful did not 'do away with him' - that is, simply drive him out of the village or kill him, or perhaps just beat him (procedures which have been used by the powerful against the lower orders often enough). Unlike other exploiters of India's poor - landlords, landlord money-lenders, village headmen - the small-scale money-lender had no political base in the village. Unlike other exploiters of India's village rich as well as poor - absentee landlords, politicians, larger merchants, and corrupt police officials - he had no political base outside the village. What protected him? The money-lender's physical survival despite his villainy implies that he was necessary to the village and, curiously, that people saw reason not only for tolerating him but also for tolerating the 'outrageous profits' which he made. The third peculiarity, the money-lender's survival in the face of 'low cost' competition, implies that in some sense the money-lender's prices were not outrageous, that he did give something of value which others - the co-operative movement, for instance - did not. How can one account for the long-term survival of one regarded as a villain when his victims had the opportunity and the power to dispose of him - how, unless they needed him badly? It is certainly true that the money-lender had money to lend, and that people came to him to borrow; but other people in the villages were wealthy and, for productive purposes, the co-operative societies were there to provide cash and the government was there to provide takkavi loans in kind.

It is to the mystery, or at least the question, of why the money-lender survived that this essay addresses itself, and in the process presents the hypothesis that many of the relationships between rural and urban India depended upon and were conducted by a variety of people in social roles to which the literature of anthropology has attached the rubric 'culture broker';[6] that the culture-brokering characteristics of these roles were often more important to the relationships existing between villagers and others than were the specific functions implied by the administrative or occupational titles of the brokers; that some of the developmentally ineffective responses to the

The Role of the Broker

stimuli of British rule, with its commercial and contractural outlook, were a result of the need for intermediating culture brokers; and that some further understanding of the difficulties modern developmental services experienced in the rural areas is to be gained by realizing that it was, among other things, as culture brokers that extension and development officials failed.

Unlike the Indian marriage-broker, or other brokers found operating in both the Indian and western economies, the culture broker's peculiar expertise is not in supplying a particular item or service, although he does that, but in being able to operate in two different cultures or subcultures because he understands the folkviews and cognitive maps of both. He is thus able to give each culture *access* to the other. He is a link between two cultural worlds and might better be called a 'social translator' than a middleman or a broker.

Culture-broking roles have formal resemblances and some matters of substance in common with western middlemen and with some of our service industries and financial institutions, but their primary function and the source of their strength are different. Middlemen and brokers exist in western societies because, in varying proportions, they speed the flow and reduce the costs of information; they perform a specific economic function more cheaply than their clients could provide it for themselves; they possess an expertise which most people cannot be expected to master; or they fulfil a role given by the institutional structure of society. Real-estate brokers and estate agents illustrate the first sort of function, as do employment agencies. Stockbrokers, wholesalers, and savings associations and building societies exist because they can perform more cheaply than those they serve; and financial firms, such as stockbrokers or building societies, provide a technical expertise their clients lack - how to write a contract of sale or a mortgage. Lawyers similarly provide a technical expertise, but they also derive their role from the presumed impartiality of our courts and consequently institutionalized arm's-length relationship of suitors to judges and juries. Banks, while performing the same functions as savings associations and building societies, also and importantly exist as middlemen because our laws and institutions give them something close to a monopoly of the power to create money. In each case it is not that the two parties to a possible transaction or relationship cannot understand each other or deal with each other if they come face to face. Sellers and buyers of houses or stocks, savers and borrowers, and plaintiffs and defendants understand each other's aims; and if by chance they come face to face with each other, they are often capable of carrying through the transaction more cheaply than they could by employing a broker. Even in the case of plaintiffs and defendants, it is not lack of mutual comprehension that requires the lawyers, but rather the system of courts which requires the lawyers; and the system of courts is required to prevent blood feuds and to enforce decisions, not to introduce the parties to a dispute to each other.

Perhaps the best example, in modern western history, of a broker *in cultures* - as opposed to the sorts of brokers discussed above - is the ward or precinct boss of American politics during the late nineteenth and early twentieth centuries. The newly-arrived immigrant had no idea of where to go to complain about a landlord, no idea of how to get admitted to a city hospital, no idea of how to deal with a desk sergeant at a police station - and was often terribly afraid to try. He faced a person with power who asked incomprehensible questions and gave incomprehensible directions. If one did not do as one was told, one failed; and how could one follow directions if the directions made no sense? Conversely, the confusions, ignorances, and fears of the immigrant were often a mystery to those born and bred in the U.S.A. Immigrants raised in a society whose rules and perceptions were not American appeared ignorant, stupid, incompetent, demanding, whining, violent, unco-operative - in fact, different. The precinct boss understood the needs and the fears of the immigrants and knew how to talk with them to find out what they wanted. He also knew how to get admitted to a hospital and how to soothe a policeman. And he would lend five dollars in an emergency. In 'exchange', gratitude and the need to keep such bosses and their superiors in office guaranteed the votes of the newly naturalized. While language could be a barrier, the important function of the boss was to overcome the cultural barrier.

The importance of the culture broker has been recognized in the literature of anthropology, where a number of different kinds of such brokers has been identified. For instance, Silverman's central Italian

brokers were (a) members of the village community, and
(b) from patron families of long standing in their
villages.[7] Wolf's Mexican brokers were from outside
the old communities and were members of the new group
of politician-entrepreneurs who ruled the country.[8]
According to Geertz, the Javanese kijaji who added
'political brokering' to their former religious brokering role were honoured members of the community
and commanded local support.[9] Among those in rural
India who could be described as culture brokers, only
the village headman and, more recently, the elected
members of the institutions of panchayati raj had political roles or could be likened to patrons. Certainly
the village money-lender lacked both characteristics
of the Italian and Javanese culture brokers: he was
far from being a member of the ruling group and he
certainly did not command a loyal local following,[10]
unless, of course, he was also a landowning member of
the dominant caste.[11]

Indian village money-lenders and the men who were
both money-lenders and merchants filled one of several
culture-brokering roles, albeit their primary function
may have been the economic one of providing credit and
goods from outside. Other brokerage roles included
village headmen, lawyers, and politicians.[12] All survived, although disliked and distrusted, because they
were necessary links between village and town, villager
and official, villager and court, villager and state.

The Indian economy was long 'segmented', meaning
that policies and procedures effective in the organized or modern sector had little effect upon the unorganized, largely rural sector. Thus interest rates
charged in the cities had virtually no effect on
interest rates charged in the countryside, while the
distribution of acreage among crops was only marginally
influenced by the relative crop prices existing in the
centres. There were linkages between village and town.
Of necessity there had to be linkages: because of marketing of commercial crops and some marketing of
staples; the payment of land revenue; and the enforcement of laws about landed property and tenant rights.
After the turn of the twentieth century there were
increasing efforts to increase the number and improve
the effectiveness of the linkages, culminating in the
intensive efforts of community development and other
services after independence. But until the 1970s
these linkages remained weak. Partly they remained
weak because the rural economy could function with

little dependence on the urban economy, while the
urban economy could function with little dependence on
the rural economy so long as commercial crops and some
staples continued to flow from the rural areas. Tea,
coffee, and later rubber provided examples of the
urban, organized sector assuring the flow of commercial
crops quite independently of the village agriculture.
But partly the linkages remained weak because there
was a cultural barrier between the two segments. Culture brokers arose to provide links where there were
none, or only weak ones.

What did Indian culture brokers do? The moneylender provided the wherewithal - money - essential to
transactions in the commercial sphere. The headmen
collected the revenue and turned it over to higher
authorities while enjoying the support of higher authorities in enforcing law and order and in pursuing his
own aims within the village. The rural lawyer - that
tout so looked down upon by British administrators as
well as so distrusted by villagers - took the villagers
into the courts to plead cases, explained (if not too
accurately) the rights, powers, and so on that the law
gave to plaintiffs and defendants, and got such documents drawn and registered as the villager might need
or want. The Congress Party 'constructive worker'
tried to organize the villagers to support the national
independence movement and then to mobilize votes for
Congress Party candidates. He was also supposed to be
- with what effectiveness opinions differ - the eyes
and ears of the Congress Party in the villages, and in
consequence it was through him that villagers dealt
with the Party and with legislators.

What each of these brokers had that other villagers did not have was *access*. In the case of the
money-lender, it was access to the urban money-lenders
and bankers and to the urban wholesale merchants. He
had access because he knew how to talk to bankers and
wholesale merchants, he knew what they could and could
not do, and he knew what they were willing to do under
various specified conditions. The villager also had
access in the physical sense. He could find the location of an urban establishment; he could walk in the
door and ask for what he wanted - but he did not know
how to ask for help or to argue over terms in a way
that was comprehensible, trustworthy, and persuasive
to the person he would then be addressing. Conversely,
the urban banker and merchant were unable to deal with
this strange peasant - although, of course, they did

The Role of the Broker

not describe the peasant as 'strange' but rather as 'poor, simple, ignorant', and so on. What the urban commercial person and the peasant needed was a go-between and the money-lender fitted here between the town and the needy peasant. The needy peasant rarely went into the urban bank or wholesale establishment, while the urban banker and wholesaler seldom if ever went to the village. In a way the money-lender was a 'drummer' for the more organized (and, in our terms, more sophisticated) financial sector of the economy, but he differed from the 'drummer' in our society in that the problem was not finding potential borrowers in the villages. The problem was organizing and administering the borrowing and lending business in the village in terms, through procedures, and in a vocabulary of discourse and of obligation which the villager understood. To say here, 'the villager understood', does not mean that he understood the accounting system used by the money-lender, or that the money-lender taught him household and farm finance. What it means is that the procedures and proposals as put to the villager by the money-lender were ones which made sense to the villager and that the villager knew how to talk to the money-lender and what to expect of him - in short, how to do business with him. In F.G. Bailey's expressive way of describing how the political agent worked,[13] the money-lender was a man who knew how to wear a dhoti in the village and trousers in the town.

In effect, what is suggested here is that we look upon a 40 per cent rate of interest charged by a money-lender as consisting of 10 per cent for the money plus 10 per cent for the expenses of collecting debts plus 10 per cent for wearing a dhoti plus 10 per cent for wearing trousers. If one accepts this proposition, then one should not argue that 40 per cent was an outrageous rate of interest for money (that rate was a mere 10 per cent), but rather that 20 per cent was an outrageous wage for intercultural transvestism. It may have been outrageous; it may not have been outrageous - who knows the just price for simultaneous translation between cultures? - but the 40 per cent fee should not be compared with commercial rates of interest.

The major points of contact between the village and the larger world were the use of the monetary system and monetary devices by the villagers; the collection of land revenue by the government; the use of the police and the courts by the state, the villagers, and others; and the efforts of political parties to organize village support. The untrustworthy and, in academic and village folkview, even villainous headman, zamindar, talukdar, jagirdar, money-lender or money-lender-merchant, petty lawyer, and politician were the inside-outsiders (or outside-insiders), each of whom had a brokerage role corresponding to one of the points of contact (kinds of events) which linked the villager with the nation and the world. To convey attitude, rather than information, one might assert that these people 'did not exploit the villager' but that they 'exploited an opportunity provided by the differences between the social systems and attitudes of the towns and the social procedures and beliefs of villagers'.

It is peculiarly revealing that the degree of contempt, although perhaps not of dislike, in which the linking brokers were held was, if only roughly, *inversely proportional* to the degree to which the linking brokers were participants in the events of village life *independently* of their roles as linking brokers. If it was true that the respect/contempt rankings here suggested corresponded with that village hierarchy of values which placed agriculture above all other activities (except, in principle, holy ones), it was also true that the rankings correlated with the degree to which the person's daily round of activities was integrated with the common daily round of village activities. Since the daily round was largely agricultural, those engaged in agriculture were involved in many of the 'multiplex' relationships of a 'simplex' village society and hence villagers regarded them as village agriculturists rather than as linking brokers.[14] Also, as a consequence of this integration with the village, the more 'inside' of the linking brokers - such as a resident landlord-headman - spoke and acted in the terms of the village folkview more fluently and completely than did the others. Their activities were therefore more comprehensible to the villager and the individuals themselves appeared to be more trustworthy. The result was that, even though hatred for resident landlords and money-lenders may have exceeded hatred for lawyers and politicians, the latter two were held in greater contempt. As between landlord and money-lender, there is no doubt that the money-lender was the more contemptible - no doubt that in fact the landlord, whatever else he may have been, was not an object of contempt. A wealthy landholding resident

The Role of the Broker

of the village who was also a money-lender was held in greater respect, and even disliked less, than the pure money-lender or the money-lender who also engaged in trade but not in agriculture. Similarly, members of the new local legislative bodies under panchayati raj were often given more respect than were the members of the state legislative assemblies.[15] It was probably because they were drawn directly from the village populations that those elected to these bodies were held in greater esteem.

Much has been made of monetary profits gained in brokering roles. Money was certainly one of the rewards for undertaking a brokering role, and for the money-lender in particular the major reward; but it was not the only reward, and for the headman-zamindar money may well have been less important than the power which came from contacts with the police and revenue officers of the urban-based culture. By emphasizing the monetary rewards of brokering roles observers and reformers have perceived and therefore classified problems and conflicts arising from the existence of brokering roles as 'economic'. This has led to explaining the roles, the motives of the brokers, the situations in which the brokers operated, and the consequences of brokering in economic terms. Because economic analysts do not worry about subcultural differences in perceptions (and are strongly inclined to regard institutional variations as 'non-economic', if not downright idiosyncratic), the possibility that brokers survived and even throve to serve other ends than profit and the supply of goods or money has been overlooked. The situation misclassified, the problems have been misunderstood. A narrowly economistic view of what was happening led to solutions which were not solutions, and from thence to critiques of public programmes which missed the point.

To by-pass and to subvert the 'exploitative' position of middlemen-brokers the government of India, both before and after independence, sent several kinds of lower level officials into the villages: co-operative society secretaries, extension officers, village level workers, and panchayat secretaries. Disappointment followed: money-lenders continued to thrive while co-operative societies failed, or at best expanded slowly; new techniques and tools were adopted much more slowly than had been hoped; the members of the dominant castes who had supplied the headmen and run the old caste panchayats took over the management of co-operative societies and new organs of local government. Along with disappointment came charges of incompetence and corruption. Certainly a significant number of lower level officials were technically poor at their jobs. They did not know enough about the *whats* and *hows* of agricultural techniques, did not understand how the individual measures of improvement must be fitted together to make an economically worthwhile whole, and did not grasp the scientific bases of the improved technologies. But this was only a part of the problem: when right, when technically competent, when knowledgeable about why the improvements should be made, these officials were nevertheless often unable to convey the ideas and unable to teach the cultivator how to acquire and to use the new techniques. The reasons, I submit, were not the ignorance or stupidity of cultivators - and, in any case among social scientists, this interpretation has been largely dropped in the last two decades [16] - nor by any means entirely a failure to appreciate some one or more specific elements in the local situation (although such was frequently the case), but rather that the extension officer operated and discoursed in the modes and phrasings, and with the perceptions of cause-and-effect and of reward and punishment, of the modern urban world. The cultural idioms as well as the procedures of the urban world were by no means wholly meaningful in the world of village India, and this lack of meaningfulness reinforced villagers' already well-developed distrust of government agents.

Reformers and developers assumed that what was needed to develop the villages and to change the villages was access to more resources and new techniques at lower costs. They were right in that without more wherewithal of inputs and more knowledge of how-to-do there would be no development. But they were in error in thinking that *access* meant the establishment of modern institutions willing to provide credit, information, tools, cement, and services at lower cost than money-lenders and merchants had been charging. Like nitrogen for plants, new inputs for villagers must be in an 'available form'. Brokering is putting resources and extra-village organizations into an 'available form'. When the organizations are structured in a modern mould and staffed with personnel who live, or try to live, or want to live, only in the modern style, then the new elements of modern scientific society are not transmitted to the participants in the small, village societies. Furthermore, insofar as people entering a brokering role did have the trust of the villagers, '... in virtually all cases this trust [was] withdrawn if the broker [was] seen to be a missionary for modernization'.[17]

Indian leaders and administrators conceived of extension officers and panchayat and co-operative secretaries as efficient, honest, 'economic' middlemen, but the officers and secretaries failed in these roles in significant part because what was needed were brokers who could translate new knowledge and opportunities into the social idiom and perceptions of the villagers. In the absence of new officials good at brokering the new technologies and organizations, 'private entrepreneurs-in-folkview-translation' continued to thrive: men who could operate in two subcultures became political brokers who effectively took over the substance of the roles of the panchayat and co-operative secretaries while the money-lender still lent at 40 per cent to villagers who would pay 'extra' for access on terms understandable and acceptable in their own view of how-the-world-works.

Were this the whole story the efforts at development would have been a complete failure: but, in fact, they were not. Quite the contrary. The long-run rise in agricultural output since the 1950s, at about three per cent per year, was ample evidence of more than minimal success. Furthermore, while results were always less and later than planned, the extension efforts of the Indian government did contribute to change in the villages and to the creation of effective linkages between the sectors. One might liken the process to the effect of water pounding upon the lip of a waterfall: nothing appears to happen until suddenly a large piece gives way. Similarly, there appeared to be no revolutionary change in rural India for 15 to 20 years after independence, and then the 1970s saw many changes.

One of the first evidences of change was corruption in the development services. Curiously, from the viewpoint presented in this essay, one important way in which extension officers were corrupted involved brokering. Bribing officials could occur only because cultivators wanted the new inputs, but if corruption in the development services was a mark of the success of the services in creating demand for new inputs, it was also a measure of the failure of the services to create properly *public-service* brokers. This failure was manifested in that common form of corruption whereby a development officer held up validation and transmittal of forms for government subsidy or for the supply of new farm inputs until a few rupees found his pocket. The way in which this kind of transaction was conducted illustrates the importance of brokering: the villager often did not himself go to the official, but rather a manufacturer or seller of inputs himself approached the validating official. This seller had already reached an agreement with a villager who wanted the new inputs and had already helped the villager to fill in the forms.[18] He too was a broker who could deal with both the villager's culture and the bureaucracy's culture.

There have been other changes reducing the need for culture brokers and the opportunities for culture brokering. The village headman or zamindar is no longer the focal point for revenue collection. During the 1960s the members of district zilla parishads and members of the legislative assemblies became the people who represented the villagers to officialdom.

The efforts of community development officers over 20 years and experience of political activity at block, district, and state levels, reinforced by the opportunities provided by the Green Revolution, changed the villagers, or at least those villagers who had accustomed themselves to the new technologies and expanding markets. Sugar farmers in Maharashtra and wheat and now rice farmers in Punjab, Haryana, and western U.P. are not only willing and able to approach representatives of the modern or urban culture - they even barge into the offices of professors of agriculture. The village money-lender is now facing effective competition from the banks, which have, since nationalization, been required to achieve lending targets in the rural area. Perhaps legal necessity was the mother of cultural invention by bank managers, but similar instructions to the State Bank of India 15 years earlier were not nearly so effective. More likely the 'lead banks' - one in each district responsible for seeing to it that the banks in the district do lend the target amounts - have met a more responsive clientele. In either case, the money-lender is being replaced by the banks when loans are wanted for productive purposes.

It is possible that culture brokers will survive for some time yet because there is still a lot of difference between the world as understood by the landless labourer and the Harijan and the world as understood by development administrators and the political organs of the nation and the states; but it is perhaps equally likely that political and labour organizations will eliminate the need for culture brokering between the dispossessed and the rest of Indian society.

Culture brokers arise when two groups wish to deal with each other but find that they 'word the world'[19] so differently that they cannot reach mutual accommodations. The culture broker always has a substantive function - the achievement of one of the mutual accommodations which the two groups wish - but the key to his position and power is not his technical expertise in the substantive function but his ability to word the world differently, and intelligibly, to the members of the two groups. In India he often appeared corrupting and exploitative because he enjoyed more income or power than seemed justified by the particular accommodations - loans, access to officials - he made possible; and because he violated the law or the ethics of one or both of the cultures he served to connect. He was certainly corrupting of the administration and was probably exploitative of the villagers with whom he dealt - at least, he certainly took advantage of his position and was less than averagely sensitive to the standards of law and equity as commonly understood in India. However, such behaviour was necessarily inherent in his role, which was to act between and therefore outside as well as inside both cultures, and therefore to some degree independently of the ethical standards of both. It is understandable that he tried to maintain his role in the face of the efforts of reformers, adminstrators, and statesmen to replace him with other, less costly and more equitable agencies. If some of his gains were ill-got, not all were; for the very situation of cultural diversity must share some of the blame.

The Indian brokers' roles originated in the difference, in a phrase popular in the 1950s, between the 'little traditions and the great tradition'. In particular, as British commercial practice and law became more important in India, the numbers, wealth, and powers of the culture-brokering money-lender and lawyer grew. It has only been very recently, perhaps only in the last decade on any significant scale, that the village farmer and those representing the city and the nation have come to understand each other's cultural idiom well enough to do without culture brokers.

NOTES

Neale, 'The role of the broker in rural India'

The line of argument in this essay originated in a paper of the same title delivered to the Annual Meeting of the American Association for the Advancement of Science, New York City, 30 December 1967.

    1. Fourth edition (London 1947).
    2. Bombay 1954.
    3. That many or all money-lenders did these things was probably true; but the point of the argument which follows is that these facts do not exhaust the important truths about money-lenders (or about other rural brokers).
    4. The point was made at the SOAS Conference in December 1980 that a great deal of lending in India's villages was by richer villagers to poorer villagers in kind, especially in foodstuffs; and that such lending probably constituted well over half of total lending within India's villages - perhaps, it was suggested, amounting to three-quarters of all village lending. The Report of the All-India Rural Credit Review Committee(Bombay: Reserve Bank of India 1969), p.100, says that professional money-lenders provided 43.8 per cent and traders and commission agents 6.1 per cent of the total borrowings by rural households in 1950-52. The comparable figures for 1962 are 12.7 and 10.1 per cent. Landlords and 'agriculturist money-lenders' provided 26.8 per cent in 1950-52 and 34.6 in 1962 (relatives provided 14.4 and 8.8 per cent). But, because no one knows either the total amount of lending nor the amount in kind, it is impossible to state with any precision the 'proportional importance' of the money-lenders' activities within the villages. However, the point of this essay does not depend on the relative importance of the money-lender, but only upon the fact that he did have a significant role - and if his lending amounted to only a fifth of total lending, his role would still have been significant. The much reduced proportion of rural credit attributed to the money-lender in 1962 may reflect the decline in the importance of his role as culture broker, a decline discussed toward the end of this essay.
    5. Henry S. Maine, 'Prices and Rents', in *Village Communities in East and West* (3rd, author's edition,

Notes to pages 164-7

New York 1876).
6. I believe that Eric Wolf introduced this concept. See his 'Aspects of Group Relations in a Complex Society', *American Anthropologist* 58 (December 1956), pp.1065-78.
7. Sydel F. Silverman, 'Patronage and Community-Nation Relationships in Central Italy', *Ethnology* 4 (April 1965), pp.172-91.
8. Wolf, op.cit., pp.1071-2.
9. Clifford Geertz, 'The Javanese *Kijaji*: the Changing Role of a Culture Broker', *Comparative Studies in History and Society* 2 (April 1960), pp.228-49. The literature on culture brokers is larger than the citations here might indicate. However, an effort at much wider citation or further illustrations does not seem necessary, or even advisable, in this essay, in which I wish to borrow the concept and offer it as a possible explanation of some of the traits of those dealing with Indian villagers. Those interested in further discussions of the meaning, significance, types, and case studies might consult B. Kapferer, ed., *Transaction and Meaning* (Philadelphia: Institute for the Study of Human Issues 1976), especially the references in A.P. Cohen and J.L. Comaroff, 'The Management of Meaning: On the Phenomenology of Political Transactions' (pp.87-107), pp.105-7; or Irwin Press, 'Ambiguity and Innovation: Implications for the Genesis of the Culture Broker', *American Anthropologist* 71, 2 (April 1969), pp.205-17, which relates the concept of the broker to the concept of 'the marginal man'.
10. In his discussion of the seemingly analagous roles of Indian politicians and officials, Bailey says that these people 'are not ... "culture brokers" in the sense of providing a communication of ideas and a meeting of minds: on the contrary .... By providing pragmatic contacts they render unnecessary normative communion'. F.G. Bailey, 'The Peasant View of the Bad Life', *Advancement of Science* 23 (December 1966), pp.399-409. However, it seems possible to view Silverman's broker as making commercial and legal understanding unnecessary, and Geertz's broker as making orthodox understanding of Islam unnecessary (opp.cit.).
11. See Adrian C. Mayer, 'Patrons and Brokers: Rural Leadership in Four Overseas Indian Communities', pp.167-88, in Maurice Freedman, ed., *Social Organization: Essays Presented to Raymond Firth* (Chicago 1967), which contrasts the broker with the patron as 'ideal types': 'The patron recruits followers by his power to

dispense favours. The broker, on the other hand, is a middleman attracting followers who believe him able to influence the person who controls the favours .... [W]hereas the client of the former is only interested in his relation with the patron, and does not care about the source of the patron's power, the client of the latter has a relation with the person with whom the broker is in contact, and indeed has called in the broker to influence that relation to his advantage' (pp.168-9). The point is important in respect to roles, for both roles can be adopted by a single person in respect to another person. Silverman's brokers (op. cit.) illustrate how patrons can use knowledge as well as favours-to-grant, and be both patrons at home and brokers with the outside world. The culture broker in India, as argued in this essay, not only influences relations with outsiders - there may be only the most tenuous relations with outsiders in the absence of a culture broker.

12. See F.G. Bailey, *Politics and Social Change: Orissa in 1959* (Berkeley 1963), pp.136-57, for a discussion of politicians.

13. Bailey, 'The Peasant View of the Bad Life', p.404.

14. I am indebted to F.G. Bailey for the proposition that in 'simple' societies relationships are 'complex', whereas in 'complex' societies relationships are 'simple'.

15. I have not seen such statements in the scholarly literature but Indian officials and MLAs made this 'complaint' and some other people familiar with rural India have expressed agreement.

16. At least in its overt form; but I suspect that it has crept back in the covert forms of 'the importance of education' and 'investment in human capital'.

17. Bailey, 'The Peasant View of the Bad Life', p.405.

18. I know of no literature which supports this assertion with citations of specific cases, but Indian and foreigner alike, who have worked in community development blocks, agree that this was a common form of corruption - as did sellers of such equipment whom I have interviewed.

19. For this phrase too I am indebted to F.G. Bailey, in comments he made at the Interdisciplinary Conference on Processes of Change in Contemporary Asian Societies at the University of Illinois at Champaign-Urbana, 5-7 November 1970.

TWO KARNATAKA VILLAGES AND THE OUTSIDE WORLD:
INTERNAL CHARACTERISTICS, MOVEMENT LINKAGES,
AND STATE OF DEVELOPMENT

H.G. Hanumappa and John Adams

Introduction

For over one hundred years India's villagers have been increasingly drawn into and had their lives affected by external developments. In the late nineteenth century railroads were laid down, the road system was repaired and extended, port and dock facilities were put in place, and telegraphic links were established within India and overseas. These infrastructural improvements were associated with an increased use of money and the spread of product and factor markets, and these phenomena were in turn connected to the dramatic gains in exports and imports of the 1860-1910 period.[1] It is still an open question as to whether there was any uptrend in average incomes during this time, but there is no doubt that the degree of economic, social and political change in the villages was profound. These forms of change, and the concomitant expansion of the infrastructure and market system, have continued to move in tandem right down to the present.

From the village perspective, rather than that of the economic historian, the interactions of village life and these external dimensions of change have been catalogued and assessed by several generations of field workers.[2] These anthropologists and other researchers provide ample documentation of the myriad changes in the villages. They usually describe the physical and infrastructural setting with care, stating precisely how far roads, rail stations, market towns, and other features of importance are from the villages and what links there are to them. What is often deficient in these studies, however, is the failure to expound in any detail upon the frequency with which villagers utilize these aspects of the village's external environment. Nor is there any systematic analysis of which strata of villagers use which external features and for what purposes. There is thus a yawning hiatus between the carefully sketched infrastructure on the one side and the copiously depicted pattern of village structure and change on the other. Actual connections and movements between these two spheres are described

only anecdotally or in a fragmented way.[3] An interest of this paper is to use the method of reversing the usual anthropological procedure and to quantify and analyse movement patterns at the village level, as the first emphasis, with village conditions being described only when relevant.

Evidence collected in detail as part of a large sample survey of the villages of Tumkur district, Karnataka state, and via field visits provides considerable insight into the nature of movements and interactions between two South Indian villages and the outside world as tangibly manifested in neighbouring villages, hobli and district headquarters and market centres, and the state capital, Bangalore.[4] Furthermore, it is possible to relate the frequency of visits from each of the two villages to these various places to the social and economic characteristics of the travellers. It is also feasible to sort visits by purpose. Although two villages cannot be used as a basis for wide generalizations about patterns over all India, or even within Tumkur district, the novelty of this exercise makes it of intrinsic interest and may serve as a stimulant to parallel investigations.

Movement patterns in rural India take many forms. People may migrate permanently to other villages or exit from the rural sector to towns and cities. The concern here is, however, with transient movements of short duration, after which the visitor returns to the home village. Such movements may be habitual, as going into town to work each day, or essentially sporadic, arising out of special needs, interests, or circumstances. Whether habitual or sporadic, the frequency and purpose of external movements are likely to be closely related to a number of factors. The physical and economic base of the village and its occupational and demographic structure will influence a settlement's mobility patterns. The movements of a village's residents will be affected by its level of development, the location of the village in relation to neighbouring markets, administrative centres, educational facilities, clinics, extension offices, and other things such as cinemas or co-operative offices. The quantity and quality of bus, road, and other infrastructural links will condition the frequency and timing of such visits. Political involvement and the aggressiveness of local leadership in seeking extension or other contacts will be important. Kinship ties, such as those involving marriage networks, and the pull of religious centres may shape travel patterns. Insofar as possible the impact of these various influences on the movements of villagers in the two selected Tumkur villages will be assessed. Following the example of Epstein and others who have used a comparative methodology, the two villages were chosen because they had different characteristics. It will be shown how these differences are related to the quite striking contrast in movement patterns between the two.

While a tracing of the elaborate movement patterns of two sets of Indian villagers, viewed against the backdrop of their respective ecological, economic, and demographic milieux, is not a trivial gesture, it would be overly mechanical and simplistic if matters were left thus. The argument to be made is not only that movements are outgrowths of the underlying village conditions but that they are connected with salient social and political features of the villages. In particular, many movements follow lines of social and political interaction between key village groups and individuals and the outside world. These connections to the larger political and administrative system of the region, state, and nation are highly instrumental in changing the economic base and ultimately the level of development of a village. Or, where such connections are weak or absent, the village base is static or eroding. A key intervening variable may be styled 'leadership' or 'manipulative ability', which is associated with a particular caste structure. There is, in sum, a triangular relationship among movement, the economic base and its development, and political and administrative gamesmanship. Infrastructural links, the village's ecological base and resources, basic demographic patterns, are conditioning factors but are not decisive.

The Setting: District, Tahsil, and Village Characteristics

Karnataka state may be divided along two axes into north-south and west-east dichotomies.[5] The northern zone features black soils utilized extensively for cotton. The south is typified by ragi, small stock, and little irrigation. The west, along the coast, is a high rainfall, rice-oriented area.[6] Although it falls in the southern and eastern regimes, Tumkur district is not an extreme case of either melange of characteristics. Still, ragi occupies about 29 per cent of the net area sown and is the most widely cultivated crop.[7] Sheep and goats are significant in the rural economy.

The two villages chosen are located in Sira and Tiptur taluks. The economies of these two microregions of Tumkur district have somewhat different features, although they share the limitations of light Deccan rainfall. Figure 1 shows the locations of Karnataka, Tumkur, the two taluks, and Biligere and Changavara villages, located respectively in Tiptur and Sira taluks. Railways and major roads are drawn in. The two taluks, which form the immediate economic and political context for life in the two villages, represent variations on the traits typical of Tumkur. About 62 per cent of the area of Tiptur is cultivated, versus 47 per cent in the district and only 27 per cent in Sira. About one-third of the arable in Tiptur is devoted to ragi, which is about the district average; this contrasts with only 12 per cent in Sira. The chief sharply-defined aspect of Tiptur is that 28 per cent of its cultivated land is in coconut plantations. Sira has a diversified agriculture, because of canal, well, and tank irrigation covering 19 per cent of its arable. Minor millets are grown on one-quarter of the land, and pulses occupy 21 per cent. Cash cropping takes the form of groundnuts (11 per cent), coconut (3 per cent), and areca nut (3 per cent). About 23 per cent of the district's sheep are in Sira taluk.

The two villages, Biligere of Tiptur taluk and Changavara of Sira taluk, were selected in part because they represent the modes of agriculture of the region. Table 1 shows the land-use patterns in Biligere and Changavara. For reference, the respective populations of the two villages as of 1971 were 1538 and 1765. Despite their rough equality in population numbers, Changavara has over three times the total area of Biligere, but the large area unsuited for agriculture, and scant irrigation, mean that Changavara must focus its agriculture on dry cropping. In contrast, the farm land of Biligere is 30 per cent irrigated from tanks and wells and over 40 per cent of the gross cropped area is devoted to wet land and garden agriculture, with coconut tracts dominating. Ragi is the most important grain crop in Biligere; there are smatterings of other millets and pulses. Ragi is important, too, in Changavara, but there is an even more diverse mix of various millets and pulses. Some irrigated paddy and dry and irrigated tobacco are grown.

In addition to their agricultural contrasts, Biligere and Changavara have exhibited radically different demographic trends in the 1951-71 period. According to table 2, over the two census periods, India, Karnataka, and Tumkur district have all experienced positive population growth in the range of 19 to 25 per cent. Tumkur district is at the bottom end of this range, but Biligere is toward the top. The divergent case is Changavara, where growth at about one-third the district's rate in the 1951-61 interval was followed by an absolute and rapid decline of 19.4 per cent in 1961-71. For this reason Biligere can be called a 'growing' village and Changavara a 'declining' village; of course, these designations do not imply anything about average income trends although they may be related to them.

The demographic structure of the two villages is broken down in table 3. In Biligere, the uptrend in population is more or less matched by an expansion of households, although there is a rise in average household size from 5.0 to 5.8 persons. The male/female ratio has climbed between 1951 and 1971, perhaps reflecting some in-migration of males. The shrinking village has experienced a decline in the number of households from 336 to 218. The sex ratio has risen somewhat but the source here may be high female infant mortality connected with dimmer local prospects rather than selective in- or out-migration. A particularly interesting phenomenon is the elevation of household size from 6.1 to 8.1 persons with most of the increase coming in the last decade of falling population. Either small domestic units have found it easier to emigrate, or having fewer resources have been more driven to. The lack of scheduled caste out-migration on a proportional basis, however, weakens both of these propositions because their household size would normally be low. Since the availability of housing would be enlarged as population shrivels, this could be presumed to lead to some domestic fragmentation and dispersion. In Changavara, however, a number of houses stand empty suggesting that social or economic factors are controlling household size, rather than a shortage of housing.

The taluk and village agricultural bases do not permit any easy generalizations about relationships between the economy and demographic and mobility patterns. The irrigation of a high proportion of village land and concentration on coconut farming has provided an impetus to population growth above the regional average for Biligere. The dry farming of Changavara has been less successful. It is clear, however, that other factors need to be considered in order to ascertain why emigration has been so high in Changavara. It may be anticipated that transient movements will also differ, reflecting the known differences in the ecological and economic situations of the two villages.

Biligere and Changavara should manifest differences typical of growth and expansion on the one hand and stagnation and decline on the other. This supposition is confirmed by obvious differences in literacy and in the amenities available in the two villages. Tables 4 and 5 summarize these contrasts. The literacy rate is a good measure of childhood contact with educational institutions in rural India. Looked at dynamically, a high and rising rate indicates that villagers are reaching out for educational opportunities and possible economic advantages. In turn, educational exposure may make villagers more open to outside ideas and more able to cope with the increasing demands of a modernizing society. Such developments are of high salience and influence when women's education is involved. The literacy rate in Biligere has been high and rising during the 1951-71 period (see table 4). Changavara's people had low literacy rates through 1961, after which some gains are noticeable. The position of women in Biligere rapidly shifted in the nontraditional direction after 1951 so that their literacy rate is actually as high as that of Changavara's men. Female literacy in Changavara is quite low although some gains have been made in the last decade. These findings imply that Changavara is at once more conventional, less receptive of educational involvement, especially for girls, and not as participatory in the ladder of schools of the region.

The labour participation rates for 1961 and 1971, included in table 4, do not convey much insight. Definitional changes make strict comparisons between the censuses impossible, but for the two years Changavara has higher male participation rates. The female workers of Changavara appear to have been marginally employed in agriculture in 1961, and with the definitional change of the 1971 census this peripheral activity was not sufficient for them to be counted as workers.

To highlight further the image of Biligere as more progressive and more involved in interaction with regional economic and political developments, the facilities or amenities available in the villages are identified. The argument is put in terms of a reciprocal interaction between an outward-looking village and its milieu, the result being progressive or modern behavioural patterns. Conversely the declining village is less keyed into surroundings - there is less social, political-administrative, economic interaction - with the result that it is less progressive or modern. Its residents may face more 'leave-for-good-or-else' decisions once dead-ends are reached. They lack the ability and opportunities for more complex responses to India's changing rural setting. Superior amenities in Biligere are both a sign of wider involvement and more successful manipulation and a base for the expansion of a village's relationships with the outside world.

Table 5 makes amply plain the superior development of facilities achieved by Biligere, a differentiation especially notable given that both villages are of roughly the same size. While both have electricity, Biligere has piped water, a primary health centre, and a family planning clinic. Changavara does not even have a small dispensary. The consciousness of the desirability of piped water and of the benefits of medical attention, not to mention receptivity to family planning, attest Biligere's orientation towards the securing of manifestations of modernity, valued either for their own sake or as tokens. Post-secondary education is even available in Biligere itself in the form of a junior college. Changavara has the usual amenities of an Indian village in 1980: wells, electricity, schools, road and bus services, and a post office. Biligere has gone beyond what has become the usual to have such novelties as chlorinated water, superior health facilities, and a junior college.

Movement Patterns: Interaction with the Outside World

On balance, it is accurate to say that Biligere has somewhat better access to its taluk headquarters (Tiptur) than Changavara does to its (Sira). Biligere is also near the Bangalore-Poona railroad. The villagers of Biligere enjoy somewhat easier access to Tumkur, the district headquarters, than do those of Changavara, and can also more easily visit Bangalore, the capital of the state. Nonetheless, these advantages are not so significant as to account for the dynamism of one village and the retrogression of the other. The economic resources of a village are susceptible to management and it is unclear why a previously adequate base should have declined to the point that out-migration would have been forced on so many, as has happened in Changavara. There is a considerable scope to push beyond these undeniably important but still not fully convincing factors to others.

On the basis of its more cash-oriented economy centred on the coconut, and because of its long-standing interest in securing better education and better facilities for itself, it may be argued that Biligere will have a wider network of contacts with outside centres than Changavara. Such connections will involve not only market links, but also visits to relatives, religious centres, and political seats. Rural Indians build alliances and seek support through a variety of relationships; they receive information about technology, occupational opportunities, and political payoffs through many channels. Visits to relatives or religious sites must not be seen merely as leading to frivolous or purely social encounters. Similarly, travel to markets may involve much socializing, casual political action, and information-gathering and idea-exchanging.

Table 6 illustrates visits of the residents of Biligere and Changavara to their relatives over four different distances. As expected, the rate of visitation is lower the greater the distance involved. Not only cost and time are relevant, because the distribution of kin must be considered. Since the two villages are of roughly equal population size, the number of visits is a reasonable raw measure of interaction with the outside world (for kin, physically 'outside' even if socially 'inside'). Regardless of distance, the villagers of Biligere far exceed those of Changavara in travelling to meet with kin. Two anomalies concerning Changavara require some explanation. Changavara is located at the western edge of Tumkur district but is still close to Andhra Pradesh on the east. Visits to kin draw villagers outside the district to the west and into Andhra on the east; hence, the number of such journeys within the state exceeds the number within the district and the number of visits outside the state is higher than for Biligere.

The total number of visits to kin is 2,022 for Biligere and 481 for Changavara or a difference of over 4.2 times. More persons (556) travel for this purpose from Biligere than the number (248) from Changavara, although the ratio is only 2.2. At all distances the frequency of visits per person is higher for Biligere than Changavara, with the total averages being 3.6 and 1.9 visits per person respectively. Not only does Biligere have more people visiting relatives in and outside the taluk, but they do so almost twice as commonly.

Visits to religious centres have their own intrinsic motives, but also afford opportunities for political and economic opportunism and for discussions with caste or sect peers. Such visits require some affluence and manifest religious fervour and a traditional outlook. These several influences are reflected in table 7, in which the less progressive, declining village is found to have made more religious visits in one year than did the other. Only three of these visits took residents of Changavara outside the district, however, compared to 68 such visits (49 per cent) for Biligere. The average frequency of visits per pilgrim is about one per year in all cases. The villagers of Biligere may be typified as somewhat less disposed to religious travels than those of Changavara, but true to form their inclination is to longer distances. These results show a more parochially-oriented exposure to regional religious visitation on the part of Changavara and more cosmopolitan participation in pilgrimages by the villagers of Biligere.

Many young rural Indians must, every morning and afternoon, make the trip to and from school. Indians of any age, and at virtually any time, are on the roads and tracks between villages and local markets. Table 8 summarizes the movements to and from educational centres for the two villages. Given its endowment of educational insitutions, Biligere's children largely remain within the village, but 40 students voyage within the taluk or further to attend schools (the response concerned 'daily' travel but the longer distances may necessitate weekly or other periodic movement). Changavara does have some students who are being educated outside the village, but its low overall commitment to education is consistent with its low literacy rate and lack of advanced facilities.

Both villages have products - coconut in one case and tobacco, small stock and ragi in the other - that must be taken to market; and, both villages need to purchase consumption goods and agricultural inputs. Table 9 shows the monthly frequency of market visits and their purpose for the two villages. Insofar as the purchase of consumption items is concerned, Changavara actually exceeds Biligere in the number of visits outside the village. Biligere's location on a main road between the taluk and district headquarters, and its nearness to a north-south road and the Bangalore-Poona railroad, have encouraged the establishment of shops. Purchases of consumer items in the village are convenient and longer trips are unnecessary. Differences between the two villages in movements for marketing become more acute when farm sales are examined. Biligere does more travelling for farm sales than does Changavara; the same is true when the purchase of farm inputs is the purpose. The vitality of the coconut economy of Biligere and its related non-farm activities shows up clearly in the large numbers of visits to taluk headquarters for the selling and buying of farm and non-farm products. Most marketing for both villages is done at the taluk headquarters, which is an interesting comment on their efficacy as regional economic centres - both appear capable of bearing the demands placed upon them by client villages. While there is not by any means a trivial degree of market interaction between Changavara and the outside world, Biligere has a quantitatively greater rate of market participation and that participation covers a broader array of activities.

Apart from education and marketing, the kind of work a villager does, and the place where it is done, will guide regular movements outside the village. The occupational structures of the two villages are given in the first four lines of table 10. The chief differences in the two villages are that Changavara has more agricultural labourers but fewer small and medium farmers. This contrast is not of great import, however, since landholdings in a wetter village are likely to be smaller than in a dry village. The greater variety of occupations in Biligere is shown by a somewhat larger number of workers in the 'other' category, which includes shopkeeping, modern crafts, carting and driving, and metal work. All in all, the occupational structures of the two villages are not radically different. Once again, however, the greater regional involvement of Biligere is shown by the number of workers who live in the village but spend some appreciable part of their typical workday some distance away. There peripatetics are drawn not only from the more mobile artisans and other groups but from middle and other farmers. The ability of these farmers to cultivate lands outside their own village, lands in some cases that are even outside the district, is testimony both to their managerial and entrepreneural abilities and to their skill in handling the often difficult role of outsider in a foreign village community.

The caste composition of the two villages varies profoundly. Changavara has quite diverse social divisions. The major landholding castes are the Kuruba and Golla households, 45 in number.[8] Nineteen each of Lingayat and Vokkaliga families have land. There are 42 scheduled caste and 33 scheduled tribe families. The larger landowners are from all three of the farm household groups and smaller landowners are mostly Kurubas and Gollas. In Biligere, there is a patently dominant group of Lingayat farmers, who are formed into 144 households with small and middle-sized holdings. There are 44 scheduled caste and 14 scheduled tribe families. In both villages there are representative artisan, service, and twice-born castes. In Tiptur taluk, where Biligere is situated, almost 40 per cent of the population identifies with the Lingayat group so the village is tied into the locally most numerous castes. Only 15 per cent of the population calls itself Vokkaliga and this is the second lowest proportion in the district's 11 taluks. In Sira taluk, about 31 per cent of the population is Vokkaliga and only 2.2 per cent is Lingayat. This district does have the largest Golla-Kuruba proportion in the district at about one-fifth. Changavara's population is not clearly affiliated with its taluk's plurality caste, the Vokkaligas, although its Gollas and Kurubas would appear to have some comparatively strong external attachments within the district. Changavara has an untypically high share of scheduled caste and scheduled tribe families, and particularly many of the latter disadvantaged group. There is therefore a sharp contrast between the classically shaped social structure of Biligere, featuring as it does a cluster of Lingayat farmers in the midst of a regionally numerous and influential amalgam of castemates, and that of Changavara, showing another face of rural India, namely a village with no clear elite and a large number of socially marginal families. These contrasting caste distributions, and the potentials for extra-village connections that they stimulate or inhibit, contribute to the differential ability of each village's population to interact effectively with its social and political surroundings. The identification of a common interest or interests and the leadership of Changavara's diverse array of people is more likely to be a formidable, if not impossible and fruitless task, while Biligere offers a situation ripe for the emergence and management of an effective caste spokesman, unless lineage or other rivalries disunite the preponderant Lingayats.

A summary of movement patterns by occupational group is provided in table 11. Since the occupational ranks are associated with caste status, inferences about differences across castes may be made. This large table provides a synthetic overview of extra-village visits. The evidence firmly reinforces the line of argument being developed: that the more extensive and more frequent contacts of Biligere tie it into intertwined social, political, and economic networks in the region and state; that these movements are important evidence of this progressive village's efforts to gain information, secure economic advantages, and enhance the village's payoffs from the taluk, district, and state political-administrative systems; that the declining village, Changavara, has been less skilful in forging such links, with consequent backwardness in education and amenities.

The parochial nature of Changavara's connections is exhibited in the dominance of visits per month to neighbouring villages rather than more distant targets. A total of 682 visits by 153 persons to nearby communities was made in an average month for a per person visit rate of 4.4. This rate is pretty well constant across occupational categories. Biligere visits neighbouring villages less commonly but more persons (191) make such visits, albeit at the low average rate of 1.9 visits per person. So, in a given month fewer of Changavara's people will travel to other villages and, while they will do so with double the frequency, they are therefore as a group less exposed to the circulation of ideas and information in their immediate vicinity than those of Biligere. The pattern is much the same for 'within taluk' travel: movement within the adjacent rural areas rather than to regional economic and political centres, carried on by a few relatively active people in Changavara, and more numerous, but less frequent travellers from Biligere.

H.G. Hanumappa and John Adams

Final Evidence and Conclusion

The two villages are remarkably at variance in the frequency with which their residents visit regional centres: the hobli, taluk, and district headquarters. No single part of the evidence more reinforces the view of Biligere as actively pursuing its interests through systematic manipulation of the local economy and political system. The broad pattern is that more of Biligere's villagers, from more occupational groups, visit these centres more regularly than do those of Changavara. One hundred people of Biligere visit their hobli headquarters for every one from Changavara. Four times as many people make four times as many visits to the taluk headquarters; 40 people average 1.8 visits per month to the district headquarters, versus three people making three visits from Changavara. The occupational differences in mobility between the two villages are revealing. Wherever the numbers are large enough to mean anything, each of Biligere's work groups makes more visits on average than do Changavara's. For Biligere, it is the medium farmers that dominate in absolute numbers the movements to regional centres. *Most critical, however, is the telling observation that for each of the three centres the size of holding and higher social status and greater political power in the village are perfectly correlated with the frequency of such visits.* On an annual basis large farmers who make such journeys undertake 30 visits to the hobli headquarters, 36 visits to the taluk headquarters, and 29 visits to the district headquarters. Middle and small farmers in the aggregate make more total visits to the three types of centre but their rates of doing so are lower. The villagers of Biligere visit the state capital more than do those of Changavara, further demonstrating their aggressive reaching out for gain and advantage.

Field visits to the two villages have provided further support for the thesis attributing Biligere's growth to the interaction of favourable internal economic conditions, an aggressive, questing, and manipulative leadership, identifiable with the farming groups (but not exclusively), better education and facilities, and a modestly advantageous location in relation to infrastructure. Biligere has a group of local leaders that in the last 15 years has been responsible for the obtaining of a junior college, a primary health centre, and piped water. The village's

location on the state highway has been exploited at
every possible opportunity by this leadership. A
favourite ploy has been to meet with political figures
and senior government officials passing up and down
the road, encouraging them to detour into the village
proper. This behaviour is largely absent in Changavara where there is an absence of such local initiative.
Consequently, schooling and other amenities are un-
developed and there has been demographic decline
through permanent out-migration. The more isolated
location of Changavara and its dependence on extensive
dry-land farming are doubtlessly factors in its population recession, but it is undeniably further disadvantaged by poor human resources, a weak orbit of contacts throughout its region, and a dearth of entrepre-
neurial and manipulative farmers.

Throughout its recent history Biligere has been
led by a remarkable and sagacious panchayat chairman.
He has vigorously pursued caste and village interests
and has been responsible for the bringing of many
amenities and development schemes into the village.
He has been chairman of the taluk development board
and in an oversight position for local planning and
distribution of resources. He has made a full life-
time commitment to the idea that payoffs are to be had
by capturing and manipulating the local political and
administrative apparatus and using it for the benefit
of the village. Recognizing that it is not a perfect
system, this is nonetheless how rural India is supposed to work and how in the present institutional
setting a village is supposed to develop itself in
alliance with external powers and aid. This village
leadership is provided by an individual who happens
to be in the neighbourhood of 75 years old. Whether
his sprat of a protégé (who is about 40) will ultimately continue this adroit management is not certain,
but conditions are favourable.

The identification and analysis of extra-village
contacts focus attention on a measurable behavioural
dimension of the process of change and development in
south India. Too often villages have been analysed
only by the description of internal economic, political, and social relationships. The infrastructure
has been regarded as important and it is frequently
specified and mapped at the beginning of village sur-
veys; market towns and administrative centres are
normally mentioned. The evidence from Biligere and
Changavara convincingly demonstrates, however, that a

detailed examination of interactions between village populations and their regional context can shed considerable light on internal development patterns, including their demographic profiles, and the availability of electricity, schooling, and other beneficial elements.

The finding that the farmers, especially the large farmers, are more intensively involved in the interchange between village and local economic and political centres, is consistent with much recent discussion of rural India. Large and middle farmers are perceived as the leading groups in more progressive areas in reaching out to, manipulating, and even 'capturing' local political and administrative agencies capable of providing farm inputs such as seeds or fertilizer, irrigation and power, extension advice, credit, or public goods such as schools, roads, wells, or clinics. A question not opened in this discussion of such links is whether these activities lead to a skewing of these benefits in favour of the already comparatively rich and powerful. The breadth of Biligere's ties to the outside world, encompassing as it does all occupational groups, implies there is at least some catholicism in the process, but this issue cannot be faced with the evidence in hand.

Insofar as the future is concerned, further development and modernization, along with deepening politicization of the rural populace, will enchance the importance of the kinds of personal contacts nurtured by Biligere. To some extent the transient migrations of Biligere - to work as well as to bring benefits to the actors and the village at large - may be perceived as a substitute for permanent out-migration of the type found in Changavara. Facilitating, anticipating, and determining how to control - rather than being controlled by - such transient and opportunistic migration and movement may be essential for an administration desirous of working effectively and achieving its particular mission in the Indian rural setting. The lesson of Biligere is that an alliance between capable village leadership and local development agents can put into place effective schemes in such fields as schooling, health and family planning, dairying and modern farming, clean water and sanitation, and others. The lesson of Changavara may be that a divided village lacking caste consensus and leadership may have significant difficulty in reaching out to local political and administrative networks. Able and achieving

Two Karnataka Villages

individuals in such circumstances may opt out via education and migration. Changavara has generated a number of college graduates but most have moved away, one as far as Canada where he practises medicine. If Changavara is to restore any dynamism to its economy, very strong pressures and positive opportunity creation from outside may be required.

TABLES

1. AGRICULTURE STRUCTURE IN ACRES

	Biligere		Changavara	
	Area	%	Area	%
Total area	1948	–	6540	–
Area not available for cult.	199	–	633	–
Total cultivable area	1749	100.0	5907	100.0
Irrigated area	526	30.1	424	7.2
Unirrigated area	708	40.5	4844	82.0
Cultivable waste area	515	29.4	639	10.8
Gross cropped area	1234	100.0	5268	100.0
Dry land	708	57.4	4844	92.0
Wet land	83	6.7	323	6.1
Garden land	443	35.9	101	1.9

Sources: 1. Census of India, District Census Handbooks, Tumkur District, 1951, 1961, 1971.
2. Personal field visits.

2. GROWTH OF POPULATION, 1951 to 1971: PERCENTAGES

Decades	India	Karnataka	Tumkur Dist.	Biligere	Changavara
1951-1961	21.5	21.6	18.8	23.7	5.9
1961-1971	24.8	24.2	19.0	24.4	-19.4

Sources: Census of India, District Census Handbooks, Tumkur District, 1951, 1961, 1971; General Population Tables, Part IIA(i), All India, 1961, 1971.

3. DEMOGRAPHIC STRUCTURE: BILIGERE AND CHANGAVARA

Year	Households Total	% Change	Male	Fem.	Males / Fems.	Population Total	% Change	SC/ST (%)	H'hold size (av.)
BILIGERE									
1951	198	-	500	499	100	999	-	NA	5.0
1961	234	18.2	652	584	117	1236	23.2	14.1	5.3
1971	262	12.0	814	724	112	1538	24.4	14.7	5.8
CHANGAVARA									
1951	336	-	1079	990	109	2069	-	NA	6.1
1961	370	10.1	1158	1033	112	2191	5.9	14.1	5.9
1971	218	-14.1	956	809	118	1765	-19.4	14.7	8.1

Key: NA Not available SC/ST SC/ST population to total population
Source: Census of India, District Census Handbooks, Tumkur District, 1951, 1961, 1971.

4. LITERACY AND PARTICIPATION RATE IN BILIGERE AND CHANGAVARA

Year	Male	Female	Total	Male	Female	Total
BILIGERE						
Literacy				*Percentages*		
1951	167	42	209	33.40	8.42	20.92
1961	337	117	454	51.69	20.03	36.73
1971	485	246	731	59.58	33.98	47.53
Workers				*Participation rate*		
1961	362	154	516	55.52	26.37	41.75
1971	442	84	526	54.30	11.60	34.20
CHANGAVARA						
Literacy				*Percentages*		
1951	190	16	206	17.61	1.62	9.96
1961	200	8	208	17.27	0.77	9.49
1971	174	351	425	34.70	9.15	24.08
Workers				*Participation rate*		
1961	1320	547	1320	66.75	52.95	60.25
1971	599	64	663	62.66	7.95	37.56

Source: See table 2.

5. AMENITIES BASE

Amenities	Biligere	Changavara
1. *Drinking Water*		
Wells	Yes	Yes
Piped Water	Yes	No
Tanks	-	-
2. *Electricity*		
Domestic	Yes	Yes
Irrigation	Yes	Yes
3. *Health*		
Primary Health Centre	Yes	No
Dispensary	-	No
Family Planning Centre	Yes	No
4. *Education*		
Primary School	Yes	Yes
Middle School	Yes	Yes
Secondary School	Yes	Yes
Junior College	Yes	No
Others	-	-
5. *Roads*		
Type of Road	'Pucca'	'Pucca'
Bus Stop	Yes	Yes
6. *Post Office*	Yes	Yes

Source: See table 2; field survey.

6. VISITS TO RELATIVES (ANNUAL)

	Visits (No.)		Persons (No.)		Frequency per person	
	B	C	B	C	B	C
Within taluk	1023	362	236	163	4.3	2.2
Within district	550	25	170	20	3.2	1.2
Within state	438	73	146	48	3.0	1.5
Outside the state	11	21	4	17	2.7	1.2
Total	2022	481	556	248	3.6	1.9

Key: B Biligere C Changavara
Source: Tumkur District Study.

7. VISITS TO RELIGIOUS SITES (ANNUAL)

	Visits (No.)		Persons (No.)		Frequency per person	
	B	C	B	C	B	C
Within district	71 *51*	162 *98.2*	63 *52.5*	142 *98*	1.1	1.1
Within state	53 *38.2*	3 *1.8*	43 *35.8*	3 *2*	1.2	1.0
Outside the state	15 *10.8*	–	14 *11.7*	–	1.1	–
Total	139 *100*	165 *100*	120 *100*	145 *100*	1.1	1.1

Note: Figures in italics are percentages.
Source: See table 6.

8. MOVEMENT FOR STUDY (REGULAR)

	Persons (No.)	
Places	Biligere	Changavara
Within village	354	61
Neighbouring villages	–	5
Taluk headquarters	7	–
Within taluk	2	–
Within district	17	12
Within state	14	6
Total reported	394	84

Source: See table 6.

9. TRAVEL FOR MARKETING (PER MONTH)

	Sale of prods.				Purchases (I)				Goods for Consumptn.	
	Farm		Non F		Farm		Non F			
	B	C	B	C	B	C	B	C	B	C
Within village	–	6	–	3	2	17	9	1	82	24
Within taluk	144	93	141	2	116	83	200	7	123	154
Within district	–	3	2	–	–	3	3	–	1	3
Within state	1	–	1	–	–	–	–	–	–	–
Total	145	102	144	5	118	103	212	8	206	181

Key: B Biligere   C Changavara   F Farm   I Inputs
Source: See table 6.

10. MOVEMENT FOR WORK BY OCCUPATION GROUPS (REGULAR)

Occupations		a	b	c	d	e	f	Oth.	Tot.	Row %
Total.	B	68	30	43	77	170	26	89	503	100
		13.5	*6.5*	*8.5*	*15.3*	*33.8*	*5.2*	*17.7*	*100*	
	C	137	25	40	38	105	40	50	435	100
		31.5	*5.7*	*9.2*	*8.7*	*24.1*	*9.2*	*11.5*	*100*	
Within vill.	B	66	24	37	65	130	21	75	418	83.1
		15.8	*5.7*	*8.9*	*15.6*	*31.1*	*5*	*17.9*	*100*	
	C	135	23	38	36	100	40	46	418	96.1
		32.3	*5.5*	*9.1*	*8.6*	*23.9*	*9.6*	*11*	*100*	
Neigh. vill.	B	–	2	3	4	13	–	3	25	5.0
	C	–	–	1	–	2	–	1	4	0.9
Taluk HQ	B	–	–	–	–	2	1	1	4	0.8
	C	–	–	–	–	–	–	1	1	0.2
Within taluk	B	1	–	1	2	4	–	5	13	2.6
	C	–	2	1	–	3	–	1	7	1.6
Within dist.	B	–	–	1	–	9	1	3	14	2.8
	C	–	–	–	–	–	–	–	–	0
Within state	B	1	4	1	6	12	3	2	29	5.8
	C	2	–	–	2	–	–	1	5	1.2

Note: Figures in italics are percentages.
Key: B Billigere   C Changavara   a labourers   b artisans
       c marginal farmers   d small farmers
       e medium farmers   e large farmers
       Oth. others   Tot. total
Source: See table 5.

Two Karnataka Villages

11. VISITS TO DIFFERENT PLACES BY OCCUPATIONAL
    GROUPS (MONTHLY)

Occupations	Visits		Persons		p.Per		Visits		Persons		p.Per	
	B	C	B	C	B	C	B	C	B	C	B	C
	Neighbouring Villages						Hobli Headquarters					
Labourers	59	240	22	55	2.7	4.4	80	–	50	–	1.6	–
Artisans	46	22	15	6	3.1	3.6	36	2	16	1	2.2	2.0
Marg.Fmrs	29	83	17	21	1.7	3.9	44	–	29	–	1.5	–
Small Fmrs	52	90	32	18	1.6	5.0	63	–	45	–	1.4	–
Med. Fmrs	127	134	81	28	1.6	4.8	135	1	74	1	1.8	1.0
Large Fmrs	17	73	9	15	1.8	4.8	30	–	12	–	2.5	–
Others	15	40	10	10	1.5	4.0	91	1	55	1	1.6	1.0
Total	376	682	191	153	1.9	4.4	479	4	281	3	1.7	1.3
	Taluk Headquarters						District Headquarters					
Labourers	7	12	5	8	1.4	1.5	–	–	–	–	–	–
Artisans	18	1	10	1	1.8	1.0	–	–	–	–	–	–
Marg.Fmrs	28	6	15	5	1.8	1.2	–	3	–	3	–	1.0
Small Fmrs	64	4	38	2	1.7	2.0	3	–	3	–	1.0	–
Med. Fmrs	167	20	75	12	2.2	1.6	33	–	18	–	1.8	–
Large Fmrs	24	9	8	7	3.0	1.3	12	–	5	–	2.4	–
Others	88	43	47	20	1.9	2.5	22	–	14	–	1.6	–
Total	396	95	198	55	2.0	1.7	70	3	40	3	1.8	1.0
	Within Taluk						Within District					
Labourers	1	28	1	6	1.0	4.6	–	–	–	–	–	–
Artisans	–	4	–	1	–	4.0	–	–	–	–	–	–
Marg.Fmrs	1	4	1	1	1.0	4.0	1	1	1	1	1.0	1.0
Small Fmrs	5	7	5	2	1.0	3.5	2	2	2	2	1.0	1.0
Med. Fmrs	8	–	5	–	1.6	–	–	–	–	–	–	–
Large Fmrs	–	–	–	–	–	–	–	–	–	–	–	–
Others	–	1	–	1	–	1.0	–	–	–	–	–	–
Total	15	44	12	11	2.4	4.0	3	3	3	3	1.0	1.0
	Within State						State Capital					
Labourers	–	–	–	–	–	–	–	–	–	–	–	–
Artisans	–	–	–	–	–	–	–	–	–	–	–	–
Marg.Fmrs	–	–	–	–	–	–	2	–	1	–	2.0	–
Small Fmrs	1	1	1	1	1.0	1.0	4	2	3	1	1.3	2.0
Med. Fmrs	1	1	1	1	1.0	1.0	22	1	10	1	2.2	1.0
Large Fmrs	–	–	–	–	–	–	8	2	4	1	2.0	2.0
Others	–	–	–	–	–	–	27	2	12	2	2.2	1.0
Total	2	2	2	2	1.0	1.0	63	7	30	4	2.1	1.4

Key: B Biligere C Changavara p.Per Visits per person
    Marg. Marginal Med. Medium Fmrs Farmers
Source: Data collected through field visits and from
    the Institute for Social and Economic Change,
    Bangalore.

NOTES

Hanumappa and Adams, 'Two Karnataka villages and the outside world: internal characteristics, movement linkages, and state of development'

The authors wish to thank the authorities of the Tumkur Project, the Institute for Social and Economic Change (ISEC), for permitting them to use data from that study in writing this paper. Hanumappa has worked as a member of the team conducting this on-going project. Professor V.K.R.V. Rao, Honorary Director of the project, has provided general guidance to all aspects of its research and early recognized the importance of examining rural movement patterns. The authors are thankful to Professor V.M. Rao of the Rural Economics Unit, ISEC, and Dr S. Seshaiah of the Sociology Unit, ISEC, for comments on a draft of the paper. The authors remain responsible for the interpretation and analysis of evidence in the study.

1. Vera Anstey, *The Economic Development of India* (London 1936), chs.VI, XII, and XIV, remains for better or worse, the best overview. Also see John Adams and R. Craig West, 'Money, Prices, and Economic Development in Late Nineteenth Century India', *Journal of Economic History* XXXIX (March 1979), pp.55-68.

2. The standard comprehensive bibliography is *Village Studies, Data Analysis and Bibliography, Vol.1: India, 1950-1975* (Brighton 1976), compiled by Mick Moore, John Connell, Claire M. Lambert, edited by Claire Lambert; also see, for a description of some of the older studies, John Adams and Uwe J. Woltemade, 'Studies of Indian Village Economies: A Bibliographical Essay', *Indian Economic and Social History Review* VII (March 1970), pp.109-37.

3. This is true of even detailed studies recognized to be among the most thoughtful and comprehensive of their type. Examine F.G. Bailey, *Caste and the Economic Frontier* (Manchester 1957), T.S. Epstein, *Economic Development and Social Change in South India* (Manchester 1962), S.C. Dube, *Indian Village* (Ithaca 1955), or M.N. Srinivas, 'The Dominant Caste in Rampura', *American Anthropologist* LXI (February 1959), pp.1-16, and his related papers.

4. The Tumkur survey covered 252, or 10 per cent of the district's villages and over 30,000 rural

Notes to pages 182-90

households. The villages were randomly selected but for each village all households were surveyed. Hanumappa visited the two villages selected for study several times in the summer of 1980 to check and expand the originally gathered material. Hanumappa was at the University of Maryland in 1979-80; Adams visited ISEC in 1980.

    5. R.L. Singh, ed., *India: A Regional Geography* (Varanasi 1971), pp.791-828 and 907-31.

    6. John Adams, 'Regional Patterns of Development in Karnataka', *The Journal of Developing Areas* 12 (July 1978), pp.439-48.

    7. Data on Tumkur district and Sira and Tiptur taluks employed in this and the next few paragraphs are drawn from Government of Karnataka, Bureau of Economics and Statistics, *Tumkur District at a Glance, 1974-75*, issued by the District Statistical Officer, Tumkur, n.d. For a survey of the distribution of castes in Tumkur district, and their association with landholding, quality of housing, and other economic factors, see John Adams and H.G. Hanumappa, 'Caste and Economic Structure in Tumkur District, Karnataka state, India', presented at Association for Asian Studies, Southeast Regional Conference, Columbia, South Carolina, 25 January 1980; issued as working paper 12 (1980), Department of Economics, University of Maryland; also in the *Annals*, vol.II, Association for Asian Studies, SERC, 1981, pp.74-81.

    8. Village data are taken from field notes and the Tumkur survey. Taluk and district data are based on the survey. See Adams and Hanumappa, op.cit., for a summary of caste distribution by taluk.

'DECENTRALIZED' PLANNING IN A CENTRALIZED ECONOMY: A STUDY OF SARVODAYA PROGRAMMES IN A TALUKA

Ghanshyam Shah

More often than not anthropologists and sociologists have studied Indian villages and tribes 'Behind Mud Walls' - in isolation from the outside world. With a few exceptions, their description is ahistorical, as if mud walls were stronger than walls made of cement and concrete, were iron curtains steadfastly facing hurricanes generated by outside forces. 'Governments may come and governments may go but village society remains undisturbed' is an oft-quoted phrase used to explain the resilience of rural society.[1] Social scientists have theorized about the uniqueness of the Indian social system, namely the caste system, which is governed by the ideology of homo hierarchicus as against the ideology of homo equalis that characterizes the Western society. According to them, caste hierarchy maintains harmony in the village society.[2] Some of the scholars plead for the protection of village society from the onslaught of 'Western' culture and industrialization. That is possible, they hold, only through 'decentralization' of political power and economy. Some others emphatically hold that it is only through decentralization that local people can be involved in 'development' programmes, and thereby strengthen the Indian democracy.[3] The concept of decentralization is in vogue among theoreticians, policy-makers and administrators in contemporary India.

To Mahatma Gandhi and his apostles 'decentralization' is the panacea for all the ills afflicting India. Gandhi wrote, 'I suggest that, if India is to evolve along non-violent lines, it will have to decentralize many things. Centralization cannot be sustained and defended without adequate forces .... Rurally organized India will run less risk of foreign invasion than urbanized India, well-equipped with military, naval and air force'. Without decentralization 'human happiness combined with full mental and moral growth'[4] is impossible to attain. Gandhi pleaded for building a village 'republic', that is, a self-sufficient and autonomous village. The village should be self-sufficient as far as its basic needs - food, clothing and other necessities - are concerned. Its economy should be planned

'Decentralized' Planning

with a view to provide full employment to all the adults of the village, so that no one is forced to migrate to towns. Gandhi opposed industrialization with a view to counter exploitation on the one hand, and to provide full employment to all on the other. He held that large-scale production requires marketing, which means profit-seeking. That develops an exploitative mechanism. Industrialization also replaces man-power and hence it adds to unemployment. Gandhians, therefore, mainly favour the development of village and cottage industries. Along with decentralization of the economy, comes that of the polity. All major decisions relating to every village should be arrived at in the village itself rather than in the state and national capitals. The policy-makers and planners of India have accepted the Gandhian concept of rural society - at least in principle. Several programmes have been launched by the government during the last three decades for 'building the roots of a tree'.[5]

On the other hand, the world economy is predominantly capitalist. So is India's economy which gives 'a lot of initiative to private capital'. As India is economically a backward country, it faces the problem of capital formation for the growth of its economy. This calls for centralized economy for the management of investment, accumulation, production and consumption. It invariably involves the countryside in production, not for use, but for exchange. It develops a nationwide market economy, linking the village market with the international market in which the latter generally dominates the former. The political system that India has adopted is also centralized and is conducive to the development of capitalist economy. Though India is a federal state, political authority is constitutionally centralized in New Delhi. Elections, political parties and administration link New Delhi with all the villages in all the parts of the country.

This creates a paradoxical situation for the Gandhian workers. They shoulder the responsibility for building a self-sufficient, self-reliant and self-governing village community in a centralized economy over which they cannot exercise any control worth the name. There are three types of Gandhian workers. One: the political workers, engaged in political activities; they are divided into various non-communist political parties. Two: constructive or Sarvodaya workers; they carry out 'constructive', that is, socio-economic, programmes to ameliorate the condition of the masses.

They do not directly participate in the activities of the political parties. Three: constructive-cum-political workers; engaged in constructive as well as political work. In 1948, after the assassination of Gandhi, the constructive workers formed the Akhil Bharat Sarva Seva Sangh. Its aim is to bring about social change, especially in rural India, through the voluntary efforts of individuals and communities. Since its inception, the Sangh has provided a platform and organizational-support base for constructive as well as political workers of Gandhian leanings. There are numbers of Gandhian voluntary associations, working in various parts of the country for the reconstruction of rural society. One of such associations is the Valod Group in Surat district, Gujarat. Though it has been primarily engaged in implementing socio-economic programmes, it is not averse to participation in political activities. We give below a descriptive account of the constructive programmes that the Valod group formulated and carried out in a relatively backward area. While doing so, we shall highlight the role local initiative and local resources play in such activities on the one hand, and the influence outside forces exert in the formulation and the implementation of the programmes on the other hand.

Background

The area in which the Valod Group has been active for the last three decades is the Valod taluka of Surat district in Gujarat, Western India. It is a cluster of 40 villages with a population of 51,999. The land is rocky and sandy, eroded in many places by heavy rains. Though there are three rivers in this taluka, they provide little irrigation water for agriculture in summer. The rivers flow from east to west. They are small, narrow and seasonal. They are flooded in the monsoon and become mere rivulets during the summer.

Scheduled tribes and non-tribals are two major social groups of the taluka. The former account for more than three-fourths of the total population. They include Chaudhri, Gamit, Halpati and Dhodia tribes. Caste Hindus include Brahmans and Banias, the higher castes; Patidars and Kolis, the middle castes; and Suthars, Hajams, Darjis, the intermediate castes. Bhangis, Chamars and so on belong to the lower castes. There are also some Muslims residing in this area. On the

'Decentralized' Planning

whole, the dominance of higher and middle-caste Hindus is striking. High-caste Hindus own a large proportion of agricultural land. Banias, in particular, were traditionally (and are still) engaged in trade and money-lending. Patidars and Kolis are neo-traders and money-lenders. Among the tribals, 20 per cent are landless, 46 per cent own less than five acres of land and 24 per cent own more than five acres of land. [6]

Contacts between the tribals and the non-tribals of this area can be traced back for three centuries. In the past, the caste Hindus and Muslim traders, forest contractors and money-lenders, took away the land belonging to the tribals and enslaved them; they were reduced to the status of agricultural labourers. They appropriated farm and forest products. Though the non-tribals had no desire to better the lot of the tribals, the latter were influenced by the religious beliefs and the life-styles of the former. The bhakti movement of the seventeenth and eighteenth centuries influenced the upper stratum of the tribals who adopted the rituals and the life-styles of the caste Hindus.

The tribals came closer to the high-caste Hindus during the freedom movement. A few disciples of Gandhi coming from other parts of Gujarat settled in the village of Vedchhi in the 1920s to carry out Gandhi's constructive programmes. They started a residential school or ashrama to provide education for the tribal boys. At the same time, they introduced the production of khadi as part of their programme to encourage self-reliance as far as clothing was concerned. They also tried to induce the tribals to give up liquor and non-vegetarian food. The tribals were also mobilized and encouraged to particpate in political activities directed against the British raj. [7]

After independence the activities of the Vedchhi ashrama became systematized. As early as 1948, the ashrama hosted the all-India training camp for senior 'constructive' workers. The camp was sponsored by the Gandhi National Memorial Fund, New Delhi. The participants resolved that the development of the country was possible along strict Gandhian lines. They decided to concentrate their efforts on developing villages accordingly. The camps prepared a development programme for the village Vedchhi, 'which if successfully implemented would be transferred to every village throughout India'. The Vedchhi plan emphasized the importance of utilizing 'local resources and talent'. However, it is beyond the scope of this paper to analyse the plan and the method of its implementation or to assess how far it was successfully carried out. Suffice it to say, that the ashrama has continued to carry out several socio-economic and educational programmes during the last three decades.

The Valod group is an off-shoot of the activities of the Vedchhi ashrama, though initially it developed independently. It was formed by some of the natives of Valod, the headquarters of the taluka, which is about four kilometres from Vedchhi. The group consists of six persons. Born in the late 1920s, they all belong to the same age-group. They played and studied together in the schools situated in and outside the village. They are the sons of Banias and Brahmins whose fathers were absentee landlords or money-lenders-cum-traders. Like many school boys of those days, they were influenced by Gandhi and the freedom movement. They organized student activities, such as distribution of books, performances of drama, cleaning of the streets, and celebration of Gandhi Jayanti (Gandhi's birthday). Like many other Gandhian youths, they romanticized village life and decided to settle in Valod itself to reconstruct the village according to the Gandhian model.

However they could not afford themselves to engage in full-time voluntary work without financial support. Hence they had to take to some employment to enable them to earn their livelihood. For this purpose they could either take up the traditional family occupation - agriculture, business and money-lending - or they could become teachers in the village school. Business and money-lending were automatically ruled out, because the young boys thought that these occupations were exploitative. On the other hand, they lacked the knowledge and experience which are necessary for pursuing agriculture as an occupation. The only other alternative was service in the village school. Teaching would give them a living and at the same time enough leisure to enable them to pursue constructive activities.

There was only one primary school in the village, managed by the District School Board. The three members of the Valod group approached the office-bearers of the Board and offered their services. The Board were convinced about their ability and sincerity in wishing to develop the school, and were willing to appoint them as teachers. But the local village leaders did not want competitors in the public life of Valod and therefore succeeded in preventing the Board from giving over the responsibility of running the school. At this juncture one of the leaders of the Vedchhi ashrama, Jugatram Dave, who was in touch with the young men, came to their rescue. He invited them to join the ashrama as teachers. Two members of the Valod group immediately accepted the invitation and joined the ashrama in 1948. The other four joined at a later stage. While working in the ashrama, they received lessons in Gandhian ideology and programmes. The ashrama helped them to establish contacts with Gandhian workers who were taking part in the constructive and political activities in various parts of the country. Slowly, the Valod group began to feel that their employment as teachers did not offer them a wide enough field of activities. They were, therefore, in search of an opportunity to get involved in rural economic development programmes.

At this time (1951), the Planning Commission prepared the first five year plan for the whole of India. The plan adopted the Community Development (C.D.) and the National Extension Service (N.E.S.) programmes for rural reconstruction. The first programme owes its origin to the West. It was influenced by the 'extension work' programme of the U.S.A. and the 'village uplift' movements of Great Britain. The programme is based on 'self-help' and on the utilization of local human and natural resources.[8] It had been started symbolically on Gandhi's birthday, 2 October, in 1952, with 'American Technical and Financial Assistance'.[9] The Khadi and Village Industries Commission, managed by Gandhian constructive workers and financed by the government, launched the Intensive Area Planning Scheme adopting the Gandhian version of the C.D. approach in fourteen blocks. One of them was Vedchhi, where the Commission handed over the project to Jugatram Dave, the leader of the ashrama. Dave asked the Valod group to carry out the project. Under the guidance of Jhaverbhai Patel of the Khadi Commission, the Valod group accepted this responsibility in 1954. Later on, in 1957, the Valod group set up the formal organization known as the Vedchhi Intensive Area Scheme (V.I.A.S.) under the chairmanship of Jugatram Dave. Under the main Scheme, the Commission provided the funds necessary for the payment of the salaries of the full-time workers. It also provided a small fund for undertaking economic programmes. The Scheme ended in 1961. Thereafter the Vedchhi Scheme itself prepared five-year plans for the taluka, plans entitled 'Building from Below'. To date three such plans have been prepared and put into execution, and the fourth (for 1980-85) has already started.

The five-year plans have, by and large, coincided with
national plans. The Planning Commission, in New Delhi,
postponed its planning exercise at one stage; so did
the Valod group. The Planning Commission prepared a
'rolling plan' for 1977-78; so did the Valod group.
The Vedchhi five year plans set targets for the taluka
as a whole. The basis of planning that the Valod group
claimes to have adopted is *janashaktini jagruti*, that
is, consciousness of people's power. The plans aim at
using local resources and mobilizing people for participation in the execution of the programme. It is an
attempt at 'establishing a decentralized co-operative
economy' and thereby at building a sarvodaya society on
the Gandhian model.[10]

Before we discuss the programmes, a word is in
order about the status of the Valod group and the influence it has been wielding in and outside the taluka.
From the beginning, the members of the Valod group were
associated with the Congress party. They took part in
the various activities of the Congress in the 1960s and
continued to do so till the mid-seventies. One member
became the president of the district Congress committee.
Another member of the group was the personal assistant
to the president of the state Congress committee. A
third one was appointed as the Chairman of the State
Khadi Board. One more member holds an executive post
in the Khadi and Village Industries Commission. (As
mentioned, Jhaverbhai Patel, their mentor, who taught
them the techniques of planning, was a member of the
Commission. Later, he was also a member of the International Labour Organization, Geneva.) The group has
contacts with academics in Bombay, Ahmedabad and Amsterdam, whose guidance and assistance were made available
in the preparation of the Vedchhi plans. After the
introduction of panchayati raj in 1964 one of the
members of the group became the president of the taluka
panchayat. Through its organizational network, the
group maintains links with village sarpanches (presi-
dents). The Valod group enjoys considerable influence
in the taluka, and carries weight with the administration as well as in the politics of the area.

Programmes

The Valod group has undertaken a variety of programmes
with a view to 'build rural society from below' during
the last two and a half decades. Space does not allow

'Decentralized' Planning

us to examine all the programmes in detail here. We shall, therefore, discuss in brief, only a few of the important ones to show the relationship between local and outside centres.

Education. The Gandhians believe that education is the agent of social change. Gandhi believed that 'a right type' of education was essential for building the new society of his dreams and for its maintenance. He formulated a new educational system known as *nai talim*, that is, basic education, to counter Macaulay's system of education, which was imparted in government schools. The nai talim puts great emphasis on education through work.[11]

The Valod group entertained the ambition to start a nai talim school. However, whatever may have been Gandhi's ideals, starting any kind of school requires capital to buy a piece of land, and construct a building on it which is big enough to house the students and equipment, as well as income to pay the salaries of teachers and other employees. The Valod group thought of two ways of collecting funds. One was voluntary donations by individuals or institutions, local or outside. The second was to get finance in the form of grants from the government. The group did not make any effort to tap local resources. It felt that because the inhabitants of the area were poor, it was 'impossible' to raise funds locally - for recurring and non-recurring expenses. The possibilities of raising funds by way of voluntary donations from outside the taluka were also limited, because in the 1950s, the group's contacts with outside donors were confined to friends and relatives of members. The group, therefore, turned to the government for financing its educational efforts. But the government had to work according to its own rules and procedure. Hence there was no scope for starting another primary or secondary nai talim school, as there was already one at Vedchhi - a village in the taluka. But the group found that there was a possibility of getting a grant for starting a high school on the traditional lines; all that was required was a building. At that time, the Valod group was in charge of the Intensive Area Planning Scheme, under which there was provision for constructing a godown. The group made use of this provision. It purchased a piece of land and immediately constructed a small building for which it obtained the Scheme's financial support. The building was then treated as a godown for the Scheme and also as a school as far as the education department was concerned. The V.I.A.S. utilized its connections with the district education department and secured permission and a grant to start a high school. The school was opened in Kalam Kui in 1960.

To be eligible for the recurring government grant, a school must have, on its rolls, a 'minimum' number of students prescribed by the government from time to time. But the population of the villages around Kalam Kui is predominantly tribal, and not many of these tribals had completed the requisite primary education. The number of students who could attend the high school was below the 'minimum' prescribed by the government. Efforts were therefore made to attract the required number of students from distant villages. But these students needed lodging and boarding facilities. The V.I.A.S. did not command financial resources which could have enabled it to offer these to the students. It was, therefore, again forced to look to the government for help. It found that there was an arrangement for matching grants, whereby government offered three-fourths of the funds needed for the construction of a building, provided the voluntary organization raised the remaining one-fourth as a 'people's contribution'. The V.I.A.S. did not have at its disposal even that much, nor had it the confidence and patience needed to raise the required funds from local people. It, therefore, had to seek external support. Through some friends in Ahmedabad, it came into contact with international organizations which were financing 'development' work. The V.I.A.S. presented its case to Community Aid Abroad, Australia. It emphasized that if Community Aid were to agree to give Rs.15,000, the Indian government would give Rs.45,000 for the construction of the hostel building. Community Aid agreed, and the V.I.A.S. treated the fund as a 'people's contribution' and received the matching grant from the government. Similarly, the V.I.A.S. received more funds from different foreign agencies to start four other high schools in different parts of the taluka.

The V.I.A.S. realised that it had failed to start a nai talim high school; it, therefore, introduced in the curriculum some subjects like agriculture, spinning and craft, which have a Gandhian bias. However, as the number of subjects taught in schools is fixed, the V.I.A.S. schools gave less weight to English, mathematics and science. But this was not appreciated by the local population. Some of the tribal students and their guardians who wanted to compete with the non-

'Decentralized' Planning

tribal students resented the fact that they had to study subjects which have a Gandhian bias. They realized that it is necessary to learn English and science, for taking up higher studies. They openly said that they knew agriculture, and that they had no desire to take to cultivation after they completed their education: 'We want to become Sahebs (bosses) in government offices just like other non-tribals'. They alleged that non-tribals are seeking deliberately to perpetuate the low positions of tribals by giving them education in subjects like agriculture and crafts, training for manual and not for 'office' work. This charge levelled by the tribals reveals that well-to-do tribals are attracted to the education offered by non-Gandhian schools located in towns. Slowly but surely, as the years roll by, smaller and smaller numbers of students from the taluka join the schools run by the V.I.A.S.

The V.I.A.S. wanted the schools not only to impart education on Gandhian lines, but also to become centres of village development work. Each school has adopted a few villages in its vicinity for carrying out 'intensive' development programmes. School teachers are considered to be village-level workers also. They are expected to visit the villages and implement development programmes. The V.I.A.S. made its expectations clear to the teachers at the time of recruitment. But all teachers do not work according to the V.I.A.S.'s expectations. And the V.I.A.S. is helpless, as the teachers' service conditions are determined by the government department, which also pays their salaries; the V.I.A.S. has little control over them. In fact, even some of the senior teachers who have been with the V.I.A.S. for many years are now reluctant to take part in village development work. Thus, the role of these schools as extension centres is also declining with the passage of time.

Agricultural Development. Since its inception the V.I.A.S. has tried to implement an agricultural programme on a continuous basis in addition to its work in the field of education. Agriculture is the main source of livelihood for the rural people. More than 95 per cent of the working population of the taluka are either cultivators or farm labourers. Besides, on the whole, Indian agriculture was backward in the 1950s. Tribal areas were more backward, and faced many more constraints than the non-tribal areas. Additionally, as elsewhere in India, agriculture in the Valod taluka faced institutional, infrastructural and input problems.

Most of the non-tribal 'agriculturists' - Banias, Brahmans, Patidars and Muslims - were absentee landowners and many tribals were their tenants. The non-tribals also owned a high proportion of the total cultivable land. During the 1950s the state government passed several laws with a view to abolishing absentee landlordism and giving land to the tillers. Though the Valod group was sympathetic to the 'radical' land legislation, it did not directly participate in the implementation of these laws. It was rather the leaders of the Vedchhi ashrama who made the tenants conscious of their legal rights and helped them to get land from the landlords. Because of these efforts, a few tribals became owners of the land which they were cultivating as tenants. But that has not brought significant change in ownership, as far as the tribals and the non-tribals are concerned. The non-tribals even now own a far larger acreage than the tribals. The Valod group did nothing to change this state of affairs. What it did in the 1950s as a part of the Intensive Area Planning Scheme, was to build up the infrastructure - by the levelling of land, construction of embankments and irrigation. And these activities proved to be beneficial mainly to the non-tribal landowners.

On the other hand, as the government rhetoric became shriller, the western aid-givers became apprehensive of land reforms. The Ford Foundation's Report on India's Food Crisis and Steps to Meet It (1959) asserted that India would have to increase the production of food-grains by 200 to 300 per cent. The report implicitly criticized the entire approach which treated institutional change as the keystone of an agricultural strategy. It favoured a technocratic approach based on offering price incentives to individual farmers to enable them to go in for higher (private) investment in modern inputs, especially fertilizers. The Draft Outline of the Third Five Year Plan, therefore, projected a very large increase in the outlay on fertilizers - from less than Rs.30 crores in the Second Plan to Rs.240 crores in the Third Plan.[12] The government adopted a 'package' for agricultural development which involved the utilization of numbers of modern agricultural practices - improved seeds, chemical fertilizers, and pesticides - in selected areas which had a potential for growth. Surat was one of the districts selected for the implementation of this 'package'.

The Valod group found the 'package' very useful from their strategic view-point. It therefore decided

'Decentralized' Planning

to take it up even though the group did not know what the response of the farmers to modern technology and input would be. This is reflected in its first five year plan (1961-66) for the taluka prepared under the guidance of Jhaverbhai Patel, then associated with the Planning Commission. It hesitantly projected the use of some 1610 tonnes of different varieties of chemical fertilizers. However, the response of the local farmers to modern technology was greater than the V.I.A.S. expected. At the end of these five years farmers of the taluka used up almost three times the amount of chemical fertilizers recommended in the plan. Similarly the use of high yield variety seeds also increased considerably.

The distribution of these inputs - fertilizers, high-yield seeds, insecticides - has been arranged through the government departments. The V.I.A.S. has worked as a co-ordinating agency between the farmers and the government. In the 1970s the V.I.A.S. received aid for the distribution of improved seeds, and diesel or electric pump-sets for irrigation from Community Aid Abroad, Australia. The V.I.A.S. is now directly involved in distribution work. The field workers of the V.I.A.S. provide technical expertise regarding 'modern' commercial crops. Consequently, the area under food crops has decreased and the area under commercial crops has increased during the last ten years. Also, agricultural yield per acre has increased in the taluka, as it has increased elsewhere in Gujarat.

But the V.I.A.S. failed to organize the market to the advantage of small and marginal farmers. It made unsuccessful attempts to organize marketing co-operative societies so as to offer 'reasonable' prices to the farmers for their agricultural products. Such societies incurred losses, failed to compete with individual traders, and had to be closed. On the other hand, the V.I.A.S. did not put its weight behind the implementing of the Land Ceiling Act (1973) and Minimum Wages Act (1972). It may be noted that during this period the Valod group was close to the ruling party. However, it complained that since the farmers did not get 'reasonable' prices for agricultural produce, it was uneconomical for them to pay the minimum wages laid down by law. It opined: 'Our planners demand justice from the farmers, but deny the same justice to them. In the absence of this justice in the form of fair prices to the farmers, the implementation of the Minimum Wages Act would just squeeze the farmers to the extent of making farming uneconomic'.[13] The V.I.A.S. felt helpless in this matter and left the problem of doing 'justice' to the planners in New Delhi. It opted for the softer course, and tried to develop non-farm economic activities to supplement the income of small farmers and farm labourers, or to change their occupation.

Khadi. When the Vedchhi ashrama was started 50 years ago, the production of khadi was adopted as the main plank of its programme. The ashrama persuaded people to spin and weave, and it also imparted training for the purpose. In the beginning, the programme was devised with a view to serving the national aim of attaining independence through developing self-reliance, at least in the matter of clothing. Later on, khadi became an occupation which enabled some people to earn their livelihood. By the time the Valod group started working independently, the enthusiasm for khadi as a means of achieving self-sufficiency in clothing declined. It became a commodity, like any other, to be sold in the market.[14]

In order to boost the production of khadi, the Union Government formed the Khadi and Village Industry Commission - an autonomous organization - in 1952. The state governments also appointed Khadi Boards in their respective states in the early 1960s. During the 1950s the Khadi Commission gave grants to the V.I.A.S. for the purpose of encouraging spinning activity. It also gave charkhas (spinning wheels) at subsidized rates and offered marketing facilities as well. The government also subsidizes khadi to boost its sales. The V.I.A.S. distributed charkhas either free or at a subsidized price to the spinners. It also distributed ambar charkhas, an improved model of spinning wheel, to increase the productive capacity of labour. With the financial support from the state Khadi Board, the V.I.A.S. conducted several training courses for the spinners and weavers.

Despite such a huge effort, financial support and managerial skill, the khadi programme has not taken off in Valod even after 50 years. At the end of the last decade the number of spinners had not increased by more than four hundred. Their number also fluctuates from year to year. For instance, there were 106 spinners in 1974-75 in village Algadh, where the V.I.A.S. had organized the Khadi Centre in 1956. In 1977-8 the number of spinners had gone down to only 52. Every year, some spinners were recruited but some dropped out. Very few have continued to work as spinners for many years. The spinners who dropped out reported that they could not spare any time for spinning. Almost all the spinners have been, and are, cultivators. They can spin only in their spare time. 'Why don't you take to spinning?' we asked the agricultural labourers. Their invariable reply was that it was tiring as they had to spin alone in the house. Moreover, farm labour was more remunerative than spinning, and, in contrast to a spinner, a farm labourer could hope to secure a loan from the farm-owner in case of need. During the year 1975-6, a spinner in Algadh earned, on average, only Rs.102, whereas in Degama a spinner earned Rs.705 per year. The difference between Degama and Algadh arises from the fact that the spinning wheels supplied to these two villages were not of the same model. In Degama the spinners used the ambar charkha, whereas in Algadh they used the traditional spinning wheel. Moreover, the V.I.A.S. started a workshop in Degama, where all the spinners spin together under one roof for eight hours a day. Their work is supervised, and the spinning wheels are repaired as soon as they go out of order. (Despite these facilities of supervision and organization, a spinner does not earn even a subsistence income.)

Weaving is linked with spinning, as it depends on the availability of yarn. Spinners in the taluka do not spin regularly, and do not produce enough yarn to provide employment to many weavers. Like spinning, weaving is also not an attractive occupation as it does not provide even a subsistence income. The weavers who worked in their spare time earned, on average, Rs.379 in 1978-9 in Algardh. In Buhari where they worked as full-time weavers, they earned, on average, Rs.1,349 in a year. Consequently, weaving is not an attractive substitute for agriculture. In the whole of the taluka one could never find even 50 persons who had taken to weaving as a full-time occupation. In fact, there is no full-time weaver today. The V.I.A.S. has brought weavers from Maharashtra to keep the organization running. It has now extended spinning and weaving activities to neighbouring talukas and districts so as to maintain the production centre. The consumption of khadi has also declined in the taluka. Though old freedom fighters continue to wear it, young persons prefer to go in for mill cloth. The V.I.A.S., however, exports khadi to Amsterdam, London, Aden and Geneva through its contacts with aid-giving agencies.

Dairy. Development of the dairy industry was on the agenda of the V.I.A.S. from the very beginning.

During the 1950s, thanks to its strong Gandhian orientation, it emphasized the development of cows, more than of buffaloes. The programme however remained on paper, as financial assistance was not forthcoming to enable the group to buy cows of good quality. Moreover, there was no incentive for local farmers to take to the production of milk as a market for milk did not then exist. Though there were three co-operative societies in Surat which supplied milk to urban consumers, their activities were confined to Surat and the area around it. None of them had any means of bringing milk from distant villages to the city.

During the 1960s, the Milk Co-operative Society of Kheda district, known as the AMUL, came into prominence. Following the establishment of the Amul, attempts were made in Surat to merge the three existing co-operative societies and to start a huge milk processing plant. The result, in Surat, was a dairy named Sumul in 1968.[15] During the 1960s, the V.I.A.S. made efforts to organize Milk Co-operative Societies and to bring more milch animals into the taluka. Its first two five year plans put a modest target - the distribution of 215 and 400 buffaloes in the taluka in the first and the second plans respectively. The targets remained unfulfilled. The taluka purchased 65 cows as against its target of 125 during the first plan period. In the second plan it purchased 32 cows against the target of 100 cows. The gap between the plan and the performance became glaring.

However, the National Dairy Development Board launched the Operation Flood I Programme in July 1970. Its aim was to develop the dairy industry in four metropolitan cities and the milk-supply areas surrounding them. This obviously gave a fillip to a small dairy like the Sumul Dairy which launched a programme of expansion. Between 1968 and 1975, the village co-operative milk societies attached to the Sumul increased from 14 to 445. The Sumul built a chilling plant at Bajipura in Valod taluka in 1975, and this facilitated the collection of milk from the surrounding area. On the other hand, the Small Farmers Development Agency of the government started giving a 50 per cent subsidy to small and marginal farmers to enable them to buy buffaloes. The other 50 per cent came from the nationalized banks as a loan. Community Aid Abroad, Australia, also gave financial assistance to the V.I.A.S. to enable it to advance loans to farmers who were unable to get advances from the banks for buying buffaloes. The workers of the V.I.A.S. organized milk co-operative societies in villages to collect milk from the producers for the Sumul.

The V.I.A.S. carried out a cross-breeding programme in the taluka similar to one which had been implemented successfully in Maharashtra. With financial support from a foreign agency, an effort was made to cross-breed the Indian cows with exotic breeds like the Jersey. This programme faced several difficulties. The crossbred cows require good care and fodder which the farmers of the taluka could not provide. Hence the milk yield did not increase significantly. Moreover, artificial insemination was not properly carried out in time, and much of the semen brought over long distances was spoiled. The programme remained a non-starter in the 1970s, though the V.I.A.S. hopes to make it successful in the 1980s.

As a result of the efforts of the V.I.A.S., the number of buffaloes has almost doubled during the last ten years. However, the quality of the milch cattle has not yet improved. And despite the distribution of fodder and the provision of veterinary services, production of milk per buffalo has not increased significantly. On an average, it is less than one pound per buffalo per day. Consequently the economic returns are not satisfactory. On an average a milk producer gets less than Rs.700 per year. He spends between Rs.300 to Rs.400 on fodder alone. The net profit is thus found to be almost nil, even without allowing the farmer some minimal return for his labour. What he gets is the psychological satisfaction that 'ownership' of milch cattle may provide. Moreover, prices of green, dry and concentrated fodder have increased during the last few years, whereas the price of milk has not increased correspondingly. Further, with an increase in the number of milch cattle, the supply of milk has increased, but the buying capacity of the urban consumers has not. Hence, the Dairies have started facing a problem of marketing their surplus which may become acute in the 1980s. Obviously, the V.I.A.S. can exercise no control over these market forces.

Lijjat Papad. The V.I.A.S. organized the Sales and Purchase Co-operative Society in 1962. Its objectives were to purchase farm products from the farmers at a 'reasonable' price and sell them in the market at a competitive price. In 1968, the co-operative society purchased a large quantity of udad (a legume), paying a slightly higher price than the merchants used to pay to the farmers. But by the time it had stocked up, the market registered a sharp decline in the price of udad. The society found that it would not be able to recover even its purchase price; loss was imminent. The V.I.A.S. contacted a friend of theirs who was associated with the Shri Mahila Griha Udyog Lijjat Papad (M.G.U.), Bombay. Udad is an ingredient of papad, which is prepared by the M.G.U. on a commercial basis. The papad is a wafer-thin, dry, round product which has a diameter of about seven inches. It is crisp, salty, and hot in taste. It is either roasted directly on a charcoal fire or fried in an edible oil. It is eaten by the middle-classes and the rich with their meals.

The V.I.A.S. processed the udad with a view to selling it to the M.G.U. They would not buy it, however, as its quality was different from that of the udad they had been using. To convince the M.G.U. that their udad was not inferior, the V.I.A.S. prepared samples of papad and sent them to the M.G.U. for approval. The M.G.U. not only approved of the sample, but also agreed to provide technical expertise and equipment to the V.I.A.S. to enable them to organize a co-operative society for the manufacture of papad. Later, the Valod Papad Society became a branch of the M.G.U. and thus the problem of marketing papad was solved. The M.G.U. invested Rs.1,000 and the V.I.A.S. Rs.500. Community Aid Abroad, Australia, gave financial support through the V.I.A.S. to enable the purchase of a delivery van.

Though the Valod M.G.U. started with a small group of seven members who prepared papad, it was able to employ 150 members at the end of only six months. The number increased nearly three-fold, to 410, by the end of 1976-7. In the first six months, the sale of papad fetched Rs.42,000. After ten years the sale of papad fetched a sum of Rs.2,812,000. The society distributed Rs.10,000 as remuneration during the first year. During 1976-7 the remuneration amounted to Rs.608,000. The Lijjat Papad at Valod, now has an impressive two-storied building - much more imposing than any of the other buildings of the village. It has a number of vehicles at its disposal and its members are provided with other amenities besides.

The Lijjat Papad, Valod, drew its membership from all the social strata, though the proportion of members drawn from different castes varies. It has been able to recruit more members from high-caste Hindus than from the tribals and the scheduled castes. In 1977-8, 40 per

'Decentralized' Planning

cent of its members were Muslims and 23 per cent were tribals; the rest were caste Hindus.[16] However, only one per cent belonged to the lowest castes, the Harijans, known as untouchable. The Lijjat Papad, Valod, has opened a sub-branch at Golan, a tribal village, with a view to enrol tribals. In 1977-8 it had 43 members. More than 50 per cent of them, however, were non-tribals. The reason is that papad does not form part of the meals of tribals. Moreover, unlike caste Hindus, tribal women work on farms.

The average income of a woman worker was Rs.708 in 1968-9; it increased to Rs.1,470 in the year 1976-7. The average remuneration of an employee works out at Rs.4·90 per day.[17] A woman has to work for at least seven hours a day to earn this remuneration which is slightly more than a farm labourer earns. Middle-class women who are generally not engaged in any economic activity, take up the preparation of papad as a sparetime occupation.

The V.I.A.S. is however not happy with the functioning of the Lijjat Papad, Valod. It has mainly a commercial approach. The V.I.A.S. tried to persuade the M.G.U. to extend the papad-making industry to tribal villages, but the latter turned down the proposal, because the M.G.U. is concerned about marketing the product. The V.I.A.S. resented the high salaries paid to the managerial staff of the Lijjat Papad, Valod. The M.G.U. recently declared through the press that the Lijjat Papad, Valod, had no organizational or any other relationship with the V.I.A.S. It is now centrally administered from Bombay.

Diamond Cutting and Polishing. The V.I.A.S. invested its man-power and financial resources in the diamond cutting and polishing industry during the mid-1970s. The diamond industry is directly linked with the international market. The production of raw diamonds and their marketing are monopolized by a handful of international companies based in London, Amsterdam, Tel Aviv, New York and Antwerp. Raw diamonds have to be cut and polished before they are used in machinery or as jewels. The diamond cutting and polishing industry developed in India after 1960. Labour is costlier in the European cities than in India. After the devaluation of the rupee in 1966, Indian labour became cheaper still. On the other hand, during the 1960s India entered the world diamond market for the first time, as a lot of princely jewellery was put up for sale - one piece of jewellery was worth as much as

Rs.1 crore. A market for such costly jewellery existed only abroad. In order to promote exports, the Government of India set up the Gems and Jewellery Export Promotion Council in 1966. Against the export of jewellery the government allowed the import of raw diamonds. They were to be cut and polished in India and then re-exported. The demand for diamonds increased in foreign markets in the mid-1970s, as people lost faith in paper currency and there was a buying spree in gold, silver and diamonds. This boosted the price of gold. Consequently, exports of cut and polished diamonds from India rose sharply between 1970 and 1978. The exports which were of the order of Rs.28 crores in 1970-71 reached Rs.82 crores by 1975-6. The figure for 1977-8 was as much as Rs.43,522,000.[18]

Bombay is the only centre for the export of diamonds. As Gujarat is quite near Bombay, and as the Gujaratis enjoy a monopoly in the diamond business, the work of cutting and polishing of diamonds has developed mainly in Gujarat. Ninety per cent of all the diamonds processed in India are from Gujarat. More than 80 per cent of the diamond-processing units came into existence in Surat between 1966 and 1975.[19] With the spectacular rise in exports between 1973 and 1976, small entrepreneurs started diamond cutting and polishing units even in rural areas, including fifteen villages of Valod taluka. They employed about 2,000 workers, a majority of whom came from taluka other than Valod. These units were owned by non-Adivasis. This development had nothing to do with the activities of the V.I.A.S.

The V.I.A.S., however, did not want to be left out. In 1978, it claimed: 'having been involved in decentralized small scale village industry through its development work in the past 25 years, it decided to encourage in every way possible the growth of this particular industry, and especially for the poorer groups and in the more remote villages'.[20] It helped several individual entrepreneurs to get loans to start one or two units. It started one co-operative unit, and one unit exclusively for women.

However, before these units were off the ground, the diamond industry in India faced recession. De Beers Consolidated Mines, the biggest owner of diamond mines, raised the surcharge on rough diamonds by as much as 40 per cent. Moreover, the Diamond Trading Company of London which holds a world monopoly in the trade of rough diamonds not only raised the price of diamonds, but also arbitrarily cut the supply of diamonds to

India. The Company started developing new and alternative centres like China and Singapore for the processing of diamonds. Consequently, Indian exports of cut and polished diamonds fell to Rs.22 crores in December 1978 from 43 crores achieved in the previous month.[21] Many of the small diamond-cutting units which had sprung up in the previous five years had to shut down because of the crisis. As many as 1.5 lakhs of people lost their jobs owing to the closure of diamond units. This unprecedented reversal in this export business marked the end of the great diamond boom started in 1975. The diamond processing units of Valod faced the same fate. All the units started by the V.I.A.S. were closed down within six months. The V.I.A.S., however, is waiting for an opportunity to revive them.

Paper Mill. The V.I.A.S., a protagonist of cottage and labour-intensive industries, started manufacturing hand-made paper in 1958 with financial support from the Khadi and Village Industries Commission in the form of 50 per cent loan and 50 per cent subsidy. The total investment in the industry was around Rs.50,000. On an average it provides employment to eighteen persons - including the manager and salesmen. The average pay of an employee was only Rs.979 in the year 1974-5; that is, it was no more than the income earned by a farm labourer. The production capacity of the hand-made paper plant is, however, limited. On the other hand, the demand for paper for cultural (printing and writing) and industrial uses (craft and other packing material) has increased considerably during the last three decades. The per capita consumption of paper was 0.7 kilogram in 1951. It had increased to 18 kilograms in 1977. The production of paper has not increased to a corresponding extent. During the period of the first five-year plan ending in 1966, there was a shortfall of 153,000 tonnes of paper. Therefore, in order to boost paper production, the Indian government de-licensed the industry producing paper boards and strawboard paper used by the packaging industries in 1966.

Slowly, the number of paper plants in general and mini-paper plants in particular increased in the 1970s. Recently, 'there has been a sudden rush of proposals for putting up mini-paper plants with daily capacity ranging from 10 tonnes to 30 tonnes of paper and paper board. The government has so far (1979) issued 129 letters of intent and industrial licences for a total capacity of 821,265 tonnes per year for such paper

mills. These schemes are based on raw materials, such
as paddy straw, wheat, husk, jute waste, bagasse, rags,
linter and waste paper.'[22] Since paddy is one of the
main crops in Surat district, paddy straw is available
in plenty. Even in Valod, the area under paddy crop is
around 8,700 acres yielding 27,000 tonnes of straw.
Moreover, the scheduled commercial banks have also
started advancing loans to the paper and paper board
industries. They advanced Rs.19,704,000 to the paper-
manufacturing plants at the end of June 1977.[23] Thus
with delicensing, the availability of advances from
banks and of raw materials, eight mini-paper plants
came into existence in Bardoli taluka, the taluka adjoining Valod, by the end of the year 1978. They are
controlled by rich and middle non-Adivasi peasants.
The growth of paper plants in surrounding areas and
their profitability attracted the V.I.A.S. It may be
mentioned that 'between 1973-4 and 1975-6, the profitability of the [paper] industry remained above the
average profitability ratios for all industries'. But
the V.I.A.S. did not have the necessary capital to invest in paper plants and the Adivasi farmers were not
economically so well off as to be able to raise the
needed share capital.

 The Netherlands Organization for International
Development Co-operation came to the rescue. One of
its associates encouraged the V.I.A.S. to prepare a
plan for a mini-paper plant. The V.I.A.S. immediately
collected preliminary information from the existing
factories of Bardoli taluka. It also hired the services
of an expert and assigned to him the task of preparing
a project. The Netherlands Organization immediately
sanctioned a sum of Rs.18 lakhs. With this working
capital the V.I.A.S. proposed to establish the Valod
Antyodaya Sahakari Paper Mills Limited at Dumkhal,
four kilometres from Valod. It procured a loan of
Rs.61 lakhs from a commercial bank. Thus, the total
cost of the project came to Rs.79 lakhs. The paper
plant which thus came into existence has a production
capacity of ten tonnes a day. It aims at providing
employment to 500 persons when the plant starts working
at full capacity.

 Within two years land was purchased, the building
was constructed and machinery installed. Production
was started in April 1980. This mini-paper plant
represents a major change in the approach of the V.I.
A.S. to rural development. It has now started establishing capital-intensive industries. At this juncture

'Decentralized' Planning

it would be hazardous to answer the question as to whether the mini-paper plant of the V.I.A.S. will be able to face the competition offered by the larger plants which produce as much as 80 per cent of the paper produced in the country. But if the experience gained in running this plant is favourable, the V.I. A.S. may perhaps be tempted to go in for still bigger projects.

Conclusions

The foregoing analysis of the rural development programmes pinpoints many theoretical issues related to economic planning and political authority in a 'backward' society. It also highlights the futility of the so-called Gandhian approach to rural development aiming at 'building from below' in a centralized economy. But at the moment I shall refrain from discussing these issues. Here, let us draw some conclusions regarding the linkages between the 'localized' rural society and the larger society of which it is an undoubted part. The present-day Indian rural society does not function - for good or bad - in isolation, notwithstanding the Gandhian ideology and efforts the Gandhians put in to build village 'republics'. A tiny tribal hamlet is linked with the district, the state and the national capitals through political institutions and administrative machinery. Production and consumption in village society have increasingly been linked with the market economy governed from metropolitan areas.
The local intermediaries - the Valod group is a case in point here - work as active agents (though sometimes as catalysts) in the process that increasingly establishes links between the local rural society and 'outside' forces. The 'outside' forces are not monolithic. They are complex and often pull in opposite directions. The intermediaries do not get swept away by all kinds of outside forces. They try to be selective and strengthen certain forces. They dilute or modify some and ignore others. Their selection is guided by their 'ideology' and subjective interests. If the ideology is not well-defined or if it is utopian the intermediaries become more vulnerable to subjective interests and the forces conducive to them.
Precisely this has happened to the V.I.A.S. The V.I.A.S. was greatly influenced by national and international forces - the government policy, market and

the availability of financial assistance in formulating the programmes - whether for khadi, or a paper plant. Their preferences and priorities have been dictated by the market, though in the 1950s they resisted it without success. The V.I.A.S. had limited options in the selection of the programmes. Whenever it tried to ignore the market forces, the programmes came to a standstill soon after they were launched; or they remained non-starters. Besides the market forces, the response of the local people also influenced the V.I.A.S. programmes. In the beginning the local people did resist the change which resulted from the operations of forces operating from outside village society. But once they realized the economic advantages that were made possible by the new opportunities, they began to take advantage of these opportunities. Thus, their resistance against the outside forces was slowly weakened. In fact, during the 1960s and thereafter the people of Valod gave a cold response to programmes which tried to keep them within the village boundaries. Hence, the V.I.A.S. had no option but to accommodate itself to the forces working outside the taluka. And it has successfully accomplished that, within the limits imposed by the given resources, constraints and response of the local people.

NOTES

Shah, '"Decentralized" planning in a centralized economy: a study of Sarvodaya programmes in a taluka'

This paper is a part of the study on Vedchhi Intensive Area Scheme, partly financed by NOVIB, Netherlands. H.R. Chaturvedi is a collaborator in the project.

1. See B.H. Baden Powell, *The Indian Village Community* (London 1896); Louis Dumont, 'The Village Community from Munro to Maine', *Contributions to Indian Sociology* (December 1966).
2. See McKim Marriott (ed.), *Village India* (Chicago 1955); M.N. Srinivas, *India's Villages* (Bombay 1960); Oscar Lewis,*Village Life in Northern India* (New York 1965).
3. Rajni Kothari, *Politics in India* (Delhi 1970); S.K. Sharma and S.L. Malhotra, *Integrated Rural Development* (Columbia 1977).
4. M.K. Gandhi, *Sarvodaya* (Ahmedabad 1954), p.36.
5. Ghanshyam Shah, 'Gandhian Approach to Rural Development', *Ideas and Action* 125, 6 (1978).
6. Ten per cent of the heads of households are engaged in non-agricultural occupations.
7. I.P. Desai, 'Vedchhi Movement', in I.P. Desai and Banwarilal Choudhary, eds., *History of Rural Development in Modern India* II (New Delhi 1977).
8. Norman Long, *An Introduction to the Sociology of Rural Development* (London 1977).
9. Francine R. Frankel, *India's Political Economy, 1947-77* (Delhi 1978).
10. Vedchhi Sanghakshetra Samiti, *Valod Mahal Kshetra Ayojan* (Gujarati), Valod, V.I.A.S. 1962; Jhaverbhai Patel, 'The Constructive Approach', in *Building From Below, Third Five Year Plan 1975-79, Valod Taluka* (Vanasthali, Sarvodaya Planning and Training Centre, n.d.).
11. M.S. Patel, *The Educational Philosophy of Mahatma Gandhi* (Ahmedabad 1953).
12. Frankel, op.cit.
13. Jhaverbhai Patel, op.cit., p.12.
14. I.P. Desai, op.cit.
15. Babubhai D. Desai, *A Socio-Economic Study of the Milk Producers of South Gujarat* (Surat: Centre for Social Studies (Mimeo.) 1979).

16. Bhikhu Vyas, 'Participation of Rural Women in Income Raising Group Activities' (mss.), Valod, V.I.A.S., n.d.
17. Ibid.
18. Diamond Company, *The Economic Times*, 7 August 1978.
19. K.M. Desai, 'Hirane Paher Padavana Udyog - Surat Ane Navsari Vistar no Ek Abhyas', Surat: South Gujarat University 1979, (unpublished Ph.D. Thesis).
20. V.I.A.S., *Planning for Industry in Valod Taluka*, Kanjod: Sarvodaya Planning and Training Centre, 1978, (Mimeo.), p.22.
21. Indra Gidwani, Diamond Industry, *Economic Times*, 16 December 1978.
22. 'Paper Industry: Position and Prospects III', *State Bank of India, Monthly Review*, March 1980, p.110.
23. Ibid.

INTERNATIONAL RICE RESEARCH AND THE PROBLEMS OF RICE GROWING IN UTTAR PRADESH AND BIHAR

Paul R. Brass

It is widely asserted that the 'green revolution' in India has been far more successful for wheat than it has been for rice. In fact, the use of the high yielding varieties (H.Y.V.s) in rice, with their associated technology, has also produced impressive results in the Punjab and south India. However, in the great paddy-growing belt of northern and eastern India, stretching from the eastern districts of Uttar Pradesh (U.P.) into the Bengal delta and Orissa, virtually no increases in productivity have occurred in the last 20 years. Whereas, between 1960-2 and 1972-4, the average yield of paddy for those three-year periods increased in south India from 2,007 kilograms per hectare to 2,582 and in the Punjab, Delhi, and Himachal Pradesh from 1,470 to 2,930 kg./ha., there was only a marginal increase in yields in Orissa and West Bengal from 1,427 to 1,513 kg./ha., in Bihar from 1,260 to 1,309 kg./ha., and in U.P. from 1,123 to 1,192 kg./ha. Yet, this region of northern and eastern India produced 44.11 per cent of the paddy harvested in the country, amounting to 26.6 million metric tons.[1] More rice is produced in this region of India than in any country in the world outside of India, except for the People's Republic of China.[2] In this area, the H.Y.V.s in rice were not widely sown. Only 30.19 per cent of the acreage sown with H.Y.V.s in rice in 1974-5 was accounted for by the rainfed areas of northern and eastern India.[3]

Many people who know little about agriculture and think they know a great deal about the different peoples of India are quick to jump to conclusions, based on these bare facts, such as that the farmers of the northern and eastern Indian paddy belt are less energetic, innovative, and willing to take risks than the proverbially enterprising Punjabi peasantry and the nearly as proverbially clever Tamils. In fact, however, many farmers in this region have adopted the new H.Y.V.s in wheat and have extended considerably the acreage sown to wheat during the past decade. For example, wheat acreage in Bihar increased from 809,000 hectares in 1966-7 to 1,815,000 in 1975-6, with the percentage under H.Y.V.s going from 3.1 to 96.4. In U.P., wheat acreage increased from 4,394,000 to 6,103,000 hectares, with the percentage under H.Y.V.s rising from 8.3 to 73.7 in the same period.[4]

Moreover, the problems of northern and eastern India paddy-growing are common to three-quarters of the paddy-growing areas in Asia. When it became clear in the late 1960s and early 1970s that the adoption of the new seeds and the associated technology had peaked, in terms of coverage, at approximately 25 per cent of the rice-growing areas of Asia, it was generally assumed that the principal limiting factor in the spread of the H.Y.V.s in paddy was the availability of irrigation which also was confined to 25 per cent of the cultivated paddy acreage in Asia. Although rice scientists at the International Rice Research Institute (IRRI) and elsewhere argue that the new H.Y.V.s in paddy will do better than traditional varieties even in the upland and drier areas, provided that fertilizers and pesticides are applied, it was clear that farmers were not willing to take the risks involved in applying expensive inputs for limited increases in yields in agricultural zones where either the absence of irrigation or inadequate water control already made paddy-cultivation a high-risk enterprise. In fact, it is believed at IRRI that many farmers in northern and eastern India are using the H.Y.V.s and applying fertilizer in the rabi season and getting good yields, but 'are not putting an ounce of fertilizer in the field(s) during the wet season' when the risks of flood and/or drought threaten to wipe out all investments in such high-cost inputs.[5] These impressions are also held by persons in the Indian Council of Agricultural Research, who point out that the major increases in rice production and in rice yields in India have occurred 'in non-traditional rice areas or in non-traditional rice seasons'[6] when irrigation can be applied and water-logging is not a problem. However, in the rainfed areas and in the kharif season, both the great risks of total crop loss and the somewhat less catastrophic risks of fertilizer loss through leaching after heavy rains make the use of H.Y.V.s in rice, with the associated technology, unattractive to most peasants. Moreover, in the Philippines, farmers were using the H.Y.V.s on irrigated land, but were not achieving the yields expected. These problems in India, in the Philippines, and elsewhere suggested that the association between irrigation and the adoption of H.Y.V.s and between absence of irrigation and the use of traditional varieties did not necessarily imply a simple causal relationship such that the spread of

The Problems of Rice Growing

irrigation would necessarily lead to the adoption of H.Y.V.s. Consequently, in the early 1970s, IRRI launched a research programme, led by its economists, on constraints in the adoption of the new technology in rice in order to discover precisely what were the limiting factors in the further spread of the H.Y.V.s.[7]

At the same time in India, agricultural policy makers concerned about the same questions and also about questions being raised by political leaders as to why there had as yet been no 'rice revolution' began to turn their attentions to the special problems of the predominantly rice-growing rainfed areas of Bihar, Orissa, and West Bengal. Then, in 1977, when the Janata party came to power, with its principal base of support lying in north India and including all the principal rainfed areas in that part of the country, and with a clear commitment to give the highest priority to agricultural and rural development, the time was clearly ripe to assist the farmers of northern and eastern India.[8] In September 1977, at the suggestion of the Director-General of the Indian Council of Agricultural Research,[9] an IRRI team of economists and rice scientists visited India and joined with a Government of India team to tour the paddy-growing areas of eastern India and to prepare a report on the strategies required to increase rice production in those areas. That team found that, in villages they visited, 'a negligible portion of the land' was sown with H.Y.V.s except in irrigated villages where H.Y.V.s were sown in the rabi season.[10] The failure to adopt H.Y.V.s in eastern India in the main kharif season was attributed to the fact that the H.Y.V.s were simply unsuitable to most of the region because of problems not only of availability of irrigation, but of water control generally. For example, rapid flooding in north Bihar would quickly submerge the stiff and short-stalked IRRI type varieties. In other areas of eastern India, drought, rather than excessive water, was a frequent problem. Some areas often experience both flood and drought conditions in alternate seasons. In areas where canal irrigation was available in the kharif season, it was found that its use caused 'excessive silting in farm fields'.[11] Because of the short monsoon in this part of India, the H.Y.V.s, which flower in September-October, and, therefore, require watering when the monsoon is finished, are unsuitable for much of the region, which requires instead 'short duration, non-photoperiod sensitive varieties'[12] that flower early even under monsoon cloud cover. In general, the IRRI study team was impressed by the heterogeneity of environments under which paddy was grown in this region, ranging from drought to high water. Finally, given the high-risk farming in most of these environments, especially during the kharif season, and given the relatively high price of nitrogen and the low market price of paddy, the team found it not at all surprising that neither the H.Y.V.s nor large quantities of inputs were being used.

The team found it possible to identify what strategies needed to be followed in eastern India, but was not particularly sanguine about the likelihood of success in the near future. What was required, the team suggested, was adequate water control, the replacement of photoperiod sensitive with short duration non-photosensitive varieties in large parts of the region, and an emphasis on high-stability rather than high-yielding varieties in these high-risk farming areas. However, adequate water control in much of this region is hundreds of millions of rupees and many years ahead because such control involves large-scale construction of flood prevention and canal systems. With regard to the development of new varieties suitable to 'the drought and flood conditions common in Eastern India', the IRRI team suggested that insufficient research was being done to produce such varieties, that where potentially suitable varieties were available at research stations, adequate mechanisms were not available for their 'field testing', multiplication, and 'rapid and wide dissemination'. Moreover, it was found that the development and release of new varieties of rice in India took ten years, rather than the five years normally required in the Philippines, and that, even after ten years, once a 'variety is released, there is no assurance that seed will be made available to farmers'.[13] In other words, the adequacy of both agricultural research and the linkage between research and the distribution system in India was questioned.

Phrased in simple language, the report of the IRRI-Government of India team could lead to only one conclusion, namely, that there is not yet available for most of the paddy-growing region of northern and eastern India a suitable technology to increase or even stabilize yields.[14] This rather sobering conclusion raises several broad questions of strategy both for international rice researchers in general and for Indian agricultural policy makers in particular. First, given

The Problems of Rice Growing

the difficulties in the rainfed areas and the unlikelihood of dramatic improvement in the near future, does it make sense to divert resources to those areas that might be used to increase production further in the irrigated areas? If increased production is deemed necessary to feed the population of India and Asia, then why not continue to concentrate resources on improving results in the irrigated areas through the application of more inputs or of inputs applied with ever more precision? It is estimated at IRRI, for example, that only 17 to 50 per cent of the technology that is available for the irrigated areas, including fertilizers, pesticides, weedicides, and the like, is actually being used and that the fuller utilization of already available technology in the irrigated areas might lead to a bigger increase in production than efforts devoted to the rainfed areas. In fact, insofar as India is concerned, the concentration of agricultural development resources in irrigation and inputs in the Punjab has made it possible for farmers in the Punjab, already famous for their output of wheat, to produce substantial quantities of rice. The rices grown in the Punjab are principally Java and IR-8. The latter, which is not highly regarded because of its poor taste, flavour, and texture, is not eaten in the Punjab, but is shipped through the central government procurement system to be processed and marketed in the food-deficit paddy-growing regions of eastern India. In this way, the prosperous Punjab farmers are benefited, the urban residents of Calcutta are fed, and the small paddy-farmers of eastern U.P. and Bihar continue to struggle along at a bare subsistence level, producing high quality, but low-yielding grains that they are often unable to market even if they should produce a surplus because either the price is too low or marketing facilities are not available. The value choice here then becomes one of deciding whether or not to divert financial and other resources to maintain the poor subsistence paddy growers of U.P. and Bihar when production and consumption needs might be better met and the political dangers of discontented urban populations be more easily warded off by a policy that maximizes the potential for immediate production increases. Such a policy accepts that it may be necessary to introduce inequalities into the agricultural economy to prevent the greater evil of an inadequate food supply. For example, a policy maker at the Indian Council for Agricultural Research, frustrated over the criticism that the Intensive Agricultural District Programme introduced into India in the 1960s under the sponsorship of the Ford Foundation enhanced rural tensions between those farmers who acquired irrigation and those who did not, responded:

> But then ... we have got 650 million people. We have got to feed them also. So, those who make these comments do not understand that we must also have enough food for everyone.[15]

If there is a single basic value assumption in international agricultural research that underlies the overall strategies that are followed and that sets the boundaries for specific decisions and alterations in policy, it is that increasing agricultural production must take precedence over all other considerations. The whole world is familiar with the Malthusian arguments that justify the production orientation. Those arguments have been so powerfully and widely presented that they go virtually unchallenged as a basic premise of agricultural research and policy making. Yet, it is not at all clear that production, rather than distribution, is the more serious problem in the world as a whole or in Indian agriculture in particular. For one thing, there is no doubt at all that there was enough grain in America, Australia, and the Soviet Union to feed the people of the Sahel during the recent terrible drought there. As far as India is concerned, American food imports for 20 years filled the estimated gap between production and consumption needs there. However, it is quite likely that there has nearly always been sufficient food or production capacity in India in the past two decades to feed the people of the country provided either that all barriers to the free movement of grain were removed or that governments were willing or able forcibly to procure grain from surplus areas to distribute to deficit areas. However, since both policies presented political and/or economic costs that the Government of India was not willing to pay, it proved to be politically easier and also cheaper economically to transport wheat from Kansas to Bihar than from Punjab to Bihar and rice from Louisiana to Calcutta than from Tamil Nadu to Calcutta. When the Punjab began to produce a large marketable surplus in both wheat and rice, the Government of India found it politically expedient and financially easier to procure grains at controlled prices from the

The Problems of Rice Growing

Punjab to ship to eastern India rather than either to allocate the resources necessary or to provide the marketing facilities and price incentives to make it possible for the paddy growers of eastern U.P., Bihar, and Bengal to feed themselves and to provide a surplus for Calcutta.

The strategy of importing grain and procuring it within India at a low price kept prices within reasonable bounds in India, thereby also preventing political instability. It also benefited the production and profit-oriented wheat farmers of Kansas and the Punjab. The latter would have benefited even more from an open-market policy in India, but they at least were permitted to hoard surplus stocks and maximize their price by the unwillingness of the government to squeeze them through a harsh procurement policy. The production and import strategy also ensured the dependence of India upon the United States and of Bihar upon the Punjab.

Both the scientists and policy-makers at IRRI and in India are well aware of the dilemma in which an exclusively production-oriented strategy places them. On the one hand, the IRRI scientists confront the realization that the technology they have developed is irrelevant to at least 60 per cent and possibly 75 per cent of the rice farmers of Asia, but that a major diversion of their own research efforts to developing an appropriate technology for the rainfed areas might not pay off for many years and that the ultimate pay-off will, in any case, probably not be as great in terms of yield increases as has already occurred and might still be possible in the irrigated areas. On the other hand, it is estimated that further efforts in developing varieties, insect control and fertilizer use might lead to production increases of a ton or two tons per hectare in the irrigated areas with the existing H.Y.V.s. Moreover, a decision to shift a substantial part of its resources to work on the diverse environments of the rainfed areas raises considerable problems for IRRI and carries greater risks. Although IRRI is financially well-endowed and has adequate resources to carry on research that is highly focused on a single, ideal environment for rice-growing, it does not have the resources to duplicate its research effort for a number of different and less-than-ideal environments. Moreover, although it is possible to create an ideal environment for rice-growing on a single research site in the Philippines, it is not possible to create several sets of adverse conditions that would duplicate the varied environments in which rice is grown throughout Asia. Consequently, any major shift of emphasis at IRRI towards research on the problems of rice-growing under adverse conditions must involve IRRI much more in collaborative research in different locations in Asia.[16] In the face of these facts, IRRI policy makers insist that the production emphasis was valid when IRRI began and will continue to be valid in the foreseeable future.

> The accusation that IRRI spent its early days working on irrigated rice exclusively ... [is] a very appropriate statement of what should have been done because the potential for increasing production [was unquestionably in] irrigated rice. And I think if [we] were sitting here twenty years from now, we'd probably say that the potential for increased production of rice between now and twenty years from now will be still very heavily oriented toward irrigated crops, so that there's no reason why IRRI shouldn't have done this. [17]

IRRI policy makers also believe that, if adequate systems of irrigation and drainage were established in the rainfed areas, the technology that has been emphasized at IRRI would then become appropriate for these areas, though the yield potential in the rainfed areas of north India, where the cloud cover is greater than in other parts of Asia, would still be less than in areas with greater radiation. Consequently, IRRI faces a choice of whether to wait on the governments of Asia to develop the water management that is desirable or to try to develop a technology that would suit present conditions without adequate water management. Since IRRI policy makers do not foresee the widespread development of good water conservation in most Asian countries in the near future, they are

> not going down either road completely. We're still putting abut 40 per cent of our effort toward the irrigated situation and 60 per cent toward situations that might be changed but that, in some cases, will not likely be changed that much. [18]

Actually, the choices faced by IRRI scientists and policy makers are more complex than simply choosing

The Problems of Rice Growing

between research in irrigated versus rainfed areas, for the environments in which paddy is grown in Asia are extremely heterogeneous. Each distinctive environment presents different problems, potentials, and value choices. The apparently harmless, even noble goal of providing a technology to maximize production of rice in Asia, when translated into cost-benefit ratios, presents policy choices with quite different value implications. Primary emphasis on increasing production leads inevitably to favouring the already-favoured areas and paying less attention to the less-favoured areas. Moreover, since the more reliable forms of irrigation, especially tube-wells but also canal irrigation, tend to be made use of more by the larger farmers than the small farmers, the production orientation also tends to favour the bigger farmers and neglect the poorer. The solution adopted at IRRI in the face of this dilemma has been to continue emphasizing work on the technology of irrigated rice, but to supplement it with work on the problems of rice growing under adverse conditions. In general, the attitude at the policy making level at IRRI is that it is necessary and desirable that more attention be paid to research on rice cultures in the 'adverse areas', but that 'once this is done, if we find, for example, the potential ... in comparison to what you could get in irrigated and other conditions is insignificant, then you would phase out of a major input there and go ahead and put your money where it makes sense in terms of potential change in production'.[19] Moreover, the largest share of the research funds at IRRI, approximately 41 per cent, continue to be allocated for work on irrigated rice, compared to 31 per cent for the rainfed areas, and the remainder for other adverse conditions (see table, p.238). This distribution reflects accurately thinking at IRRI about where the next production increases are going to come. It is believed that they are going to come first from increasing production in the irrigated areas by improving the technology there and gaining better control over insects and diseases that affect the new varieties so that actual production will move closer to the yield potential of the new varieties. The current feeling at IRRI is that 'the feasible potential for increasing rice production in rainfed wetland areas with reasonable research inputs is second only to that in irrigated areas'.[20] IRRI policy makers believe also that their scientists will be able to develop new varieties that will produce under adverse soil conditions and that will

withstand floodwaters, thus preventing catastrophe to
the farmers in the high risk areas.[21] Through this
particular mixture of research and results, it is
believed that production in Asia will increase at a minimum of four per cent a year, enough 'to produce all
the rice that is needed'.[22]

Table: Proportions of Paddy Land, IRRI
Research Budget and Anticipated Benefits

Environment	Area Sown to Paddy		IRRI Budget	Anticipated Benefits
	Asia	India		
Irrigated	27	33	41	46
Shallow Rainfed	32	33	31	25
Intermed. Ditto	14	16		8
Deepwater	8	6	5	3
Dryland (Upland)	10	6	24	4
Other	9	6	-	13

Note: *Asia* refers to Asian developing countries except
China. The table compares the proportion of land
area sown to paddy in such countries and in India
with proportions of the IRRI research budget devoted to research on different types of rice culture and of the anticipated benefits from future
research inputs. The IRRI budget is the one for
1977; 'other' categories of environment were not
separately classified there.

Source: *IRRI Long Range Planning Committee Report* (Los
Banos, Philippines 1979), pp.20 and 45.

The allocations in the IRRI research budget have
continued to be weighted heavily in favour of the irrigated areas. Moreover, reasoning in terms of expected
returns in productivity from future research input in
different types of environments, it is argued at IRRI
that the weightage in their research allocations is an
appropriate one. The table compares the allocations in
the IRRI research budget in 1977 and the allocations
that IRRI's Long Range Planning Committee feel are
appropriate in terms of the criterion of productivity
'benefits from future research input' with the area
sown with paddy in different types of environments in
Asia. The table indicates clearly that IRRI planners
have not been willing to consider seriously any criterion other than productivity as the primary basis for
allocating research funds and that the distribution of
their research budget has continued to reflect that

The Problems of Rice Growing

orientation.

While IRRI policy makers do not deny that the benefits of the new technology have gone principally to the irrigated areas, they do not accept the criticism that the new technology has led to unevenness in income distribution or benefiting one group over another. At IRRI, the general response to this criticism is that the facts are not yet in, but that some of their own research on consequences in the Philippines suggests otherwise. However, the ultimate defence at IRRI to this set of criticisms also comes back to the production orientation, as the following quotation indicates.

> The ultimate beneficiar(ies) of all agricultural research ... are the people who eat the food and the ones that benefit the most are the low income people [who] eat that food because most of what we do ends up with a more efficient system and a lower price for food. ... And an institute like this ... that can help get these production levels up and keep those prices at a steady and reasonable level, the ultimate beneficiary is the poorest people in the country.[23]

For the Government of India, the policy choices that must be faced, given the limitations of the new technology in rice, are much more complex than those faced by policy makers at IRRI. For one thing, the Government of India must allocate research funds among different crops. The principal agency that determines the allocations for agricultural research in India is the Indian Council for Agricultural Research. It is apparent from the Research Council's current relative allocation of resources among the various crops grown in India and among the several non-crop-specific research projects it has funded that the historic neglect of rice research in India is not being rectified. Although most Research Council reports on crop improvement begin with rice and stress the fact that rice is the principal food crop in India, the relative allocation for rice research is nowhere near its relative importance in the country's agriculture. It is not easy to determine what proportion of the allocation for non-crop-specific research projects, such as those pertaining to soil management or agricultural engineering, ultimately benefit rice farmers, but there is no doubt that the proportion of funds allocated directly or indirectly for rice research falls very short of the nearly 80 per cent contribution of rice to the total area sown with foodgrains production in the country[24] or even the 27 per cent contribution of rice to the total net sown area of the country.[25] In the Fourth Five Year Plan, the allocation for rice in the Research Council budget was Rs.16,000,000, a larger allocation than for any other crop. However, this figure represented less than 30 per cent of the crop-specific allocation for food and fodder crops, less than 13 per cent of the total allocation in the budget for all crops, and less than 5 per cent of the budget for all projects.[26] In 1978, the allocation specifically for rice research in the Research Council budget was less than 3 per cent of the total.[27] Moreover, several of the crop-specific agricultural research institutes in India have been funded at higher levels than the Central Rice Research Institute, including the Indian Grassland and Fodder Research Institute, the Central Potato Research Institute, and the Institute of Horticultural Research. In general, it has historically been the case in South Asia that cash crops and specialized crops grown for export markets, nearly all of them requiring capital-intensive cultivation, have received far more research support than the main food crops, particularly rice. It is, for example, remarkable that the Central Potato Research Institute is funded at a higher level than the Central Rice Research Institute, despite the fact that only half a million hectares of land in India are sown with potatoes, whereas nearly 40 million hectares are sown with rice. Moreover, the potato is a highly capital-intensive crop, 'quite exacting in its requirements of inputs such as seed, fertilizers, fungicides and pesticides and assured irrigation'[28] and, therefore, not easily taken up by 'an ordinary cultivator', but grown mostly by specialized vegetable farmers or 'prosperous farmers'.[29]

Although rice has clearly been neglected in comparison to other crops in India and in relation to its contribution to the agricultural economy of the country, it is not a fair criticism of the Indian Council for Agricultural Research to consider only the relative allocation for rice in relation to all projects sponsored by it. It is not only that many non-crop-specific projects sponsored by the Research Council benefit rice growers, but that there is some justification for a non-crop-specific approach in general. At the Council, the view is held that 'crops all fit ...

The Problems of Rice Growing

into a system because [the] farmer's life is a whole. If he is growing wheat and rice [I] have to find a solution to both the problems.'[30] On the whole, however, it does not appear to be the case that Research Council projects are structured systematically from the point of view of the specific mixed-crop patterns of farmers in different agro-ecological regions of the country. Rather, the overwhelming bulk of such projects are either crop-specific or problem-specific, rather than being focused upon different cropping patterns in the numerous agro-climatic zones of India.

The neglect of rice has been most striking in the rainfed areas of northern and eastern India, which are only now beginning to receive substantial attention. The 1977 report on Agricultural Research and Education, after summarizing the work done on H.Y.V.s in rice in India and noting their alleged 'significant impact' in contributing to increased rice production in the country,[31] concludes, however, that 'work on the monsoon rainfed rice is being intensified as the new rice technology has not yet made a real impact in such areas'.[32] There is not much evidence, however, that such intensification has begun in earnest.

A more detailed statement of the problems of rice production in the rainfed areas was presented in another Research Council publication, titled 'Research Highlights, 1977'. In this report, it was noted that 'the productivity and production of rice in low-lying areas have remained stagnant' and that 'a large proportion of the rice-growing regions of West Bengal, Assam, north Bihar, eastern Uttar Pradesh and Orissa have so far been by-passed by the high-yield technology'.[33] Referring to the joint Research Council - IRRI study team survey of the problems of rice-growing in this region, the report pointed out that 'since the performance and profit of the existing high-yielding varieties with costly inputs are uncertain', it was necessary for scientists to 'develop a technology which combines good yield with reliability and security to profit to farmers'. Recognizing that the problems associated with the adoption of the new technology in rice are particularly severe for the small peasantry, the report went on to say that 'we need a high yield-cum-high stability technology, if small and marginal farmers are to be helped to take to such technology'. However, the report concludes in a thoroughly ambiguous manner with regard to how the new technology is to be developed and, indeed, with regard to the suitability of the existing technology for the rainfed areas. After calling for the development of a high-yield high-stability technology, the report concludes that the problems of the 'rainfed upland areas ... can be corrected with new material and technology available' and the problems of the areas subject to periodic flooding can 'also partially be corrected by popularizing flood-tolerant varieties'.[34] In order to achieve these goals, three research projects were proposed to be set up, 'one each for Bihar, West Bengal and Orissa' to 'demonstrate the potentiality of the new technology and high-yielding varieties suitable for problem areas'.[35] Since, however, it is not even clear from this report whether or not such a technology exists for the rainfed areas, one cannot help but wonder how these research projects are to be oriented and co-ordinated. In the meantime, however, while the Indian Council for Agricultural Research either makes up its mind whether or not it has the technology - or whether or not to admit that it *does not* have the technology - the extension agents of the agriculture departments of the U.P. and Bihar, who are being led to believe that there is a suitable technology for rainfed upland and flood-prone areas, are going about 'recommending varieties and techniques which, because the conditions are far from perfect, are probably going to lose the farmer money'.[36]

Another recent Research Council report, 'Present State of Research and Education in Agriculture', is more in tune with the conclusions reached by international rice research specialists in its admission that 'research has not yet been able to breed varieties for very large areas experiencing heavy rainfall and conditions of water stagnation during the rainy season to which the existing high-yielding dwarf varieties are not adapted'. The report goes on to point out the specific problems of the dwarf varieties for the rainfed areas, namely, inadequate 'resistance to pests and diseases', and vulnerability 'to high rainfall and water-logged conditions', which, when combined with 'the high cost involved in resorting to the plant protection measures recommended for these varieties',[37] make it an extremely risky venture, especially for small farmers, to adopt the H.Y.V.s in rice.

Once it is recognized that the technology is not available to make the produciton of the H.Y.V.s in rice 'reliably profitable' to the farmers[38] in the rainfed areas and as long as the primary goal continues

The Problems of Rice Growing

to be to maximize the productivity of the land, then the Government of India has three choices before it, which are not necessarily mutually exclusive. One is to allocate substantial research funds to the difficult task of developing the high-stability varieties that both IRRI and the Government of India feel are required for the rainfed areas. However, while high-stability varieties with low input requirements might please cultivators, especially the small peasants, they do not promise the dramatic increases in yield dictated by a production orientation. The second alternative is to alter the environment to suit the varieties available through massive irrigation projects. This second alternative, while obviously the most expensive one, offers the prospect of predictability of results, since it is known that the new varieties respond well to inputs if assured water is available, and maximal production increases. However, since the problems of the rainfed areas concern water control generally, including drainage and flood prevention, irrigation by itself cannot satisfy the needs of all the paddy-growers in the high-risk rainfed areas. A third alternative is to move the paddy growers to withdraw from rice cultivation and to substitute crops such as maize, soybean, and blackgram that require somewhat less water than rice. The Report of the National Commission on Agriculture has proposed, in fact, that 3.27 million hectares of land constituting nearly 23 per cent of the current rice acreage,[39] be withdrawn from rice in the rainfed upland areas of U.P., Maddhya Pradesh and Bihar. This proposal, which is supported also by the Indian Council for Agricultural Research, has as its underlying premise the goal of maximizing production by growing those crops that will give the best yield from a given piece of land. It is also based upon the assumption that, if yields of rice are increased from lands that are suitable for rice-growing, the production needs of the country can be met from a reduced acreage in rice. It is recognized at the Indian Council for Agricultural Research that rice cultivation on marginal lands arises out of a 'farming system [that is] based upon the home needs of the cultivator, not on the basis of the marketability of the produce'.[40] Before a marginal or small paddy-grower in Bihar can be persuaded to substitute soya bean, sunflower, or sorghum for rice, he must be assured that his consumption requirements for rice will be met. The ideal at the Research Council is to produce enough rice from the potentially highest yielding rice lands so that the government may procure enough rice to stock the fair price shops and thereby be in a position to provide a guarantee to the rice grower that, if he switches to another crop, he will be able to purchase his family's rice requirements at a reasonable price from the fair price shops. The National Commission on Agriculture has projected that the rice consumption needs of the country in 1990 can be met by a production of 60 to 70 million tons. It is believed at the Research Council that this projection may be too high but that, in any case, the goal can be met by bringing the yields in all the irrigated lands in India up to the Punjab level of 3 tons per hectare. Consequently, the favoured policy at the Council in relation to rice production is to increase the yields on the irrigated lands by continuing to apply and develop further the H.Y.V. technology, to substitute crops other than rice in the rainfed areas where rice is not 'the correct crop' in relation to the rainfall pattern, and to provide paddy growers who make such substitutions with rice through the fair price shops.[41] The Research Council approach, which is based upon the value of increasing production in the country as a whole by 'crop planning which will maximize the benefits of a given environment and minimize the environmental risks of that particular location'[42] conflicts with the existing values of both the small paddy-growers and several of the state governments as well, which emphasize self-sufficiency rather than maximal production. At present, the small paddy-grower does not wish to be dependent on sources other than his own land and labour to feed his family. Moreover, political leaders in Kerala and other states, where national policy favours increasing the acreage sown to plantation and other non-staple crops, do not wish to be dependent upon the central government to feed their urban populations and their rural poor.

Consequently, of the three proposals, the only one currently being pursued with some resoluteness is the second, which is the most conservative one under the circumstances. Provision of increased irrigation facilities is within the existing technological capabilities of government whereas the creation of high stability varieties is not. Moreover, it is far easier to build a state tube-well than to persuade peasants to change their cropping patterns, especially when it may not clearly be in *their* interest to do so. Provision

The Problems of Rice Growing

of irrigation facilities to enhance the possibilities of adoption of H.Y.V.s in rice also is entirely consistent with the predominant production orientation.

The second alternative of developing suitable technology for the rainfed and other difficult areas also is being pursued, with the support of the Ford Foundation, which in 1975 agreed to provide $500,000 to fund research on agricultural technology for the adverse areas, including flood-prone, deep water, dry land, upland, and insect-infested areas.[43] However, it is questionable how serious the Indian Council of Agricultural Research is about pursuing vigorously the development of technologies and new varieties for adverse areas given their already noted ambiguity about the existence of such technologies and their desire to move a substantial proportion of rice area into other crops. There is, however, no major programme to implement the latter proposal. Nor are there any published documents that even discuss the likely consequences for farmers of such a major shift and the likely receptivity of cultivators to shifting to crops other than rice.

The proposal to shift nearly 23 per cent of the rice acreage in the rainfed upland areas to other crops raises strong doubts about the validity of the goal of increasing production as a reasonable guide for agricultural policy making. The individual cultivator is not interested solely in maximizing the quantity of foodgrains or other crops that can be produced from his fields, but has many other goals in mind which vary in importance also depending upon the size of his holding. The smallest peasants are most likely to be influenced considerably by the need to produce enough food to sustain their families, but even they are likely also to be concerned about a suitable mixture of crops such as would sustain an adequate variety of desired grains and vegetables to satisfy consumption needs. The cultivator may attempt to grow all or most of the food his family requires on his own lands or he may grow a mixture of foodgrains and cash crops and use the income derived from the latter to provide for his family's food consumption and other needs requiring cash. The larger the holding, the more likely is the peasant to grow a mixture of food and cash crops and to be motivated by considerations other than consumption, such as profitability and foodgrain quality, neither of which may involve an orientation to high yields.

The Ford Foundation, in a recent grant of funds to the National Council of Applied Economic Research for research on improving rice technology in adverse areas, has attempted to encourage further research on 'farmers' rice cultivation systems to identify socio-economic constraints' to the 'adoption of new technologies' and to focus more attention on 'the objective of increasing the profitability to farmers'.[44] However, the concern appears to be not with the profitability of the peasant's total operation and with what mixture of crops will maximize his economic return from his land, but with the more specific question of the profitability of the H.Y.V.s or any improved varieties of rice in relation to such factors as the relative price of paddy in the market, the cost of inputs, and the return in terms of increased production that the peasant gets in relation to the amount of paddy he must sell to buy the fertilizer that will increase his yields. These kinds of concerns arise naturally from the monocrop orientation of international and national agricultural research, which in turn is itself related to the production orientation that focuses on maximizing yields from particular crops. However, most farmers in north India grow a combination of cash crops and staple food grains. They are as much concerned with the technology for producing high-yield cash crops as they are with the technology for H.Y.V.s in rice. They are even more concerned with the market price for their cash crops and are very sensitive to fluctuations in the price of particular cash crops. The kinds of advice they require are not just how to grow H.Y.V.s in rice, but, given the available technology, irrigation facilities, and current and predicted market prices for various crops, what particular mixture of food and cash crops will maximize their opportunities to feed their families, to bring a sufficient return to marry their daughters, and to buy inputs - in that order of priority.

Although the Government of India has, in the past, shared with international agricultural research agencies a strong orientation towards increased production as a primary goal, this orientation has been modified in practice by the government's political concern to distribute food to the urban classes at a moderate price. The government's price policy, therefore, has put a damper on increased production of foodcrops. The failure of state governments in north India to provide adequate marketing facilities also has been a disincentive to production increases in the more inaccessible districts of the region. Pressure from the less favoured regions and states for an equitable allocation of resources also has modified tendencies to concentrate resources in the more productive areas.

On the other hand, the entire orientation of India's economic development policies in the Nehru era, when rapid industrialization was the primary goal and the needs of agriculture were slighted, retarded agricultural modernization in the rainfed areas. Resources that might have been used to build extensive irrigation networks and flood control systems and to extend hydroelectric power to remote areas were directed instead to industry. In recent years, however, particularly under the former Janata government, there has been a shift in emphasis in favour of agricultural development and small-scale rather than large-scale industry. An important component of this shift was the decision under the Janata government to divert considerable resources to irrigation, including a plan to irrigate the whole of Bihar state in five years. It is difficult to believe that such a grandiose plan could be brought to fruition in the time indicated, but the goal at least was indicative of a major change in priorities.

Despite the recent indications that governments in India plan to expend significant financial resources to develop agriculture in the rainfed areas, it is not at all clear that those resources will ultimately benefit the small paddy-grower. In the first place, it is not even clear that irrigation by itself, in the absence of adequate flood control measures, would be used by paddy-growers in these high risk areas or that they would or could use the H.Y.V.s and the inputs required to get good yields from them even with irrigation. Second, it is also not clear that governments in India are prepared to devote the kind of resources necessary to confront the problems of developing the full range of technologies required to grow more paddy under the extremely heterogeneous conditions that exist *within* the rainfed areas. Finally, it is least of all clear, despite the creation of such organizations as the Small Farmers' Development Agency and the Marginal Farmers' and Agricultural Labourers Agency that the Government of India is willing to make a commitment to preserve and protect existing small farmers and to make marginal farmers viable, for such a commitment would mean a reorientation of the whole thrust of economic development policy for India away from the capital-intensive industrialization strategy and the production emphasis in agriculture to a labour- and land-intensive

Paul R. Brass

agriculture-oriented strategy with an emphasis on extending the benefits of science and technological change in agriculture to all farmers who can reasonably make use of it to improve their own well-being.

NOTES

Brass, 'International rice research and the problems of rice growing in Uttar Pradesh and Bihar'

This paper has arisen out of a project on Value Issues in Technological Innovation and Social Choice: A Case Study of U.S. Rice Production Technologies in South Asia, on which I have been engaged for the past three years jointly with Robert Anderson, Edwin Levy, and Barry Morrison. Research for the project was funded by the Ethical and Human Values in Science and Technology Division of the National Science Foundation. I am solely responsible for all statements of fact and opinion contained in this paper.

Abbreviations

ICAR   Indian Council of Agricultural Research
IRRI   International Rice Research Institute

    1. Adelita C. Palacpac, *World Rice Statistics* (Los Banos [IRRI] 1977), p.32.
    2. Ibid., p.13.
    3. Calculated from ibid., p.38.
    4. Ibid., pp.39-40.
    5. Interview at IRRI on 15 and 16 February 1978.
    6. Interview in New Delhi on 23 March 1978.
    7. Ibid.
    8. Ibid.
    9. Ibid. and interview in New Delhi on 20 March 1978.
    10. Randolph Barker, *Socio-Economic Constraints to the Production of Photoperiod Sensitive Transplanted Rice in Eastern India* (Los Banos [IRRI] 1977), p.5.
    11. Ibid., p.2.
    12. Ibid., p.11.
    13. Ibid., p.9.
    14. Interviews at IRRI on 16 and 20 February 1978.
    15. Interview, New Delhi, 23 March 1978.
    16. Interview, New Delhi, 20 March 1978.
    17. Interview, IRRI, 20 February 1978.
    18. Ibid.
    19. Ibid.
    20. *IRRI Long Range Planning Committee Report* (Los Banos, Philippines [IRRI] 1979), p.23.

21. Ibid.
22. Ibid.
23. Ibid.
24. Government of India, Ministry of Agriculture and Irrigation, 'Report of the National Commission on Agriculture' Pt.VI: *Crop Production, Sericulture, and Apiculture* (Delhi 1976), p.53.
25. Calculated from Government of India, Ministry of Agriculture and Irrigation, 'All India Report on Agricultural Census, 1970-1' (Delhi: Controller of Publications, 1975), pp.29-31.
26. Calculated from ICAR, *Agricultural Research in India: Achievements and Outlook* (New Delhi 1972), pp. 47-9.
27. Interview, New Delhi, 23 March 1978.
28. 'Report of the National Commission on Agriculture' VI, p.282.
29. Ibid., p.283.
30. Interview, New Delhi, 23 March 1978.
31. ICAR, *Agricultural Research and Education: Recent Progress* (New Delhi 1977), p.24.
32. Ibid., p.26.
33. ICAR, *Research Highlights, 1977* (New Delhi 1977), p.4.
34. Ibid., p.6.
35. Ibid., p.7.
36. Interview, New Delhi, 20 March 1978.
37. ICAR, *Present State of Research and Education in Agriculture, Animal Sciences, and Fisheries and Approach to Their Further Development During the Fifth Plan Period* (New Delhi 1978[?]), p.3.
38. Interview, New Delhi, 30 December 1980.
39. 'Report of the National Commission on Agriculture' VI, pp.65-7.
40. Interview, New Delhi, 23 March 1978.
41. Ibid.
42. Ibid.
43. Interview, New Delhi, 20 March 1978.
44. Ibid.

LIBRARY OF DAVIDSON COLLEGE

Books on regular loan may be checked out for **two weeks**. Books must be presented at the Circulation Desk in order to be renewed.

A fine is charged after date due.

Special books are subject to special regulations at the discretion of the library staff.

JAN. 29. 1988			
FEB. -4 1989			
MAR 21 1989			
MAY -5 1989			
OCT 1 0 '91			